JOHN WESLEY'S
STANDARD SERMONS

GENTLY PARAPHRASED
AND SPARINGLY ABRIDGED
VOLUME I

SERMONS 1-20

edited by
CHARLES ELTON WEAVER

CP

CHARLTONIAN PRESS

Charltonian Press
charltonianpress@gmail.com

John Wesley's Standard Sermons
Gently Paraphrased and Sparingly Abridged
Volume I

All texts by John Wesley are in the public domain. Edited versions, front and back matter in this book © Charles Elton Weaver 2024.

The scanning, uploading, reproduction, and/or electronic or other sharing of any part of this book without permission of the editor constitutes unlawful piracy. No part of this book may be used without prior written permission of the editor.

Please address inquiries about permissions and bulk sales to charltonianpress@gmail.com.

Book design by cj Madigan

Cover design and art direction by Suzanne Fox

Cover image: Portrait of John Wesley by or after a work by George Romney, c. 1789. Public domain image courtesy of the National Portrait Gallery, England.

*Volume I is dedicated to
the warm-hearted Methodist people who faithfully
nurtured me as a boy in Sebring and as a
boy-preacher in rural Mississippi and Texas*

Contents

Foreword vii

Editor's Note ix

About Wesley's Standard Sermons xi

Wesley's Preface to the First
of His Four Volumes of Published Sermons (1746) 1

Salvation by Faith 6

The Almost Christian 16

Awake, Thou That Sleepest 24

Scriptural Christianity 35

Justification by Faith 49

The Righteousness of Faith 61

The Way to the Kingdom 72

The First Fruits of the Spirit 82

The Spirit of Bondage and Adoption 93

The Witness of the Spirit (I)   107

The Witness of the Spirit (II)   119

The Witness of Our Own Spirit   131

On Sin in Believers   140

On Repentance in Believers   152

The Great Assize   166

The Means of Grace   179

The Circumcision of the Heart   196

The Marks of the New Birth   207

The Great Privilege of Those That Are Born of God   218

The Lord Our Righteousness   229

Acknowledgments   243

About the Editor   247

About the Book   249

Foreword

In early 2019, I began reading Wesley's sermons devotionally, having read many of them across the years more academically. I found myself subconsciously paraphrasing and abridging what I was reading, to make it clearer to myself. The thought occurred to me that, perhaps, I ought to commit my revisions to writing. I tried for weeks to squelch that thought. Finally, I gave in to my compulsion and began to type. I was doing it strictly for myself. I assumed that others had probably paraphrased these sermons before me, but I didn't investigate; it didn't matter to me at the time.

As I completed more and more of the sermons, I wondered if I might share them with some clergy friends or my former bishop, to see if they found any value in them. I really had no idea how many of the sermons I would complete. The idea of trying to publish them came only slowly and gradually. Though I'm a history buff by training and interest, I'm not a professional historian. And though I'm a great admirer of Wesley, and have read and studied him more than most, I'm not a professional Wesley scholar either. I'm simply a retired Methodist preacher, with an inner compulsion and some extra time. I acknowledge that a person with a background like mine might have done this work. The difference is that I have done it. It's been important to me. I hope it might prove helpful to others.

I say that I've gently paraphrased Wesley: I mean that I've let Wesley speak for himself whenever possible, letting stand his theological terms and memorable expressions. I've paraphrased mainly when words were archaic or sentence structure was overly tedious and complex, reflecting the learned style of the time. I've not attempted nor desired to make Wesley sound like a twenty-first century writer, but only to make him more understandable to twenty-first century readers. I say also that I've sparingly abridged Wesley: I mean that I've eliminated some of the wordiness that was typical of his era, which often obscures, rather than clarifies, the point being made. I've tried to clear away the underbrush so one can better walk through the forest. Wesley was a man of scripture; he could think of a dozen passages that helped make his point—and often used them all. I've used only a representative sampling. But I've left out none of Wesley's points, even when they seemed to me repetitive or even tangential to the flow of his argument.

Wesley is, of course, crucial to the wider Wesleyan world—in its Methodist, Holiness, and Pentecostal expressions; but he is also important to the ecumenical Christian conversation. Wesley wrote plainly, logically, scripturally, and with great conviction to his eighteenth-century audience; it's only because nearly three centuries separate us that he is sometimes difficult for us. If you should read these revisions, I hope that you'll use them as an aid to reading Wesley in his own words. You will not be disappointed with Wesley!

Charles Elton Weaver

Editor's Note

There is no escaping the fact that John Wesley wrote like an Oxford-educated clergyman of the eighteenth century, even though he says that he intends to convey plain truth to plain people. The modern reader will notice, even in the paraphrase, a plethora of punctuation—more commas, semicolons, and colons than we might be used to. I have retained much of it for the sake of clarity and to preserve some of the cadence. Being steeped in the classical languages, Wesley uses the subjunctive mood consistently. Since I still use it in ordinary speech, I have retained it in the paraphrase, even in certain instances where it sounds a bit stilted. Wesley does not use contractions ever. I debated this, because I believe they make spoken language smoother. In the end, though, I left them out, as a concession to the author. Finally, his use of the masculine gender to refer to humanity in general. This was not an issue for women and men in the eighteenth century; it was universally used in spoken and written English. Since modern gender issues are anachronistic to Wesley's day, I have retained his usage as being more reflective of his times and less awkward in style.

I have followed the format of the 1872 edition, from the Wesleyan Methodist Book Room, London. I have retained Wesley's system of numbering paragraphs, for ease of cross-referencing back to the original. Introductory paragraphs use Arabic numerals only; each main section begins with a Roman numeral, but each paragraph within that section begins with an Arabic numeral. My three volumes preserve Wesley's sermon numbering. Sermons 1-20 appear in Volume I, sermons 21-33 in Volume II, and sermons 34-53 in Volume III.

Material within quotation marks is almost always and obviously scripture—always **KJV** for Wesley, of course, but sometimes slightly emended. Wesley rarely cited his source for brief scripture passages; neither have I. A few quotations are from prayers and homilies of the Church of England. Material within parentheses is from Wesley. Material within brackets, I have added for information or clarity.

About Wesley's Standard Sermons

Between 1746 and 1760, John Wesley published four volumes of sermons that he believed captured the heart of his preaching and defined the doctrine of the burgeoning Methodist movement. There were forty-four sermons in all. In 1763, the yearly Conference decreed that the trustees of a Methodist meeting house should allow in the pulpit only those preachers appointed by the Conference, and that those appointed should "preach no other doctrine than is contained in Mr. Wesley's *Notes upon the New Testament* and four volumes of sermons." Thus, the forty-four became "standard." When Wesley re-published these sermons in 1771, however, he added nine more, for a total of fifty-three. In these sermons, Wesley the evangelist proclaims the simple gospel of salvation to sinners (unbelievers), and Wesley the pastor challenges saints (believers) to grow into the fullness of their salvation. Like an experienced guide, Wesley leads less experienced travelers on the journey toward heaven, carefully laying out the successive stages of the journey, pointing out the dangers along the way, and encouraging faint hearts to persevere, till they reach their glorious destination.

WESLEY'S PREFACE TO THE FIRST OF HIS FOUR VOLUMES OF PUBLISHED SERMONS (1746)

1 ... The following sermons contain the substance of what I have been preaching for the last eight or nine years. During that time, I have frequently spoken in public on every topic in this collection; I do not believe that there is any point of doctrine on which I typically speak which is not included here. Every serious man who reads these will clearly see what doctrines I embrace and teach as the essentials of true religion.

2 ... But I am quite aware that these are not presented in a way that some may expect. Nothing in these sermons is elaborate, elegant, or oratorical. Even if I had intended to write like this, my leisure would not have permitted it. But, in fact, I fully intended to write as I did; I write as I speak—for the common man, for those who neither understand nor appreciate the art of oratory, but who, nevertheless, are competent judges of those truths which are necessary to their present and future happiness. I mention this so that careful readers may spare themselves the labor of seeking [in my sermons] what they will not find.

3 ... I intend plain truth for plain people. Therefore, I purposely

abstain from all pedantic and philosophical speculation, from all complicated reasoning, and, as far as possible, from all show of higher education, except in sometimes citing scripture in the original Greek. I strive to avoid all words which are not easily understood or used in common life, all technical theological terms, and all those ways of speaking which are familiar to the well-educated, but unknown to ordinary folk. I admit that I may occasionally slip those words in inadvertently, assuming that a word familiar to me is familiar to all.

4 ... My intention is to somewhat forget all I have ever read in my life, to speak as if I had never read one author, ancient or modern, except the writers of scripture. I believe that this may enable me to express more clearly the sentiments of my heart, simply following the chain of my own thoughts, without entangling them with those of others. I shall also come with fewer weights on my mind, fewer preconceived notions, to search for myself the simple truths of the gospel, or to teach them to others.

5 ... I am not afraid to expose the inmost thoughts of my heart to fair and reasonable men. I see myself as a transient creature, passing through life as an arrow passes through the air. I am a spirit coming from God and returning to God; barely hovering over a great chasm, till, in an instant, I am gone; dropping into an unchangeable eternity! I want to know one thing only—the way to heaven, how to land safely on that happy shore! God himself has graciously condescended to teach the way; for this very thing, he came down from heaven. He has written it all in a book. O give me that book! At any price, give me the book of God! I have it; it is all I need to know. Let me be 'a man of one book.'

So, here I am, far from the busy world of men. I sit down alone; only God is here. In his presence, I open and read his book for one reason only—to find the way to heaven. Is there any doubt about the meaning of what I read? Does anything seem dark and difficult? I lift up my heart to the Father: "Lord, does your word not say that 'if any man lack wisdom, let him ask of God'? That the Lord 'gives freely, and never scolds'? That 'if any be willing to do [the Lord's] will, he shall know it'? Lord, I am willing to do your will; let me know it!" I then search for and consider parallel passages of scripture, "comparing spiritual things with spiritual." I meditate on these with all the earnestness and attention of which my mind is capable. If any doubt remains, I consult those who are more experienced in the things of God; and then the passages, once dead, come to life. And what I thus learn, I teach.

6 ... Accordingly, I have written in the following sermons what I find in the Bible concerning the way to heaven, attempting to distinguish this way of God from those ways which are the invention of men. I have endeavored to describe the true, scriptural, experiential religion, omitting nothing which is crucial to it, and adding nothing which is not. It is my intention, first, to guard those who are just setting their faces toward heaven—who, having little acquaintance with the things of God, are more liable to lose their way—from formal, outward religion, which has almost driven heart-religion out of the world. And second, to warn those who know the religion of the heart, the faith which works by love, lest they totally ignore the law of God, misunderstanding the place of law in the life of faith, and thus fall back into the snare of the devil.

7 ... By the advice of some of my friends, I have included three of my sermons and one of my brother's, preached before the University at Oxford. I chose these, especially, to refute those who claim that we have changed our doctrine, and do not preach now what we did some years ago. Any fair-minded man can judge for himself, when he compares the earlier sermons with the later.

8 ... But some may say that I myself have mistaken the way, even

though I presume to teach others. It is probable that many will think so, and it is possible that I may have. But I hope that, wherever I am mistaken, my mind is open to correction. I sincerely desire to be better informed. I say to God and man, "What I do not know, teach me!"

9 ... Do you believe you see things more clearly than I do? Very likely you may. If so, treat me as you would desire to be treated, if the situation were reversed. Point me to a better way than I have known; show me by the plain proof of scripture. And if I seem to hesitate in my long-accustomed path, and am slow to leave it, just work with me a little; take me by the hand and lead me as I am willing to follow. Do not be impatient with me when I beg you not to beat me in order to quicken my pace. I can go feebly and slowly at best; if you beat me, I cannot go at all. Let me also ask you not to call me names in order to direct me into the right path. Even if I were very much in the wrong, this would not set me straight. Instead, it would cause me to run from you, and thus go farther and farther in the wrong direction.

10 ... Indeed, if you become angry, I am likely to become angry too; then there will be little hope of finding the truth. Once anger arises, the smoke will so dim the eyes of my soul, that I shall see nothing clearly. For God's sake, if it be possible, let us not provoke one another to wrath; let us not kindle this fire of hell, much less fan it into flame. Even if we could discern truth by that diabolical glow, would it not be loss, rather than gain? How far is love, even with many wrong opinions, to be preferred to truth without love! We may die without knowing many truths, yet still be carried into the arms of God. But if we die without love, what will all our knowledge avail us? Just as much as it avails the devil and his demons!

May our loving God forbid that we should ever be forced to choose between love and truth! May he prepare us to know his truth, by filling our hearts with his love, and with all joy and peace in believing!

1

SALVATION BY FAITH

By grace are you saved through faith.
—EPHESIANS 2:

1 ... All the blessings which God has bestowed on man are strictly of his grace, his lavish generosity and favor; his favor, altogether free and undeserved, man having no claim to the least of his mercies. It was God's free grace that "formed man from the dust, and breathed into him a living soul," and stamped on that soul the image of God and gave him dominion over all things. That same free grace continues toward us to this day—the source of our very lives and of all good things. There is nothing we are, or have, or do, which deserves anything from God; it is all a gift from God. And whatever righteousness may be found in man, this also is a gift from God.

2 ... How then shall a sinful man atone for even the least of his sins? With his own [good] works? No. No matter how many or holy they may be, man's works are not his own, but God's. In fact, in and of themselves, man's works [even his best works] are sinful, every one of them needing God's atonement. Only corrupt fruit grows on a corrupt tree. And man's heart is altogether corrupt, falling "short of the glory of God"; devoid of that glorious righteousness at first

impressed on his soul, in the image of his Creator. Therefore, man, having neither inner righteousness nor outward works to plead, stands speechless [helpless] before God.

3 ... So, if sinful men do find favor with God, it is strictly "grace upon grace." If God still chooses to shower fresh blessings upon us, the greatest of all being salvation, what can we say, but, "Thanks be to God for his unspeakable gift!" And it surely is [an indescribable gift]. In this, "God commended his love toward us, in that, while we were yet sinners, Christ died" to save us. "By grace," then, "are you saved through faith." Grace is the source of salvation, and faith its condition.

Now, lest we fall short of God's grace, we need to carefully consider: (1) what is the faith that saves us; (2) what is the salvation that comes through faith; and (3) how may we answer objections.

I / 1 ... What is the faith that saves us? First, it is not just the faith of a *heathen*. God requires even a heathen to believe that God exists, and that God rewards those who seek him; that God is to be sought by glorifying him as God, by giving him thanks for all things, and by carefully practicing moral virtue (justice, mercy, and truth) toward their fellow creatures. A Greek or Roman, even a barbarian, was without excuse if he did not believe at least this much: God's being and attributes, a future state of reward and punishment, and the obligation of moral virtue. This is just barely the faith of a heathen.

2 ... Second, it is not just the faith of a *devil*, though this goes further than the faith of a heathen. The devil believes that there is a wise and powerful God, who is gracious to reward and just to punish; he also believes that Jesus is the Son of God, the Christ, the Savior of the world. That miserable being believes every word which Jesus

spoke, and whatever was written by saints of old, those servants of the Most High, who showed us the way of salvation. This much, the ancient enemy of God and man believes, and trembles in believing: That God was incarnate in Christ; that Christ will overcome all his enemies; and that "all scripture was given by inspiration of God." All this the devil believes.

3 ... Third, the faith by which we are saved is not just the faith which the *disciples* had while Christ was living on earth. True, they believed in him enough to leave all and follow him; to receive power to work miracles, to heal disease, to cast out demons; and even more, to "preach the kingdom of God." [But even this is not yet saving faith.]

4 ... What then is the faith by which we are saved? First, it is faith in Christ: Christ, and God through Christ, are its objects. In this it is absolutely distinguished from the faith of *heathens*, either ancient or modern. And in this it is distinguished from the faith of a *devil:* It is not just a speculative, rational thing; a cold, lifeless assent [to doctrine]; a train of ideas in the head; but also a disposition of the heart. Scripture says, "With the heart man believes unto righteousness"; and, "If you confess with your mouth the Lord Jesus and believe in your heart that God has raised him from the dead, you shall be saved."

5 ... In this it is distinguished from the faith the *disciples* had while Christ was living on earth: It acknowledges the necessity and merit of his death, and the power of his resurrection. It acknowledges his death as the only sufficient means of redeeming man from death eternal, and his resurrection as the restoration of us all to life and immortality. Christian faith, then, is not only an assent to the whole gospel of Christ, but also a full reliance on the blood of Christ; a trust in the merits of his life, death, and resurrection; a leaning on Jesus as our atonement and our life, Jesus *given for us,* and Jesus

living in us; a surrender to him, and a desperate clinging to him, as our "wisdom, righteousness, sanctification, and redemption." In a word, Jesus Christ our salvation!

II / 1 ... What is the salvation that comes through faith? First, it is a *present* salvation. It is attainable here on earth, actually attained by believers in Christ. Paul said to the Ephesians, and to believers of every age, not "You *shall be saved* [future]," but "You *are saved* [present] through faith."

2 ... You are saved from *sin.* This is saving faith. This is that great salvation foretold by the angel, before God brought his first-born Son into the world: "You shall call him Jesus, for he shall save his people from their sins." And nowhere in scripture is there any limitation or restriction. All his people, all who believe in him, he will save from all their sins: from original sin and actual sin, past sin and present sin, sins of the flesh and sins of the spirit. Through faith in Christ, they are saved from the *guilt* of sin and from the *power* of sin.

3 ... Yes, saved from the *guilt* of all past sins. Since all the world is guilty before God, justly deserving his condemnation; and since God's law brings knowledge of sin, but no deliverance from it; now, therefore, "the righteousness of God, through faith in Christ, is revealed to all who believe." Now, "they are justified freely by his grace, through the redemption in Jesus." Now, Christ has obliterated "the accusation against us, nailing it to his cross." Now, there is "no condemnation to those in Christ Jesus."

4 ... And being saved from guilt, they are thereby saved from fear. Not from a child's fear of offending a loving Father, but from a slave's fear of offending a severe Master—the fear of punishment, the fear of God's wrath. Believers "have not received the spirit of

bondage, but the Spirit of adoption; the Spirit itself bears witness with their spirits, that they are the children of God." They are also saved from the fear, though not from the possibility, of falling away from the grace of God, and coming short of his precious promises. Thus, they have "peace with God; they rejoice in hope of the glory of God; and the love of God is shed abroad in their hearts through the Holy Spirit." And they are persuaded that nothing, absolutely nothing "shall be able to separate them from the love of God in Christ Jesus our Lord."

5 ... Again, through this faith they are saved from the *power* of sin, not just the guilt. It is often and boldly declared in I John that whoever "commits sin is of the devil"; that the sinless Christ came "to take away our sins"; and that whoever believes in Christ "is born of God and does not commit sin."

6 ... By faith, the born-again believer does not sin: (1) By any *habitual sin,* for habitual sin is sin reigning, and sin cannot reign in any true believer. (2) By any *willful sin,* for a believer's will is firmly set against all sin and hates it like poison. (3) By any *sinful desire,* for a believer continually desires the holy and perfect will of God, and, by the grace of God, stifles every unholy desire. (4) By any *infirmity* (of thought, word, or deed), for without intention, infirmities are not properly sins. And though the believer *cannot* say that he has *never* sinned, he *can* say that *now* he does not sin.

7 ... This then is salvation through faith, in this present world: A salvation from sin and its consequences, expressed in the word *justification.* Justification implies deliverance from sin's guilt and punishment, by the atonement of Christ actually applied to the soul of the sinner now believing in him; and deliverance from sin's power, through Christ formed in his heart. He who is thus justified, or saved through faith, is simultaneously *born again,* born of the Spirit into a new life, which "is hid with Christ in God." As

a new-born babe, he gladly receives "the milk of the word, and grows thereby"; going on in the Lord's might, from faith to faith, from grace to grace, until, at last, he becomes "a perfect man," transformed "into the fullness of Christ."

III / 1 ... Usual objections to salvation by faith: "Preaching salvation by faith alone is preaching against holiness and good works." We answer: It would be, if we meant a faith that was separate from these, as some do. But we mean a faith that abundantly produces good works and holiness.

2 ... A similar objection was raised in Paul's time: Does salvation by faith not "make void the law?" We answer: On the contrary. Those who do not preach salvation by faith are the ones who nullify God's law: Either by restricting or enlarging Paul's words so as to eat away at the spirit of his teaching; or by failing to point out that saving faith is the only possible means of performing the law. We, on the other hand, "establish the law," by showing its full extent and spiritual meaning, and by calling everyone to the living way of Christ, the *only* way that "the righteousness of the law may be fulfilled in them." Those who are saved by faith, though they trust in the blood of Christ alone, still use all the ordinances that Christ appointed, still do all the good works which Christ taught and exemplified, and increasingly manifest those holy and heavenly qualities which reflect the mind of Christ.

3 ... "But does preaching salvation by faith not lead to human pride?" We answer: It could, accidentally. Therefore, every believer needs to be cautioned: Because of unbelief, the natural [Jewish] branches were removed from the vine; and because of faith in Christ, the grafted [Gentile] branches were spared. An example of God's judgment and God's graciousness! If believers

do not continue in God's grace through faith, they too will face his judgment.

Paul himself answers this objection: "Where then is boasting? It is excluded"; excluded "by the law of faith." If a man were justified by his works, he would indeed have something to boast about. But there can be no boasting for him "who does not work, but simply believes on him who justifies the ungodly." Our merciful God, "even when we were dead in our sins, has brought us to life together with Christ." "By grace are you saved through faith, and that not of your own doing": Neither your faith nor your salvation comes from you. "It is the gift of God": Both faith and salvation are a free, undeserved gift of God, a gift of his good pleasure and favor; that you believe at all, and that by believing you are saved, are two instances of his grace. "Not of works, lest any man should boast": All our attempts at righteousness, *before* we believed in Christ, deserved nothing from God but condemnation; they earned from God neither faith nor salvation. Nor is our salvation based on the good works we do *after* we believe; for it is then God who is working in us. And the fact that he would reward us for what he himself has done in us, is one more instance of the riches of his mercy and leaves us with absolutely nothing to boast about.

4 ... "Will preaching salvation by faith alone not encourage men to remain in their sins, [leaving too much to God's grace]?" We answer: It could; some may think they can "continue in sin that grace may abound." But, if so, they bring down judgment on themselves. The grace of God should lead men to repentance; and it will, if they are sincere. When they realize that there is forgiveness with God, they will cry out for him to blot out their sins, through faith in Jesus. And if they earnestly cry out to God, and seek him by all the means of grace, and refuse to give up until he answers, surely "he will come, and not tarry." And God can do much work

in a short time! There are many examples in Acts, of God working this faith in men's hearts [instantaneously], like lightning striking from heaven: In the very hour Paul and Silas began to preach, the [Philippian] jailer repented, believed, and was baptized. On Pentecost, three thousand souls repented and believed, when Peter first preached. And, thanks be to God, there are many living proofs that God is still "mighty to save."

5 ... "Will men not be driven to despair, if you preach that they cannot be saved by all their good works?" We answer: Yes, they will despair of being saved by their own merits and righteousness. And they should despair of that; for none can trust in the merits of Christ, until they have utterly renounced their own; and none can receive the righteousness of God, until they have ceased pursuing their own. The righteousness which comes from faith cannot be given while they trust in the righteousness which comes from the law.

6 ... "But salvation by faith is an uncomfortable doctrine." The devil, without truth or shame, said that very thing. In fact, it is the only doctrine that can bring comfort to self-destroyed, self-acknowledged sinners: that "whoever believes on him shall not be ashamed." Here is comfort, high as heaven, stronger than death! What? Mercy for all? For Zacchaeus, a corrupt tax-collector; for Mary Magdalene, a harlot? I think I hear a sinner say, "Then I, even I, may hope for mercy!" And indeed you may, miserable sinner, whom none has comforted! God will not forget you. Perhaps this very hour, he may say, "Be of good cheer, your sins are forgiven"; forgiven, so that they will reign over you no more; forgiven, so that "the Holy Spirit will bear witness with your spirit that you are now a child of God." What joyful good news! Whatever your sins may be, "turn to the Lord, and he will have mercy on you; and to our God, for he will abundantly pardon."

7 ... When all objections have been answered, they will still argue:

"Salvation by faith should not be preached at all, but certainly not as a major doctrine." But what does scripture say? Quite the contrary. So, "whoever believes on him shall be saved" is, and must be, the foundation of all our preaching; and it must be preached foremost. "But not to everyone." What? To whom shall we not preach it? The poor? No, they have a special right to hear it. The uneducated? No, God has revealed himself to these from the beginning. The young? No, let them also come to Christ, and "forbid them not." The sinners? No, they least of all. "He came not to call the righteous, but sinners to repentance." If there were any to whom we would not preach it, it would be the rich, the educated, the reputable, the moral. And these often feel that they *should* be exempt from hearing it. But we must honor the words of our Lord: "Go and preach the gospel to *every* person." If anyone twists any part of this doctrine to his own destruction, it is his own fault.

8 ... Now, especially, do we need to preach that "by grace are you saved through faith." Never was this doctrine more needed than now. Nothing but this can so effectively prevent the increase of Catholicism among us. It is useless to attack, one by one, the errors of the Roman Church. But the doctrine of salvation by faith strikes at its root, and all errors fall as a consequence. It was this doctrine, which the Church [of England] rightly calls "the strong rock and foundation of the Christian religion," that first drove popery out of Great Britain, and this alone can keep it out. Furthermore, nothing but this can halt the immorality that has inundated our land. Can you empty the ocean, drop by drop? No; and neither can you reform the land by attacking vices, one by one. But let "the righteousness of God by faith" be established [in the hearts of the people], and the wave of immorality will be stopped. The opponents of this [foundational] doctrine may speak as sublimely of the moral law as those who have it written on their hearts by God. To hear them speak, one might think they were not far from

the Kingdom. But take them out of the law, and into the gospel of Christ and the righteousness of faith, and those who once appeared almost, if not altogether Christian, stand now exposed as men under damnation; as far from life and salvation, as the depth of hell from the height of heaven. (God be merciful to them!)

9 ... For this reason, the devil rages whenever salvation by faith is preached: He stirred up earth and hell to destroy those who first preached it; and knowing that this doctrine alone could overturn his kingdom, he called forth all his forces to stop Luther from reviving it. As Luther observed, "How it would enrage a proud strong man, fully armed, to be stopped by a little child"—stopped, overthrown, and trampled underfoot! Thus, has the Lord's strength always been "made perfect in weakness." Though you be a babe in Christ, the devil will not be able to withstand you; you will subdue him and trample him underfoot. You will march on, under the Captain of your salvation, until all enemies are destroyed, and "death is swallowed up in victory, through our Lord Jesus Christ." To whom, with the Father and the Spirit, be blessing and glory, honor and power, forever and ever. . .

Preached at St. Mary's, Oxford University, June 1738

2

THE ALMOST CHRISTIAN

You almost persuade me to be a Christian.
—ACTS 26:28

And many will go this far: From the very beginning of Christianity, many, of every age and nation, have been almost persuaded to be Christians. But since it counts for nothing with God to go only this far and no further, it is important to consider: (1) what is an *almost* Christian; and (2) what is an *altogether* Christian.

I / 1 ... Being an *almost* Christian implies, first, *heathen honesty.* By heathen honesty, I mean not only that which was recommended by their philosophers, but what was expected by ordinary heathens of one another, and actually practiced by many of them. They were taught not to be unjust; not to take away their neighbor's goods; not to oppress the poor; not to cheat rich or poor in business; not to defraud any man of what was rightfully his own; and not to be in debt to anyone, if possible.

2 ... In addition, even ordinary heathens believed that some regard should be given to the truth. They despised liars, slanderers, and false accusers; they considered them to be a disgrace to the human race and the pests of society.

3 ... Again, there was a sort of love and assistance which they expected from one another. This extended beyond those little courtesies which could be done without expense or effort. It included feeding the hungry, if they had food to spare; clothing the naked, with their own cast-off clothes; and, in general, giving to those in need whatever they did not need themselves. Heathen honesty included all this; all this is implied in being an almost Christian.

4 ... Second, being an *almost* Christian implies having *a form of godliness;* having the *outside* of a real Christian. So, the almost Christian does nothing that the gospel forbids: He does not take the Lord's name in vain; he does not curse or swear; he does not profane the Sabbath or allow it to be profaned; he avoids all sexual immorality, and even those words or looks that suggest it; he controls his tongue, neither slandering, gossiping, nor foolishly jesting—he speaks only what is edifying, and thus he "grieves not the Holy Spirit."

5 ... Furthermore, he abstains from drunkenness, gluttony, and carousing. As much as possible, he avoids strife and contention, endeavoring to live peacefully with everyone. If he is wronged, he does not seek revenge or return evil for evil. He does not berate or criticize his neighbors for their faults or weaknesses. He does not willingly wrong any man; but follows the plain scriptural rule, "Whatever you would not want done to you, that do not do to another."

6 ... And in doing good, the almost Christian does not confine himself to cheap and easy courtesies, but goes to great efforts to help as many as possible. Whatever it takes, whenever he can, he does good to all, to friend and foe alike, to good folks and bad—to their souls and to their bodies. He corrects the wicked, instructs the ignorant, confirms the wavering, encourages the good, and comforts the afflicted. He seeks to awaken the apathetic; he leads

the awakened to the fountain of forgiveness; and he encourages the forgiven to live the Christian life.

7 ... He who has the form of godliness, also uses the means of grace—all of them, at every opportunity. He is regularly at church. He is unlike many churchgoers, who enter the presence of the Most High impressed with themselves, dressed in jewels and fancy clothes; who greet their fellow churchgoers with extravagant courtesy and enter their pews with impertinent gaiety, disclaiming any pretention to even the form of godliness, much less its power. Would to God that none of us here were guilty of that; that none of us would enter church gazing about with careless indifference, even though we may pretend to utter a prayer; that none of us would fall asleep during worship, or recline in the most convenient posture for it; that none of us would whisper to each other or look around in utter boredom, as if God were not present in awesome power! But none of this describes the almost Christian: He is serious and attentive during every part of the service. And when he approaches the communion table, it is not lightly or carelessly, but with obvious reverence that silently speaks, "God be merciful to me, a sinner!"

8 ... To this, we add the practice of family devotions (to those who are heads of families), and private prayer, and a daily seriousness of behavior. He who regularly practices this *outward* religion truly has a *form of godliness*.

9 ... There is just one more thing to being an *almost* Christian, and that is *sincerity*. By sincerity, I mean a real, inward principle of religion, from which these outward actions flow. If we do not have sincerity, we do not even have heathen honesty. As an Epicurean poet said, "Good men avoid sin from the love of virtue; wicked men avoid sin from a fear of punishment." [The good man acts from sincerity; the wicked man does not.] If a heathen only abstained from evil to avoid punishment, he could not even be labeled a good

heathen. Likewise, a man of our own time, who abstains from evil *only* to avoid the loss of friends or wealth or reputation, could not yet be labeled an almost Christian—even if he did much good and used all the means of grace. Without sincerity in his heart, he is still just a hypocrite.

10 ... Sincerity is necessarily implied in being an almost Christian; a real desire to serve God and do his will, in all a man's conversation, in all his actions, in all he does or leaves undone. Sincerity runs through the whole life of the almost Christian; this is the moving principle in his doing good, abstaining from evil, and using the ordinances of God.

11 ... "But is it possible that any man living should go this far, and still be just an *almost* Christian? What more could it mean to be an *altogether* Christian?" Yes, it is possible to go this far and still be an almost Christian; both scripture and personal experience show it to be so.

12 ... Friends, let me be bold for your sakes; let me risk ridicule for the gospel's sake; let me expose my own soul. I am willing to be publicly humiliated that you may profit from my mistake, willing to be ridiculed if it advance the glory of God.

13 ... Yes, I myself was an almost Christian for many years, as many of you well know. I diligently avoided all evil; I never wasted precious time; I used every opportunity to do good to all men; I constantly used all public and private means of grace; I was appropriately serious at all times and in all situations; and (God is my witness!) I did it all in sincerity, earnestly desiring to do God's will in all things. Yet despite it all, I can testify in the Holy Spirit that all this time I was nothing but an almost Christian.

II / 1 ... "What more could possibly be implied in being an *altogether* Christian?" I answer: First, *the love of God*. God's word says, "You shall love the Lord your God with all your heart, soul, mind, and strength." Such love as this demands one's whole heart, fills one's whole soul, and requires all of one's natural abilities. He who loves like this constantly "rejoices in God his Savior," and "in everything gives thanks" to the Lord, his all in all. His heart cries out, "Whom have I in heaven but you, Lord? And there is none on earth I desire more than you!" Indeed, what can he desire more than the Lord? Not the world, or the things of the world, for he is "crucified to the world," crucified to "the desire of the flesh," and dead to pride of every kind. For love is not pretentious; he who dwells in the love of God is utterly humble.

2 ... Being an *altogether* Christian implies, secondly, *the love of neighbor.* Jesus said, "You shall love your neighbor as yourself." And one's neighbor is every man in the world, every single child of God; this includes our enemies, and even the enemies of God and goodness. But the Christian loves even these as he loves himself, and as Christ loved us. Paul described this love fully [in I Corinthians 13]: Love is patient and kind; not envious; not quick-tempered. It is not conceited, but causes him who loves to be the humble servant of all. Love does not behave badly, but seeks to relate well to all. It does not seek its own advantage, but seeks the good of all, the salvation of all. Love is not irritable, but gentle and peaceable. It does not dwell on evil; it does not rejoice in iniquity, but in the truth. Love "covers all things, believes all things, hopes all things, and endures all things."

3 ... Finally, being an *altogether* Christian implies *faith,* the foundation of everything. Excellent things are said about faith throughout scripture. John said, "Everyone who believes is born of God." "To as many as received him, who believed on his name, he gave power

to become children of God." "Faith is the victory that overcomes the world." Jesus himself declared, "He who believes in the Son has everlasting life; he is not condemned, but is passed from death to life."

4 ... But, let no one deceive himself! [As an official Homily of the Church of England states], "A faith that does not lead to repentance, love, and all good works, is not a true, living faith; rather, it is a dead faith, a devilish faith. Yes, even devils believe that Christ was a virgin-born miracle-worker, who declared himself to be God; that he died a painful death to redeem us from death everlasting; that he rose again, ascended into heaven, and sits at the Father's right hand; that he will come again to judge all men. These articles of faith even devils believe, as they believe all scripture. Yet, despite all this so-called faith, they are still devils, still damned, still lacking true Christian faith.

5 ... "The true Christian faith means, not only believing that scripture and Church teaching are true, but also having a personal trust and confidence in Christ that he will save *me* from hell; a trust and confidence that God, through the merits of Christ, will forgive *my* sins and reconcile *me* to God's favor; and this reconciliation creates in me a loving, obedient heart." *(On the Salvation of Man)*

6 ... This faith purifies the heart (by God's indwelling power) from pride and anger, from all unrighteousness and "filthiness of flesh and spirit." This faith fills the heart with a love stronger than death, both to God and man; a love that delights to do the will and works of God; a love that glories in being used by God for the sake of others; a love that endures with joy the reproach of Christ, being maliciously mocked and hated by men and devils. Whoever has this faith, working by love, is not *almost* a Christian; he is a Christian *altogether!*

7 ... But who are the living witnesses to this kind of faith? Before God, who knows the deepest mysteries and knows the human heart, I ask you, "Do *you* have this faith? Do *you* practice justice, mercy, and truth, as even the heathen require? If so, are you *outwardly* a Christian, having the *form* of godliness?" That implies that you abstain from evil, from whatever is forbidden in scripture; that you do whatever good you can, with all your might; that you use all the means of grace at every opportunity; and that you do it all with a sincere desire to please God in all things.

8 ... Are not many of you deeply convicted that you have never yet come this far; that you have never been even an almost Christian? That you do not even meet the standards of a heathen—much less the outward form of Christian godliness? Are you not aware that God has seen little sincerity in you, little desire to please him? You never intended to devote your life to his glory—your words and works, your business, your studies, your diversions! You never desired to do all things "in the name of the Lord Jesus," as a spiritual sacrifice, acceptable to him.

9 ... But supposing you had: Good intentions by themselves do not make a Christian, unless they are brought to fruition. "Hell is paved with good intentions," someone said. The important question remains: Is the love of God shed abroad in your heart? Is God your all in all? Do you desire nothing but God? Are you happy in God? Is he your glory, your delight, your source of rejoicing? Following his commandment, do you love your neighbor as yourself—every man, even your enemies and God's, as Christ loved you? Do you believe that Christ loved you and gave himself for you? Do you have faith in his blood? Do you believe that the Lamb of God has taken away your sins, has cast them into the depths, has cancelled the judgment against you, nailing it to his cross? And does his Spirit bear witness with your spirit that you are a child of God?

10 ... The Lord God, present with us this moment, knows well, that if any man die without this faith and love, it would be better for him not to have been born at all! Awake, O sleeper, and call on God while he may be found. Do not rest until you know the goodness of the Lord, his mercy and grace, his forgiveness of sins. Do not let anyone persuade you to stop short of the prize of your high calling. Cry to God day and night, the God who died for the ungodly, until you know him and claim him as your Lord and God. Do not ever give up until, with absolute certainty, you can declare to God's face that you love him, that he knows you love him!

11 ... May all of us, in this way, experience what it means to be, not an *almost* Christian, but an *altogether* Christian; justified freely by his grace, through the redemption in Jesus; having peace with God through Jesus; rejoicing in hope of the glory of God; and having the love of God shed abroad in our hearts, by the Holy Spirit given to us!

Preached at St. Mary's, Oxford University, Juuly 1741

3

AWAKE, THOU THAT SLEEPEST

Awake, O sleeper, arise from the dead, and Christ will give you light.

—EPHESIANS 5:14

In preaching on this passage, I shall try, with God's help: (1) to describe the sleepers who are addressed here; (2) to explain the exhortation, "Awake, arise from the dead"; and (3) to explain the promise, "Christ will give you light."

I / 1 ... By sleep is meant the natural state of man; that deep sleep of the soul, into which the sin of Adam has cast all those descended from him; that dull sluggishness of soul; that insensibility of his real spiritual condition, in which every man comes into the world, and continues till the voice of God awakens him.

2 ... Now, sleepers sleep at night. The natural state is a state of utter darkness. The unawakened sinner, no matter how much knowledge he may have of other things, has no knowledge of himself. He does not know that he is a fallen spirit, whose only real business in the present world is to recover from his fall and regain the image of God in which he was created. The natural man sees no need of the very thing that *is* needful: that inward change, that "birth from above," that sanctification of spirit, soul, and body, "without

which no man shall see the Lord." (And baptism symbolizes the beginning of this total spiritual transformation.)

3 ... Full of disease, the natural man fancies himself in perfect health. Imprisoned in misery and chains, he dreams that he is free. He says, "Peace, peace!" while the devil is in possession of his soul. He sleeps on, though hell's mouth is open to swallow him. A fire rages around him, and burns him, yet he is oblivious and unconcerned.

4 ... So, the sleeper is a sinner satisfied in his sins; content to remain in his fallen state, to live and die without the image of God. He is ignorant of his spiritual disease, and of its only remedy; he was never warned, or never heeded the warning, "to flee from the wrath to come"; he has never yet seen that he was in danger of hell, and has never cried out from the depths of his soul, "What must I do to be saved?"

5 ... If the sleeper is an outwardly respectable man, his sleep is usually the deepest of all. He may be the model of moderation, neither too hot nor too cold; a rational, inoffensive, good-natured man; one who practices a conventional, easy-going religion. Or he may be strict and zealous, self-righteous and judgmental in his practice of religion. [Either way, religious men are often the hardest to awake from sleep.]

6 ... The merely religious man has "a form of godliness, but not its power." And wherever true godliness manifests itself in power, this man is contemptuous, thinking it all fanaticism and superstition. Meanwhile, this wretched self-deceiver thanks God that he is not a common, low-life sinner. No, he does no harm to anyone; indeed, he does all the good he can. And he is religious: He uses all the means of grace; he is regular at church and sacrament; he even tithes and fasts. Based on the righteousness of the law, he is blameless. He lacks nothing of godliness, but its

power; nothing of religion, but its spirit; nothing of Christianity, but its truth and life.

7 ... No matter how esteemed among men such a 'Christian' may be, he is an abomination in God's sight, subject to all the denunciations leveled against the hypocritical scribes and Pharisees of old by Jesus himself. Jesus rightly compares him to a "white-washed tomb": beautiful on the outside, but inside full of dead men's bones and rottenness. He is religious on the *outside*, but *inside* the Spirit of the living God is absent. And "if any man has not the Spirit of Christ," he does not belong to Christ, but remains spiritually dead to this day.

8 ... This is another characteristic of the sleeper: He abides in death, and does not know it; he is dead to God, "dead in sins and trespasses." Scripture says: "By one man sin entered into the world, and death through sin; and so, death spread to all men," not just physical death, but spiritual death, death eternal. God said to Adam: "In the day that you eat [of the forbidden fruit], you shall surely die." You shall lose the life of your soul; you shall die to God; you shall be separated from him, who is the source of your life and happiness.

9 ... Thus was first dissolved that vital union of our souls to God, so that amid physical life, we are spiritually dead. And so we remain till the second Adam [Christ], the living Spirit, raises the dead, the dead in sin. But before any dead soul can live, he must "hear the voice of the Son of God." He is made aware of his lostness, and aware that the sentence of death hangs over his head. He realizes that he is dead to God, and to all the things of God; he has no more power to live the real Christian life, than a corpse to function as a living man.

10 ... One who is dead in sin has no spiritual senses to discern good

and evil. "Having eyes, he sees not; having ears, he hears not." He does not "taste and see that the Lord is gracious," and he has not "handled the word of life." The soul that sleeps in death has no perception of things spiritual; he understands no such things.

11 ... And having no spiritual senses, no inlets of spiritual knowledge, the natural man cannot receive the things of God's Spirit; they are foolishness to him. He is not only ignorant of spiritual things, he denies their very existence. "How," he asks, "can these things be? How can anyone really *know* that he is alive to God?" Simple: Just as you can know that your body is now alive. Faith is the life of the soul; and if you have this life abiding in you, you need no other evidence than the divine consciousness, the witness of God's Spirit, which is far greater than ten thousand human witnesses.

12 ... If God's Spirit does not now bear witness with your spirit, that you are a child of God, I pray that he may powerfully convince you that you are a poor unawakened sinner, a child of the devil still. I pray that, as I am preaching, "there may be a noise and a shaking"; that the Spirit "may breathe on these dry bones, that they may live!" Sinners, do not harden your hearts and resist God's Spirit, who even now has come to convince you of sin, "because you believe not on the name of the only Son of God."

II / 1 ... "Awake, O sleeper, arise from the dead." God is calling you now, through me; he is calling you to know yourself, to know your true spiritual state and your foremost concern here below. Arise, you sinner, call on God, that you might not perish. A hellish tempest is stirred up around you; you are sinking in the depths of God's judgments. If you would escape, you must cast yourself into them. Judge yourself [and repent], lest God judge you [and you perish].

2 ... Awake, arise! Avoid the Lord's fury; lay hold of the Lord, your

righteousness and your mighty salvation. Let the earthquake of God's threats shake you; cry out, with the trembling [Philippian] jailer, "What must I do to be saved?" And never rest until you believe on the Lord Jesus, with a faith which is his gift, his Spirit working that faith in you.

3 ... If I am speaking to any of you, more than to others, it is to you who assume you have no need of my message. Believe me, "I do have a message from God for you." I am warning you "to flee from the wrath to come." You are like condemned Peter, lying in a dark dungeon, bound with chains. The day is dawning when you will face execution. Yet, despite these dreadful circumstances, you are fast asleep; asleep in the devil's arms, on the brink of hell, in the jaws of everlasting damnation!

4 ... May the angel of the Lord come to you, and a light shine in your prison! May you feel the power of the Lord raising you and saying, "Get up quickly, throw on your clothes, put on your sandals, and follow me."

5 ... You are a spirit created for eternity; awake from your dreams of happiness in this world! God created you for himself; you will never find rest till you find rest in him! This world is not your home; you are but a stranger and sojourner here; a creature of a day, just launching out into eternity. But eternity depends on this very moment; an eternity of happiness or misery!

6 ... In what state is your soul? Were God to require it of you this very moment, are you ready to face death and judgment? Can you stand in the light of God's purity? Are you fit to "receive the inheritance of the saints in light?" Have you "fought the good fight, and kept the faith?" Have you secured the one thing needful? Have you recovered the holy image of God? Have you put off the old humanity, and put on the new? Are you clothed in the righteousness of Christ?

7 ... Have you oil in your lamp, grace in your heart? Do you "love the Lord your God with all your heart, mind, soul, and strength"? Is "the mind which was in Christ" also in you? Are you a Christian indeed; that is, a new creation? "Are old things passed away, and all things become new?"

8 ... Are you now "a partaker of the divine nature"? Do you know that God "dwells in you, and you in God"? Do you know that "your body is a temple of the Holy Spirit"? Do you have God's witness within, the first installment of your divine inheritance? Have you "received the Holy Spirit," or are you startled by that question, not sure there is such a thing?

9 ... If talk of the Holy Spirit offends you, you may be sure that you are not a Christian, nor do you desire to be one. No, you have turned the familiar collect of the Church into sin; you have mocked God by praying for "the inspiration of the Holy Spirit," when you do not really believe in such a thing.

10 ... On the authority of scripture and the Church [of England], I repeat the question: "Have you received the Holy Spirit?" If not, you are not yet a Christian. A Christian is one who is "anointed with the Holy Spirit and power." Pure religion is a participation in the divine nature; the life of God in the soul of man; Christ formed in the heart, the hope of glory; happiness and holiness; heaven begun on earth. It is not an outward thing, but righteousness, peace, and joy; the kingdom of God brought into the soul; the peace of God that passes all understanding; joy unspeakable and full of glory!

11 ... Do you not know that, in Christ, outward things (like circumcision) are marginal? What is important is a faith that is active through love, a faith that leads to a new creation. What is necessary is that inward change, that spiritual birth, that life from the dead, that holiness. And without that, no man shall see the Lord.

Are you laboring after it? Are you "working out your salvation in fear and trembling?" Are you "agonizing to enter in at the narrow gate?" Are you in earnest about your soul? Can you honestly tell God, the searcher of hearts, "Lord, you know that I love you!"

12 ... I know you hope to be saved, but what reason do you have for that hope? Is it only because you have done no harm, and done much good? Is it because, unlike other men, you are wise and honest and morally good, with an excellent reputation in the community? None of this will ever bring you to God; it is all less than nothing to him. Do you know Jesus Christ, whom God has sent? Has he taught you that "by grace we are saved through faith"? Do you believe "that Jesus Christ came into the world to save sinners"? Is that faithful saying the ground of your hope? Do you understand that Jesus "came not to call the righteous, but sinners to repentance"? Do you acknowledge that you are a sinner, a lost sheep, dead in sin and facing damnation? Do you realize all that you lack and what you really deserve from God? Are you repentant, mourning for God, and refusing all comfort apart from God? Are you the prodigal son finally come to his senses? Are you ready now to live a godly life in Christ, willing to suffer persecution and slander for the sake of Christ?

13 ... I pray that in all these questions you may hear the voice of God that wakes the dead; and feel the hammer of scripture which breaks hard hearts in pieces. Awake, O sleeper, from spiritual death, that you may not sleep in death eternal! Feel your lostness and arise from the dead. Leave your old companions in sin and death and follow Jesus into newness of life. Save yourself from this wicked world. "Come out from among them and be separate."

III / 1 ... And "Christ will give you light." How encouraging is this promise: that whoever obeys his call cannot seek him in vain! If you awake from your spiritual stupor, and arise from the death of sin, Christ has promised to give you light. "The Lord will give you grace and glory"; the light of his grace here and now, and the light of his glory hereafter. "God, who commanded the light to shine out of darkness, will shine in your heart; to give the knowledge of the glory of God in the face of Jesus Christ." And on that day, it will be said to you, "Rise, shine; for your light has come, and the glory of the Lord is risen on you." And Christ, the true light, will reveal himself in you!

2 ... God is light and will give himself to every awakened sinner who awaits him; and Christ himself will "dwell in your heart by faith." "Being rooted and grounded in love, you will comprehend with all the saints" the incredible fullness of the love of Christ.

3 ... You know what God is calling you to, my brothers. We are called to be a "dwelling of God through his Spirit"; to be saints on earth and saints in heaven. How great are the promises made by God to us who believe the gospel!

4 ... The Spirit of Christ is God's great gift, which, at different times and in different ways, he has promised mankind; and has fully given to mankind since Christ was glorified. Promises made to saints of old, God has fulfilled in the time of Christ: "I will put my Spirit within you and cause you to walk in my statutes." "I will pour my Spirit and blessing on your offspring."

5 ... You may all be living witnesses of these things; of the forgiveness of sins and the gift of the Holy Spirit. If only you believe, all things are possible. So, I ask you, in the name of Jesus, if you believe that God is still mighty to save, that he is the same yesterday, today, and forever? If so, be of good cheer: God, for Christ's sake, has forgiven you; you are now *justified* freely through faith. And

you shall also be *sanctified* through faith in Jesus and shall testify that "God has given us eternal life, and this life is in his Son."

6 ... May I speak freely to you now? Will you allow this word of exhortation from one who is little esteemed in the Church? Your conscience bears witness that what I have preached is true, if you have experienced the grace of God personally. This experiential knowledge, and this alone, is true Christianity. He who has received the Spirit of Christ is a Christian; he who has not is not. Nor is it possible to have received the Spirit, and not know it. This is the "Spirit of truth, whom the world cannot receive, because it does not see or know him. But you do know him, for he dwells with you and in you."

7 ... The world cannot receive him, but utterly rejects God's promise, contradicting and blaspheming it. Every soul who rejects the Spirit of God is no man of God; indeed, he manifests the spirit of Antichrist, which is abroad in the world. Whoever denies the inspiration of the Holy Spirit is Antichrist. And he is Antichrist who denies that the indwelling Spirit is the common privilege of *all* believers, the unspeakable gift of the gospel, the universal promise, and the criterion of a real Christian.

8 ... It does not help them to say, "We do not deny that the Spirit may sometimes *assist* a Christian; but we will not stand for talk of *receiving* the Spirit, or *being filled* with the Spirit, or *being moved* by the Spirit, or even of *feeling* the Spirit; there is no place in rational religion for any of this." But in denying these, you deny the whole of scripture, the whole truth and promise of God.

9 ... Our own excellent Church knows nothing of such verbal contortions; it plainly speaks of the powerful influence of the Spirit in the life of the believer. It teaches us all to pray for the "inspiration of the Holy Spirit," and that we may "be filled with

the Holy Spirit." Every minister is said to receive the Holy Spirit by the laying on of hands. So, to deny any of this is to renounce the Church of England and the whole Christian revelation.

10 ... But the wisdom of God always was foolishness with man. No wonder then that the great mystery of the gospel should be hidden now from the sophisticated elites, as it was in olden times; that it should be almost universally denied, ridiculed, and attacked; and that all who still profess it are dismissed as fanatics and lunatics. This is nothing but that falling away from God, that apostasy which was prophesied, and that even now has overspread the earth. Look no further than England to see the devastation of unbridled godlessness! What multiplied wrongdoing of every kind is committed daily, too often with impunity, by those who scoff at sin and glory in their shame! Who can number the profanities and blasphemies; the lies, slanders, and evil-speaking; the Sabbath-breaking, gluttony, and drunkenness; the prostitution, adultery, and promiscuity; the injustice, oppression, and revenge, which cover our land like a flood!

11 ... And even among those who are not guilty of the more serious sins, how much anger and pride; how much idleness, softness, and self-indulgence; how much covetousness and ambition; how much thirst of praise, love of the world, and fear of public opinion is to be found! And how little of true religion! Where can you find the man who loves either God or neighbor? On the one hand, there are those who have not even the form of godliness; on the other, those who have the form only. The first group have virtually no concern about religion; the second group have made religion into a lifeless form, a dull round of outward performances, without inward faith or love or joy in God!

12 ... Would to God that this university were an exception! Friends, my hope and prayer for all of us is that this place might be an island of godliness in a sea of sin. But is it? God knows, and you

know, it is not! We have not kept ourselves pure; too few of us really understand the gospel; too few worship God in spirit and truth. We are a generation that does not hold fast to God. He has called us to be "the salt of the earth; but the salt has lost its savor, and is good for nothing, but to be thrown out."

13 ... And shall the Lord not be avenged on a people like this? How soon may he take his sword against us? He has given us ample time to repent, but his judgments are abroad in the earth even now. We have every reason to expect the heaviest judgment of all, unless we heartily repent, and return to the principles of the Reformation, the truth and simplicity of the gospel. Perhaps we are even now resisting the last efforts of divine grace to save us. Perhaps we have nearly exhausted God's patience, by rejecting his pleas and ignoring his messengers.

14 ... O God, "in the midst of wrath, remember mercy!" Be glorified in our reformation, not our destruction! Let us acknowledge your judgment on our sin and let us learn your righteousness!

15 ... My friends, it is high time for us to awake out of sleep; "before the great trumpet of the Lord be blown," and our land become a field of blood. May we speedily see the things that lead to our salvation, before they are hidden from our eyes! Help us, deliver us, be merciful to us! Turn us toward you, O Lord of hosts! Let us live and never turn back from you!

"Now to him who is able to do far more than we could ever ask or think, by his power at work within us, be glory in the Church, through Christ, forever and ever." .

Preached at Oxford University,
April 1742, by Rev. Charles Wesley

4

SCRIPTURAL CHRISTIANITY

And they were all filled with the Holy Spirit.
—Acts 4:31

1 ... That same statement occurs in Acts 2: "On the day of Pentecost, they were all together, in one accord. Suddenly there came a sound from heaven, like a mighty rushing wind; tongues of fire appeared above each of them; and they were all filled with the Holy Spirit. They began to speak in other tongues," so that all the foreigners "heard them speak, in their own tongues, the wonderful works of God."

2 ... In Acts 4, we read that when the believers had been praying and praising God, "their place of assembly was shaken, and they were all filled with the Holy Spirit." There was no visible manifestation, as on Pentecost; no extraordinary gifts of the Spirit were bestowed, such as healing, prophecy, discerning of spirits, speaking in tongues or interpreting them.

3 ... Whether these spiritual gifts were intended to remain in the Church for all time, or whether they will only be restored near the end time, are questions we need not consider here. But we should notice that, even in the early Church, God bestowed them sparingly. Even then, were all believers prophets, or miracle-workers,

or healers, or speakers in tongues? No, not all—perhaps not one in a thousand. It was probably only the teachers of the Church, and only some of them. So, it was for a more excellent purpose that *all* the believers were filled with the Holy Spirit.

4 ... The fullness of the Spirit was meant to impart those things which are absolutely essential to every Christian in every age. The Spirit imparts the mind of Christ and the fruits of the Spirit ("love, joy, peace, patience, gentleness, goodness"), without which we do not belong to Christ. The Spirit fills believers with faithfulness, meekness, and temperance; he enables them to crucify their fleshly desires; and, because of that *inward* change, he enables them to fulfill all *outward* righteousness, "to walk as Christ walked."

5 ... So, without needless curiosity concerning the *extraordinary* gifts of the Spirit, let us look more closely at his *ordinary* gifts to all believers; we can be certain that these are operative in all ages. Let us examine God's great work among men, called Christianity—not as a system of doctrines, but as a living work in the hearts and lives of men. Let us consider it from three perspectives: (1) as beginning to exist in individuals; (2) as spreading from one to another; and (3) as covering the earth.

I / 1 ... First, let us consider Christianity as it began to exist in individuals. Imagine a person who heard Peter preaching repentance and forgiveness of sins; he was struck by the gospel message, was convicted of his sin, repented, and believed in Jesus. His faith itself was a gift of God's grace, the very essence of things hoped for, the irrefutable evidence of things unseen; and by this faith, the new believer instantly received the Spirit of adoption, whereby he could call Jesus 'Lord,' the Spirit convincing him that he was now a child of God. He could now truly say, "I live not, but Christ lives in me; and the life I now live in the flesh, I live by faith in the Son of God, who loved me and gave himself for me."

2 ... This was the very essence of his faith, a divine evidence or conviction of the love of God the Father, through his beloved Son, to him a sinner, now accepted in Christ. And "being justified by faith, he had peace with God," a peace beyond rational understanding, a peace that kept his heart and mind from all doubt and fear, through knowing Christ. He could now stand fast, fearing not what man could do to him, knowing that he was under God's care; fearing not the powers of darkness, knowing that God was the victor; fearing not death itself, knowing that Christ had destroyed its power over man and delivered him from its bondage.

3 ... And now, his spirit rejoiced in God his Savior—unimaginable joy in Christ, who had redeemed him by his blood, forgiven his sins, and reconciled him to the Father. He rejoiced in the witness of God's Spirit within, and (even more) in the hope of someday sharing God's glory—the hope of a full renewal of his soul in righteousness and true holiness, and the hope of receiving a crown of glory.

4 ... "The love of God was also shed abroad in his heart, by the Spirit which was given to him." Through the Spirit of his Son, the loving Father had pardoned the sinner and claimed him as his own; and now he returned that love to God as a son. God was now his whole desire and joy, in time and eternity.

5 ... He who thus loved God could not but love his brother also, "not in word only, but in deed and truth." As God loved us, we must love others. This love must embrace all humanity, including those we have never met, those we know little about (except that Christ died for them), those who are evil or irreligious, and even those who hate and persecute us for our faith in Christ. Christ himself had a special place in his heart and prayers for these—as much as for us.

6 ... God's love in the believer is never proud; it humbles every soul in which it dwells. So, this [theoretical] believer was lowly of heart, small and flawed in his own estimation. He never sought or received the praise of men, but only that which came from God. He was patient and gentle, faithful and true, temperate in all things. He was "crucified to the world, and the world to him." By God's overpowering love within, he was saved from passion and vanity, from ambition and covetousness, and from every unchristian trait.

7 ... Obviously, he who had this love in his heart would do no evil to his neighbor. He would not knowingly, purposely harm any man; he was never cruel, unjust, or unkind. He carefully guarded his lips, lest he should offend in speech; he would not lie, mislead, deceive, or defame any man.

8 ... And he was deeply conscious of his total dependence on God, of his need to be continually nurtured by God; and thus, he used daily all the ordinances of God, God's stated means of grace to man: "The apostles' doctrine," feeding his mind with sound teaching; "the breaking of bread," feeding his soul on the body of Christ; and "the prayers," offered up by the whole congregation. And thus, he grew in grace, increasing in strength, and in the knowledge and love of God.

9 ... But it was not enough to abstain from doing evil; his soul was on fire to do good. Since Jesus went about doing good, should his disciple not follow in his steps? As he had opportunity, therefore, if he could do no good of a higher kind, at least he could feed the hungry, clothe the naked, help the orphan and stranger, visit and assist the sick and those in prison. It was his joy to work and sacrifice for them; he was more than willing to deny himself in order to help them. He remembered the words of Jesus: "As you have done it to one of the least of these, you have done it unto me."

10 ... Such was Christianity in its beginning; such was a Christian in ancient times. Such was every one of those who, when threatened, lifted their voice to God, and were filled with the Holy Spirit. All the believers were of one heart and soul; the love of Christ constrained them to love one another. None clung selfishly to his own possessions, but shared them freely with his family in Christ. So fully were they crucified to the world, and the world to them! "And they continued steadfastly with one accord in the apostles' doctrine, in the breaking of bread, and in prayer." "Great grace was upon them all, and there were none among them that lacked. For the wealthy laid their wealth at the apostles' feet, and distribution was made to every man according to his need."

II / 1 ... Now, let us look at Christianity, spreading from one to another, gradually making its way into the world. It was God's will that Christianity should not be "a candle lit, then put under a basket, but that it might give light to all in the house." Our Lord had declared to his first disciples, "You are the light of the world. Let your light shine, that all may see your good works, and glorify your Father in heaven."

2 ... Can you imagine those early believers, looking out on a whole wicked world, and being unconcerned about all those for whom Christ died? Could they stand idly by, even if there were no direct command from the Lord? Would they not endeavor, by all possible means, "to pluck some of these twigs from the fire"? Surely, they would. They would spare no effort to bring back some of those poor "lost sheep to the great Shepherd of their souls."

3 ... And the early Christians did exactly this. They endeavored "to do good to all men," warning them to flee from the wrath to come; now, now to escape damnation! They declared that

God's patience was at an end; that he "now called all men everywhere to repent," to turn from their evil ways, lest iniquity be their ruin. They explained God's righteousness—the opposite of their sinfulness; and they warned of God's wrath—his final judgment on evildoers.

4 ... They attempted to speak to each person's individual need. To the careless, who lay unconcerned in spiritual darkness, they boldly thundered, "Awake, you sleeper, arise from the dead, and Christ will give you light." But to those already awakened, and groaning under a sense of God's wrath, they offered a Savior: "We have an Advocate with the Father; he is the propitiation for our sins." And those who already believed, they encouraged and challenged to a life of love and good works, and of increasing "holiness, without which no one can see the Lord."

5 ... And their labor was not in vain in the Lord. The gospel of Christ spread rapidly, mightily, gloriously! But the more it spread, the more it was opposed. The world in general was offended because the Christians condemned its evil ways. Men of pleasure were offended because the Christians claimed a higher knowledge of God, a closer kinship to God; they lived to a higher standard, shunning the world's enticements; and, what was most galling, they made converts among their worldly companions, who would no longer join them in their sinful pleasures! Men of reputation were offended, because, as the gospel spread, they declined in the esteem of the people, no longer receiving flattery and the honor due to God alone. Certain men of trade were offended when the gospel prevailed, and their goods were no longer in demand. Above all, men of religion (external, worldly religion), were offended, and complained at every opportunity about "these pestilent fellows, these who cause upheaval throughout the world." "These are the ones who teach all men everywhere against our traditional religion."

6 ... So it was that the storm clouds gathered. The more Christianity spread, the more it was opposed; more and more were enraged against these "men who turned the world upside down." Some were actually calling for the Christians' death, and believed that they who killed them were doing God's will.

7 ... Meanwhile, "this sect was everywhere spoken against"; people maligned them just as they had the prophets before them. Whatever the vicious rumor, many would believe it. In God's time, full-fledged persecution erupted. For a while, it was just shame and reproach; then, the trashing of their goods; then, trials and beatings, chains and dungeons; and finally, martyrs' deaths.

8 ... Despite the persecution, hell was being shaken and the kingdom of God continued its spread. Sinners everywhere were turned "from darkness to light, from the power of Satan to God." God gave his children an irresistible message, and their lives matched their message. But above all, it was their brave and godly sufferings, of every kind, that spoke to receptive hearts in the world. And when, having fought the good fight, they were led as sheep to the slaughter, offering their lives as a sacrifice to their faith, it was their blood that testified powerfully to the heathen.

9 ... Thus did Christianity spread across the earth. But how soon did weeds appear with the wheat, iniquity along with godliness. How soon did Satan find a place in the Church; how soon were the faithful dishonored! This sad story has been told again and again, across the generations, by faithful witnesses whom God has raised up to exhort and challenge an unfaithful Church. Yet despite its deterioration and corruption, it was evident that God "had built his Church upon a rock, and the gates of hell would not (completely) prevail against it."

III / 1 ... But shall we not see much greater things yet? Can Satan cause the truth of God to fail, or his promises to be of no effect? No, the time will come when Christianity will prevail and cover the earth. So, let us contemplate this strange sight: a Christian world! The ancient prophets searched diligently after this, and the Spirit within them testified: "In the last days, the Lord's house shall be established and exalted, and all nations shall flow to it. And nation shall not lift up sword against nation." "In that day, the Root of Jesse shall be a banner to the people. The Gentiles will be drawn to it, and his reign will be glorious." "The wolf shall dwell with the lamb, the leopard with the kid, the calf and the young lion together; and a little child shall lead them. For the earth shall be full of the knowledge of the Lord."

2 ... Similarly, the apostle Paul uttered prophetic words which have yet to be fulfilled: "Has God cast off his people Israel?" Never! "But through their failure, salvation has come to the Gentiles." "And if their humbling brings spiritual riches to the Gentiles, how much more will their exaltation?" "Consider this mystery: A certain blindness has come upon Israel until the full number of Gentiles have entered in. Then, all Israel will be saved."

3 ... Suppose that the fullness of time has come, and the prophecies have been fulfilled. What a prospect! All is peace and quiet: no armies, no blood, no destruction, no war. Nor is there any civil unrest: no brother rising against brother; no country or city divided against itself, tearing itself to pieces. Discord is at an end forever, and none is left to hurt or destroy his neighbor. There is no oppression, no extortion, no robbery, no injustice; for all are content with what they have. So, "righteousness and peace have kissed each other—righteousness flourishing out of the earth, and peace looking down from heaven."

4 ... And with righteousness, mercy is found. The Lord has destroyed the blood-thirsty and malicious, the envious and vengeful. If there were provocations, there is no one to return evil for evil; but, in fact, there are no provocations, for no one does evil, all are harmless as doves. And being filled with peace and joy in believing, and united in one body, by one Spirit, they all live and love as family, they are all of one heart and soul. No one clings selfishly to his possessions, so no one among them lacks the necessities; everyone loves his neighbor as himself and does to others as he would have them do to him.

5 ... It follows, that no unkind word can ever be heard among them; no contention, no verbal abuse, no evil-speaking. Likewise, they are incapable of fraud or guile; their love is genuine; their words are honest expressions of their thoughts; and their hearts are full of love and God.

6 ... So, where the Lord omnipotent reigns, he "subdues all things to himself," causes every heart to overflow with love, and fills every mouth with praise. "Blessed are the people who have the Lord for their God." "Arise, shine, for your light has come, and the glory of the Lord has risen upon you." "I, the Lord, am your Savior and Redeemer, the mighty God of Jacob. Violence and destruction shall no more be heard in your land." "Your people are all righteous, the vine of my planting, the work of my hands, that I may be glorified." "The Lord shall be your everlasting light, and your God shall be your glory."

Having considered Christianity as beginning, continuing, and finally covering the earth, I now close with a practical application.

IV / 1 ... First, I ask, where does this kind of Christianity now exist? Where do such Christians live? In which country are all the people filled with the Holy Spirit? Where are all of one heart and mind? Where does every man have what he needs, because all men have the love of God and neighbor filling their hearts? Where do all show mercy, humility, gentleness, and patience? Where do none offend, by word or deed, against justice, mercy, or truth? Where do all men do to others what they would have others do to them? Can any nation be called a Christian nation, unless it can be described like this? Let us be honest: There has never been such a nation anywhere, ever!

2 ... I urge you, friends, to bear with me, even if you consider me a fanatic or a fool. It is important that someone speak plainly to you, especially now. For who knows whether these may be the last times? Who knows when the righteous Judge may say, "I will no longer hear prayers for this people"? And who will speak plainly, if I do not? Therefore, I will speak, and implore you, by the living God: Do not harden your hearts against receiving a blessing, even at my hands. Do not say to yourselves that you will not be convinced by me, even though my message is convincing. Do not say, "Lord, anybody but Wesley; we would rather perish than be saved by that man's message!"

3 ... Friends, surely you would not think that way. So, let me ask you, in love and humility: Is this a Christian city? Is scriptural Christianity found here? Are we, as a college community, so filled with the Holy Spirit, as to enjoy in our hearts and to show forth in our lives the genuine fruits of the Spirit? Are all the officials of our university, all our faculty and students, not to mention the townspeople, of one heart and mind? Is "the love of God shed abroad in all our hearts"? Do all have the mind of Christ, and lives that reflect Christ? Are we all "holy as he who has called us is holy"?

4 ... I want you to observe that I am not speaking here about any peculiar notions or doubtful opinions, but rather about the fundamental teachings of Christianity, to which we all subscribe.

And so, for your answer to these questions, I appeal to your own conscience, guided by the word of God. If God, through conscience and scripture, does not convict you of falling short, then neither do I.

5 ... In the fearful presence of the great God, before whom we will all soon appear, I humbly ask you who are in authority over us, whose offices I highly regard: Are you "filled with the Holy Spirit"? Are you living representatives of him, whose authority you reflect? In your office, do you remind us of "the Lord our governor"? Are all your thoughts, feelings, and desires suitable to your high calling, your words like the words of God? In all your actions, is there both dignity and love—an indefinable greatness which can only flow from a heart filled with God, but also a humility which comes from a frank acknowledgement of one's flawed humanity?

6 ... Now, you esteemed faculty, who are specifically called to mold the pliable minds of youth, to dispel ignorance and error, to train them up to salvation: Are you "filled with the Holy Spirit" and the fruits of the Spirit, which your important office so indispensably requires? Is your heart full of God, full of love and zeal to establish his kingdom on earth? Do you continually remind your students that the one rational goal of all education is to know, love, and serve "the only true God, and Jesus Christ whom he has sent"? Do you drill into them daily that love alone never fails; that ecstatic emotions and philosophic wisdom will both vanish; that, without love, all learning is but splendid ignorance, pompous folly, and vexation of spirit? Does all your teaching tend toward the love of God and neighbor? Are your courses designed to equip your students, as young soldiers of Christ, to be bright and shining lights, reflecting and advancing the gospel of Christ, wherever they go, whatever they do? And permit me to ask: Do you give your all to the important work you have undertaken, exerting every aspect of your being, using every talent which God has lent you, to the very limit of your power?

7 ... Do not think that I am speaking as if all your students were intending to be clergy. No, I am speaking as if all were intending to be Christians. But what example are we setting, we who comfortably enjoy the fruits of our forefathers' sacrifice? Friends, do we abound in the fruits of the Spirit: in humility and self-denial; in seriousness and composure of spirit; in patience and temperance; in unwearied endeavors to do good of every kind to every man, relieving their physical needs, and bringing them to the knowledge and love of God? Is this a general description of the faculty here? I fear not. Instead, we have been accused (even by our friends, and with good reason) of pride and haughtiness, impatience and peevishness, gluttony and sensuality, laziness and uselessness. O that God would remove this reproach from us!

8 ... Many of us on the faculty are ordained to the holy ministry of God. Are we examples to the others "in speech, conduct, love, spirit, faith, purity"? Is our one aim "holiness to the Lord"? What motivated us to be ordained to the ministry? Was it for the sole purpose of serving God? Trusting that we were divinely called to this ministry, was it to glorify God and edify his people? Are we determined, by God's grace, to give ourselves wholly to this ministry? Have we forsaken, as far as we are able, all worldly cares and studies, applying ourselves completely to our ministry? Are we gifted to teach? Are we taught by God, that we may teach others? Do we know God and his Son, Jesus Christ? Has God himself "made us ministers of the new covenant"? Where then are the evidences of our ministry? Who, that were dead in sin, have been enlivened by our ministry? Do we have a burning zeal to save souls from death? Do we speak the truth plainly "to every man's conscience in the sight of God"? Are we dead to the world, and the things of the world, "laying up all our treasure in heaven"? Do we lord it over God's people, or do we have servant hearts? When we bear the reproach of Christ, does it weigh heavy on us, or do we

rejoice? When slapped on one cheek, are we angry? Or do we turn the other to be slapped also, thereby overcoming evil with good? Do we have a sharp and bitter spirit toward those who are in the wrong, or do we deal with them humbly, lovingly, appropriately?

9 ... Finally, what shall we say of you students? Do you have even the form of godliness, much less its power? Are you humble and teachable; or are you stubborn, cocky, and self-willed? Are you obedient to your superiors; or are you contemptuous of those whom you should respect? Are you diligent in your studies; do you manage your time so as to crowd as much work in a day as possible? Or must you admit that you waste your time, either in reading worthless books, or gambling, or whatever? Do you manage your money any better than you manage your time, or are you continually in debt? Do you keep the Sabbath holy; do you spend it in worship and devotion? When in church, are you truly conscious of the presence of God? Are you stewards of your own bodies; or are you guilty of drunkenness and moral laxness, even bragging about your shameful behavior? Do many of you not "take the name of God in vain," habitually, without remorse or fear? Do many of you not swear falsely? (I confess, before God and this congregation, that I myself have been guilty of this. I have thoughtlessly sworn to follow rules and regulations that I had not so much as read. I admit that it was a form of perjury, and therefore sinful. And I acknowledge that the Most High took notice of it!)

10 ... Is it not true that many of you are triflers—triflers with God, triflers with one another, triflers with your own souls? How few of you spend even an hour a week in private prayer! How few of you ever think of God, as you live your lives! Who of you have any acquaintance with the Holy Spirit, and his supernatural work in the souls of men? Are you open to any discussion of the Spirit, except now and then, in church? Would you not think, if someone initiated

such a conversation, that he was either a hypocrite or a fanatic? God Almighty, what kind of religion do you have, if you are not open to basic Christian teaching? O, my friends, how far we are from being a Christian city! "It is time for you, O Lord, to strike us!"

11 ... What possibility is there that scriptural Christianity should again become the religion of this place; that all classes of people here should speak and live as people "filled with the Holy Spirit"? And by whom should this Christianity be restored, if not by you in authority? But are you convinced that this *is* scriptural Christianity; do you truly want it restored; are you willing to sacrifice all to see it restored? [I fear not.] But supposing you did want it restored, do you have the power to do it? Perhaps some of you have made a few feeble attempts, but with little success! Shall Christianity, then, be restored by young, unknown, insignificant men [like the Methodists on campus]? I do not know whether you could stand that! You would surely cry out, "Young men, by doing this, you make us look bad!" But Christianity has not yet been restored here, and iniquity covers us like a flood. What then shall God send to restore us to our first love? Shall he send famine or plague, his most extreme messengers, to a guilty land? Or shall he send the sword—perhaps the Catholic armies [of Spain or France]? "No, Lord! Let us fall into your hands, and not into the hands of men."

Lord, save us, or we perish! Let us not sink in the mire! Help us against our enemies, for no one else can help! But, with you, all things are possible! With your great power, save us who are dying; and save us in the way you choose; not as we will, but as you will!

Preached at St. Mary's, Oxford University, August 1744

5

JUSTIFICATION BY FAITH

To him who does not work, but simply believes on him who justifies the ungodly, his faith is counted as righteousness.

—ROMANS 4:5

1 ... How a sinner may be justified before God, the Lord and Judge of all, is a question of the greatest importance to every person. It is the foundation of all our hope, since, while we are alienated from God, we can have no peace or joy, in time or eternity. What peace can there be, while our own hearts condemn us—much less the One who is greater than our hearts? And what joy can there be, in this world or the next, while "the wrath of God abides on us"?

2 ... And yet how little this question has been understood! What confused notions have many had concerning it! And not only confused, but often utterly false, as contrary to truth as light is to darkness; notions that are absolutely contrary to scripture and the whole analogy of faith. And when the foundation itself is wrong, it cannot be built upon; at least, there can be no worthy and enduring structure, but only that which is unacceptable to God and worthless to man.

3 ... In order to do justice to the importance of this subject; to save those, who sincerely seek the truth, from the pointless clatter and clutter of words; to clear the confusion into which many have

already fallen; and to give them a clear understanding of this great mystery of godliness; I shall try to show: (1) the background of the doctrine of justification; (2) what justification is; (3) who the justified are; and (4) on what terms they are justified.

I / 1 ... First, what is the background of the doctrine of justification? Man was made in the image of God; he was made holy, merciful, and perfect, just like our great Creator and Father in heaven. Man dwelt in God's love; God's love dwelt in man. God made him "an image of his own eternity," the very picture of the glorious God. He was pure, as God is pure, from every taint of sin. He knew no evil, but was inwardly and outwardly sinless and undefiled. He "loved the Lord his God with all his heart, mind, soul, and strength."

2 ... To this perfect man, God gave a perfect law, to which he required perfect obedience. He required full obedience at every point, from the moment man became a living soul, till the time of his trial was over. No allowance was made for falling short, but there was no need of any. Man was altogether equal to the task assigned, thoroughly furnished for every good word and work.

3 ... To the law of love which was written in his heart, it seemed good to the sovereign wisdom of God to add one outward law: "You shall not eat from the tree in the midst of the garden." And he added this penalty: "In the day you do eat from it, you shall die."

4 ... Such was the state of man in Paradise. By the free, unmerited love of God, he was holy and happy. He knew God, loved God, and enjoyed God, which is the essence of eternal life. And in this life of love, he was meant to continue forever, if he continued to obey God in all things. But if he disobeyed him in anything, he was to forfeit all. "In that day, you shall surely die."

5 ... Man did disobey God. He did eat from the forbidden tree and was condemned by the righteous judgment of God. The penalty he had been warned of began to take effect. The moment he tasted that fruit, he died—his soul died, separated from God, separated from the source of its life. His body, likewise, became subject to decay and death. And now being dead in spirit, dead to God, dead in sin, he hastened on to death everlasting, to the destruction of body and soul, in the fire unquenchable.

6 ... Thus, "by one man, sin entered the world, and death through sin passed on to all men." All humanity was included in the sin of Adam, the father and representative of us all. "Through the offence of one," all are dead, dead to God, dead in sin, dwelling in a body in decay, soon to die, and under the sentence of eternal death. Yes, by Adam's disobedience, all were made sinners, and fell under the judgment of God.

7 ... It was in this state that humanity found itself, when "God so loved the world, that he gave his only Son, that we might not perish, but have everlasting life." In the fullness of time, he was made man, a second representative and father of all humanity, a second Adam. And so it was that "he bore our griefs, the Lord laying on him the iniquities of us all." He was "wounded for our transgressions and bruised for our iniquities"; "he bore our sins in his own body on the tree." And through his self-sacrifice, once offered, he has redeemed me and all mankind, having "made a full, perfect, and sufficient sacrifice and satisfaction for the sins of the whole world."

8 ... In consideration that the Son of God has "tasted death for every man," God has now "reconciled the world to himself, not imputing to them their trespasses." As the *offence* of *one* man brought *judgment* on humanity, so the *righteousness* of *one* Man brought the free gift of *justification* on humanity. For the sake of

his beloved Son, of what he has suffered and sacrificed for us, God now intends to grant, on one condition only (a condition which he himself enables us to perform): the remission of punishment for our sins, our reinstatement to his favor, and the restoration of our dead souls to spiritual life—all as a down-payment on his promise of life eternal.

9 ... This then is the background of the doctrine of justification. By the sin of the *first* Adam, the father and representative of us all, we all fell short of God's favor; we all became children of wrath; "judgment came upon all men to condemnation." Likewise, by the sacrifice for sin made by the *second* Adam, also the representative of us all, God was so far reconciled to the world, that he has given a new covenant. And when we fulfill his one plain condition, "there is no more condemnation"; instead, "we are justified freely by his grace, through the redemption that is in Jesus Christ."

II / 1 ... Second, what does it mean to be justified? What is justification? It is evident, from what has already been said, that justification is not being made actually just and righteous. No, that is sanctification; which, to some degree, is the immediate fruit of justification, but is nevertheless a distinct gift of God, and of a totally different nature. *Justification* implies what God does *for us* through his *Son; sanctification* implies what God works *in us* through his *Spirit*. Sometimes, justification may be used in so broad a sense as to include sanctification; but generally, they are sufficiently distinguished from one another by Paul and the other inspired writers.

2 ... The far-fetched notion that justification clears us from the accusation of Satan is not proven by any clear scriptural text. Neither that accuser nor his accusation is given any consideration

by Paul in all that he has written of justification, either in Romans or Galatians.

3 ... The notion that justification clears us from the accusation brought against us by the law is not so far-fetched, but still difficult to prove from scripture. It is an awkward sort of argument, but it does contain this truth: We all have transgressed the law of God, and thereby deserve damnation; but God does not inflict on those who are justified the punishment they deserve.

4 ... The most far-fetched notion of all is that God is deceived about those he justifies; that God thinks we *are* what, in fact, we *are not*. It implies that God judges us contrary to the real nature of things; that he thinks us better than we really are; that he believes us righteous when we are obviously unrighteous. Surely not. The judgment of the all-wise God is always according to truth. Neither is it consistent with his unerring wisdom, to think that *I* am innocent, to judge that *I* am righteous or holy, because Christ [my Savior] is. Any reasonable man, who considers this matter without prejudice, must admit that such a notion of justification goes against reason and scripture.

5 ... The plain scriptural notion of justification is pardon, the forgiveness of sins. It is that act of God the Father, whereby, for the sake of the blood-sacrifice of his Son, he "shows forth his righteousness (or mercy) by the remission of past sins." This is the simple, natural explanation of it consistently given by Paul. "Blessed is the man to whom the Lord will not impute sin." To him who is justified or forgiven, God will not count sin to his condemnation; he will not condemn him for his sin, in this world or the next. All his past sins, in thought, word, and deed, are covered over, blotted out, not to be remembered or mentioned against him, any more than if they had never been. God will not inflict on that sinner what he deserved to suffer, because his beloved Son has suffered for him. And from

the moment we are "accepted through the Beloved," "reconciled to God through his blood," he loves, blesses, and watches over us for good, just as if we had never sinned.

In just one place, Paul seems to extend the meaning of justification further, where he speaks of it in the future tense, meaning that our ultimate justification will occur on judgment day. Jesus also mentions something similar. But generally, when Paul speaks of justification, he is not speaking of those who have already run the race successfully [past], but of those who are just setting out to run the race of faith [present].

III / 1 ... Third, who are they who are justified? Paul is quite clear: the ungodly! God justifies the ungodly of every kind and degree, and none but the ungodly. "They that are righteous need no repentance," therefore they need no forgiveness. Only sinners need pardon; only sin needs to be forgiven. Forgiveness, then, has a direct reference to sin, and nothing else. It is our unrighteousness to which the pardoning God is merciful; it is our iniquity which he "remembers no more."

2 ... This seems to be not at all considered by those who so vehemently insist that a man must be sanctified (holy) *before* he can be justified; especially by those who contend that absolute holiness, total obedience, must precede justification. This notion is flatly impossible, for without a love for God we have no holiness, and there is no love for God except from a sense of God first loving us. This notion is also absurdly contradictory to itself: It is not the saint, but the sinner, who is forgiven; God justifies not the godly, but the ungodly; not the holy, but the unholy. On what condition God does this, we will consider shortly. But whatever it is, it cannot be holiness. To assert this, is to say that the Lamb of God takes

away only those sins which were already taken away, without him.

3 … Does the good Shepherd seek and save only those who are found already? No, he seeks and saves the lost; he pardons those who need his merciful pardon. He saves, from the guilt and power of sin, sinners of every kind and degree; men who, till then, were altogether ungodly; men in whom there was no love of God; men in whom there was nothing good, nothing truly Christian, but evil only, the fruits of the flesh (pride, anger, love of the world), which means "enmity against God."

4 … Those who are sick, whose sin is intolerable, are they who need the great Physician; those who are guilty, who groan under the wrath of God, are they that need a pardon. Those who are condemned already, both by God and their own conscience, for their ungodliness (in thought, word, and deed), cry aloud for him "who justifies the ungodly," through the redemption in Jesus. Yes, it is the ungodly who are saved, those who, prior to justification, have done nothing good, nothing truly virtuous or holy, but only evil continually. For his heart is necessarily, essentially evil, till the love of God is shed abroad within. And since the tree is corrupt, so are its fruits, "for an evil tree cannot bear good fruit."

5 … It may be objected, "But a man, *before* he is justified, may feed the hungry or clothe the naked; surely these count as 'good works.'" Yes, he may do these before he is justified, and they are, in one sense, 'good works,' helpful to other men. But they are not, strictly speaking, good in themselves, or good in the sight of God. All truly 'good works' (according to the Church of England) come *after* justification; they are therefore good and acceptable to God because they spring from a true and living faith in Christ. Likewise, all works done *before* justification are not good, in the Christian sense, because they do not spring from faith in Christ—though perhaps they may spring from some kind of faith in God. It may

sound strange, but even 'good works,' not done as God wills and commands, have the nature of sin.

6 ... Why can no works done before justification be truly and properly good? The argument runs thus: (1) No works are good which are not done as God wills and commands. (2) No works done before justification are done as God wills and commands. (3) Therefore, no works done before justification are good. The first proposition is self-evident. The second is plain and undeniable, if we consider that God has willed and commanded that all our works should be done in love, in that love to God which produces love to all mankind. But none of our works can be done in this love, until the love of the Father is in us; and this love cannot be in us till we receive the "Spirit of adoption, crying in our hearts, Abba, Father." So, if God does not justify the ungodly, the ones who have done nothing to deserve it, then Christ has died in vain; and, despite his death, no man can ever be justified.

IV / 1 ... Finally, on what terms is he justified, he who is altogether ungodly and does nothing truly good? On one term alone, and that is faith: He simply "believes in him who justifies the ungodly." "He who believes is not condemned, but is passed from death to life." "For the righteousness (or mercy) of God is by faith in Jesus Christ unto all who believe." "God has set forth Christ to be the atonement for sin, through faith in his blood." "We conclude that a man is justified by faith without the deeds of the law"; without previous obedience to the moral law, which he could not, till now, perform. It is the moral law, and that alone, which is intended here: "Do we make void the law through faith? No, we establish the law." What law do we establish by faith--the ritual, ceremonial law of Moses? No, but the great, unchangeable law of love, the holy love of God and neighbor.

2 ... Faith is a divine, supernatural evidence or conviction of things not discoverable by our physical senses. Justifying faith implies not only a divine conviction that "God was in Christ reconciling the world to himself"; but a sure trust and confidence that Christ died for *my* sins, that he loved *me,* and gave himself for *me.* And whenever a sinner believes this, whether young or old, God justifies that ungodly one; God, for the sake of his Son, pardons and absolves him who, till then, had nothing good in him. True, God had given him repentance before he believed, but it was simply a deep sense of the lack of good and the presence of evil. And whatever good he has or does, from the moment he first believes in God through Christ, faith does not *find in* him, but *brings to* him. Goodness is the fruit of faith; when the tree is good, the fruit is good also.

3 ... I cannot describe faith better than in the words of our own Church: "The only condition of salvation is faith, a sure trust and confidence that God *has* forgiven and *will* forgive our sins, that he has accepted us again into his favor, for the sake of Christ's suffering and death. But we must take heed that we do not stop short with God, through a wavering faith. Peter, coming to Christ on the water, wavered in faith, and almost drowned; so we, if we begin to waver or doubt, will sink like Peter, not into the water, but into hell itself." (*Second Sermon on the Passion*)

"Therefore, have a sure and constant faith, not only that Christ died for all the world, but that he made a full and sufficient sacrifice for *you,* a perfect atonement for *your* sins; that he loved *you* and gave himself for *you.*" (*Sermon on the Sacrament*)

4 ... By affirming that faith is the condition of justification, I mean that there is no justification without it. "He that believes not is condemned already"; and as long as he does not believe, that condemnation cannot be removed, "but the wrath of God abides on him." "There is no other name under heaven," than that of

Jesus of Nazareth, no other merit whereby a condemned sinner can ever be saved from the guilt of sin; and no other way of obtaining a share in his merit, than by faith in his name. So long as we are without this faith, "we are strangers to the covenant of promise, and without God in this world." Whatever so-called virtues a man may have, whatever so-called good works he may do, it profits him nothing; he is still a child of wrath, still under the curse, till he believes in Jesus.

5 ... Faith, then, is the necessary condition of justification, and the only necessary condition. The very moment that God gives faith (and it is his gift) to the ungodly, that "faith is credited to him as righteousness." Before this, he had no righteousness at all, not even negative righteousness, or innocence. But the moment he believed, "faith was imputed to him as righteousness." It is not that God thinks him to be what he is not. But God "made Christ to be sin for us"; that is, God treated Christ as if he were a sinner, punishing him for our sins. And so, from the time we first believe in him, he counts us as righteous; he does not punish us for our sins; he treats us as though we were guiltless.

6 ... If it is hard to accept that faith is the only condition of justification, it is because you do not really understand it. Faith is the only thing without which none can be justified; the only thing which is immediately, indispensably, absolutely required. On one hand, though a man should have everything else, except faith, he cannot be justified; on the other hand, though a man lack everything else, but have faith, he will surely be justified. Imagine a sinner, totally godless, utterly incapable of thinking, speaking, or doing any good, absolutely deserving of hell. Now imagine this sinner, helpless and hopeless, casting himself wholly on the mercy of God in Christ, which he can only do by the grace of God. I assure you that he is forgiven in that moment; nothing more is required before justifi-

cation, but faith! And this has been the case for millions of souls since the beginning!

7 ... It is not proper for poor, guilty sinners, who receive whatever blessings they enjoy, (from the water that cools their tongues, to the glorious riches of heaven itself), from the free and generous grace of God, to ask him the reason he deals with us as he does. It is not right for us to question him, to demand why he made faith the only condition for salvation. Paul strongly insists on this very point: The terms of our pardon and acceptance depend, not on us, but on him who called us; God is not at all unrighteous in determining the conditions as he wills, not as we think best. God "will have mercy on whom he will have mercy"; namely, on him who believes in Jesus. It is not up to us to decide how we will be saved, or to work toward it in the way we choose. Instead, God has decided, of his own free love and unmerited goodness, to show mercy on those, and those only, who believe on his beloved Son; and those who do not believe, he leaves in the hardness of their hearts.

8 ... The only possible reason we can imagine God making faith the only condition for justification was to keep man from pride. Pride had already destroyed the very angels of God; pride motivated Adam when, desiring to be as God, he disobeyed, and brought sin and death to the world. It was worthy of God's wisdom, therefore, to choose a condition like faith to bring reconciliation to Adam's race, a condition which would be sure to bring mankind to its knees. And faith is peculiarly fit for this: He who comes to God by faith, must focus specifically on his own wickedness, on his guilt and helplessness, with no regard to any supposed goodness, virtue, or righteousness in himself. He must come simply as a sinner, inwardly and outwardly sinful, self-destroyed and self-condemned, offering nothing to God but his ungodliness, pleading nothing but his own sin and misery. It is only when he ceases to bargain with God, and

stands utterly guilty before God, that he can finally look to Jesus, as his full and only atonement for sin. Only then can he be found in Christ and receive the righteousness which is of God by faith.

9 ... You godless, helpless, miserable sinner, who hear or read these words! I urge you, in the name of God our Judge, to go to him with all your sins; do not risk your soul by trying to plead your own righteousness. No, go to him guilty and lost, destroyed and deserving hell; and you will find his favor; you will discover that he justifies the ungodly. He will bring you to the blood of sprinkling. Behold Jesus, the Lamb of God, who takes away your sins! Plead nothing of yourself: No good works, no righteousness; not even your humility, repentance, or sincerity. No! Plead only the blood of the covenant, the ransom paid for your proud, sinful soul. Do you now comprehend both your inward and outward ungodliness? If so, you are exactly the man I want for my Lord! I challenge you to become a child of God by faith! The Lord has need of you. If you feel that you are fit only for hell, then you are finally ready to experience and advance the glory of God's free grace! Come quickly! Believe in the Lord Jesus, and you, even you, are reconciled to God.

6

THE RIGHTEOUSNESS OF FAITH

Moses describes the righteousness of the law like this: The man who does these things will live by them. But the righteousness of faith is described like this: Who needs to ascend to heaven (to bring Christ down) or to descend to the deep (to bring Christ up)? No one, for God's word is very near, in your mouth and in your heart—the word of faith which we preach.

—ROMANS 10:5-8

1 ... Paul, here, is *not* setting the covenant given by Moses in opposition to the covenant given by Christ. In fact, both quotes come originally from Moses (Deut 30), speaking to Israel concerning the covenant then in effect. *Instead,* Paul is setting the covenant of *grace,* which God through *Christ* established with men in all ages (as much before and during the Mosaic covenant, as after the Christian covenant), in opposition to the covenant of *works* made with *Adam,* which many Jews treated as if it were God's only covenant with man.

2 ... Of these Jews, Paul speaks affectionately: "My heart's desire and prayer for Israel is that they might be saved. Truly, they have a zeal for God, but not according to knowledge. Being unaware of *God's* righteousness (the justification that flows from God's grace and mercy, freely forgiving our sins through redemption in Jesus), and seeking to work out their *own* righteousness (their own

holiness, prior to justifying faith, as the ground of their pardon and acceptance), they have not surrendered to the righteousness of God," which is the deadliest of errors.

3 ... They were unaware that "Christ is the end of the law for righteousness to all who believe." Through his self-sacrifice, Christ has put an end to the first law or covenant (given by God to Adam), which strictly and continuously required: "Do all this [without fail], and you shall live!" But Christ bought for us a better covenant, which graciously offered: "Simply believe, and you shall live!" Believe, and you shall be saved, saved from the guilt and power of sin, saved from sin's deadly consequences.

4 ... But how many are still unaware of all this, even among Christians? How many still have "zeal for God, but not according to knowledge"? How many still seek to work out their own righteousness, and, therefore, adamantly refuse to surrender to the righteousness of God? Surely my heart's desire and prayer for you, my friends, is that you too may be saved. So, to remove this stumbling-block, I will try (1) to distinguish the righteousness of the law from the righteousness of faith; and then, (2) to distinguish the foolishness of trusting in the law from the wisdom of submitting to faith.

I / 1 ... "The righteousness of the *law* says, The man who does these things will live by them." Constantly and perfectly do all these things, and you shall live forever. This law, the 'covenant of works,' given by God to man in Eden, required perfect obedience in every detail, as the condition for remaining eternally in the holiness and happiness in which he was created.

2 ... It required that man should fulfill *all* righteousness, inward

and outward, passive and active. Not only must he avoid every idle word and evil deed, but must also keep every thought and desire in subjection to God's will. He must be holy in heart and life, as his Creator is holy; pure, as God is pure; perfect, as his heavenly Father is perfect. He must love the Lord with all his heart, soul, mind, and strength; and must love every soul which God has made, even as God loves. By this benevolence toward all, man would dwell in God, and God in him; he would serve God and aim at God's glory in all things.

3 ... But the righteousness of the law further required that this entire obedience to God, this inward and outward holiness, this conformity of heart and life to God's will, should be perfect in degree. No allowance could possibly be made for falling short in any degree. Even if every commandment were obeyed, even if God were truly loved, but not with all man's strength, or in the highest measure, or most perfect manner, it would not be enough to meet the demand of the covenant of works.

4 ... And the righteousness of the law required one thing more: That this total obedience and perfect holiness should be absolutely *uninterrupted*, without any intermission, from the moment God breathed life into man, until his earthly trial was ended and he entered life everlasting.

5 ... To conclude, the righteousness of the law speaks like this: "O man, stand fast in love, in the image of God in which you were made. Keep the commandments now written in your heart. Love the Lord with all your heart; love, as yourself, every soul he has made. Desire nothing but God; aim toward God with every thought, word, and deed. Swerve not from him, who is your goal and the prize of your high calling. Let all that is in you praise his holy name, every power and faculty of your soul—in every instance, to the highest degree, at every moment of your existence. Do *all*

this, and you shall live. Your light will shine, your love will flame more and more, till you are received into your heavenly home, to reign with God forever."

6 ... But the righteousness of *faith* speaks like this: "Who shall ascend to heaven, to bring Christ down," as though God required some impossible task before we could be saved. "Who shall descend to the deep, to bring Christ up from the dead," as if that still needed to be done. "But what does the scripture say? God's word is very near, in your mouth, and in your heart—the word of faith which we preach," the *new* covenant which God has made with sinful man, through Jesus Christ, that he might be accepted as an heir of life eternal.

7 ... The righteousness of faith is the *one* condition of justification (and therefore, of present and final salvation, if we endure to the end) which was given by God to fallen man, through the merits and mediation of his only Son. This was partially revealed to Adam, soon after his fall, when God spoke of the "woman's offspring," who would "crush the serpent's head." It was more clearly revealed to Abraham, when God's angel promised that "through his offspring, all the world would be blessed." It was yet more fully revealed to Moses, David, and the prophets; and, through them, to many of God's people in succeeding generations. But the majority were totally ignorant of it, or understood it very poorly. Still, the promise of "light and immortality" was not revealed to the ancient Jews, as it is to us, through the gospel of Christ.

8 ... This new covenant never tells sinful man that he must live a sinless life in order to be saved. That would be as impossible as ascending to heaven, or descending to the deep, to make Christ present. If a sinless life were required, it would only mock human weakness; and man would have no benefit from all that Christ did for him. The covenant of grace, however, does not require us

to do anything toward our own justification, but simply to believe in him who, for the sake of his Son and his Son's sacrifice, will justify the sinner, imputing [crediting] his faith as righteousness. Even Abraham of old "believed in the Lord, and it was credited to him as righteousness." Thus, he became the father of all who would believe, of all whose faith would be credited to them as righteousness. What was written of Abraham was meant also for us: Faith will be credited to us as righteousness, in the place of perfect obedience, if we truly believe in Jesus, who died for our sins and was raised for our justification. For the justified sinner, there is God's gracious acceptance, an assurance of forgiveness, and a second life that has begun.

9 ... The covenant of forgiveness, of unmerited love and pardoning mercy, says, "Believe in the Lord Jesus Christ, and you will be saved." The very moment you believe, you will begin to live. You will be restored to God's favor, and in his favor is life. You will be saved from the curse and wrath of God; you will go from the death of sin into the life of righteousness. And if you endure to the end, believing in Jesus, you will never experience death eternal; but, having suffered with your Lord, you will also live and reign with him forever.

10 ... God's new covenant in Christ is plain, simple, and always available, "very near, in your heart and in your mouth," through the operation of God's Spirit. The moment "you believe in your heart and confess with your mouth" the Lord Jesus, as *your* Lord and God, you will be saved from condemnation, from the guilt and punishment of your sins, and will have the power to serve God in true holiness the rest of your life.

11 ... So, what is the difference between the righteousness of the *law* and the righteousness of *faith;* between the covenant of *works* and the covenant of *grace?* The essential difference is this: The first

supposes man to be already holy and happy, created in the image and enjoying the favor of God; and it prescribes how he may *continue* in love and joy, in life and immortality. The second supposes man to be unholy and unhappy, fallen short of the image of God, his soul now dead through sin, having the wrath of God abiding on him, and hastening on to death everlasting; and it prescribes how he may *regain* his original righteousness, may *recover* the favor and image of God, may *retrieve* the life of God in his soul, and may *be restored* to the knowledge and love of God, all of which is the beginning of life eternal.

12 ... Again: The covenant of *works,* in order for man to continue in the favor of God, required of perfect man a perfect and uninterrupted *obedience* to every point of God's law. The covenant of *grace,* in order to man's recovery of the favor of God, requires only *faith,* living faith in him who justifies the disobedient.

13 ... Yet again: The covenant of *works* required of Adam and all his children, to pay the price *themselves,* in consideration of which they were to receive all future blessings of God. But in the covenant of *grace,* seeing we have nothing to pay, God "frankly forgives us all." The only provision is that we believe in him who has paid the price *for us,* who has given himself to be the sacrifice "for our sins and the sins of the whole world."

14 ... The first covenant required what is now *impossible* for man, "conceived and born in sin"—perfect obedience. The second covenant requires only what is *possible* for man, through the grace of God. Its message is: "You are sin! God is love! You have fallen far short, but God is merciful. Bring all your sins to the pardoning God, and they will vanish away. If you were not ungodly, you would have no need of his justification. Draw near, in full assurance of faith. God speaks, and it is done. Fear not, only believe; for a just God justifies all who believe in Jesus."

II / 1 ... We now consider the *foolishness* of trusting in the righteousness of the *law,* and the *wisdom* of submitting to the righteousness of *faith.*

The *foolishness* of those who still trust in the righteousness of the law is abundantly apparent: They begin wrong; their first step is a fundamental mistake. Before they can ever think of obtaining a blessing through this covenant, they must first suppose themselves, like Adam, to be in a state of innocence. How weak must the building be, that is built on such a faulty foundation! How foolish they are to build on sand! They forget that the covenant of works was not given to man when he was "dead in trespasses and sins," but when he was alive to God, when he knew no sin, when he was holy as God is holy. They forget that it was never designed for the recovery of the favor and life of God *once lost,* but only for its continuance, increase, and completion in eternity.

2 ... Neither do they consider what kind of absolute obedience or righteousness the law requires. It must be perfect and whole in every detail, or it does not fulfill the demands of the law. But which of you can perform such obedience? Who can fulfill even all of God's *outward* commandments: Doing nothing which God forbids, and leaving undone nothing he demands; always speaking so as to "minister grace to the hearers," and doing all to the glory of God? And if you fall short of his outward commandments, how much less are you able to fulfill his *inward* commands! Is every impulse of your soul aimed at holiness unto the Lord? Are you able to love God and man with your whole heart; to pray without ceasing, in everything giving thanks? Does God, and nothing but God, dominate your every thought, desire, and affection?

3 ... You should further consider that the righteousness of the law

requires, not only perfect obedience to every command of God, but also requires it to a perfect degree. It allows no gaps in obedience; it excuses no defects; it condemns all shortcomings; it curses all offenders. It is based on strict, intractable justice.

4 ... Who can appear before a Judge who judges sin so severely? How foolish to desire to be tried in his court, according to such a covenant, where no man stands a chance of acquittal! Even if we kept all of God's commandments with all our strength, just one little slip destroys our case, just one minor offense ends our righteousness. And the guilty sinner must then face the Judge's fearsome and fiery indignation and destruction!

5 ... Is it not then the very height of folly for fallen man to seek life by this righteousness? After all, man was conceived in sin; he is, by nature, earthly, sensual, and corrupt; incapable of one good thought or deed; a mere lump of ungodliness, committing sin with every breath; whose transgressions outnumber the hairs of his head! What stupidity, what senselessness it is for such an unclean, guilty, helpless worm as this, to dream of seeking acceptance by his own righteousness, the righteousness of the law!

6 ... When we prove the *foolishness* of trusting in the righteousness of the *law,* we equally prove the *wisdom* of submitting to the righteousness of *faith.* The first step toward faith, the acknowledgement of our own unrighteousness, is nothing more than admitting the truth, the real nature of things. It is true that we have a corrupt, sinful nature; more corrupt than we know. We are prone to evil, and averse to good; we are full of pride, self-will, unruly passions, foolish desires, and vile affections. We are lovers of the world and its pleasures more than lovers of God. Our hearts have been unholy; our sins in word and deed without number. We are displeasing to the holy God, and deserve nothing from him but indignation, wrath, and death. We have no righteousness of our own, no good

works, to appease the wrath of God, or avert our well-deserved punishment. If left to ourselves, we will only grow worse and worse, sink deeper and deeper into sin, offend God more and more with our evil deeds and our carnal minds, until finally we will bring on ourselves swift destruction! To acknowledge all this is to exhibit true wisdom, to face the facts of spiritual reality.

7 ... The wisdom of submitting to the righteousness of faith becomes even more apparent when we consider that it is, in fact, the righteousness of *God himself.* God, the source of wisdom, the sovereign Lord of heaven and earth, has chosen it as his method of reconciliation with humanity. It is not for us, who are so utterly devoid of understanding, to question the mighty One, whose kingdom rules over all. It is a mark of true wisdom, of sound understanding, to acquiesce in whatever he has chosen—to say, "He is Lord: Let him do what he will."

8 ... Furthermore, it was of mere grace, of free love, of undeserved mercy, that God granted sinful man *any* means of reconciliation with himself; that God did not utterly banish us and blot us out of his memory. So, whatever method he chooses, in his merciful goodness, to reconcile obstinate rebels to his favor, it would be wise for us to accept with all thankfulness.

9 ... One thing more: It is wise to aim at the best end by the best means. The best end a fallen creature can pursue is happiness in God, by recovering the favor and image of God. And the best and *only* means for doing so, is by submitting to the righteousness of faith, by believing in God's only Son.

III / 1 ... Whoever desires to be forgiven and reconciled to God, must not say in his heart, "I must first do this or that; I must first conquer every sin, speaking no evil word, doing no evil deed, but rather doing all good to all men. I must first go to church, receive the sacrament, hear more sermons, and say more prayers. Alas, my brother! You are on the wrong road. You are still ignorant of God's righteousness, and seeking to establish your own righteousness, as the condition of reconciliation. Do you not realize that you are capable of nothing but sin, until you are reconciled to God? Do not say to yourself, "I must do such and such *first,* and *then* I will believe." No, *believe first!* Believe in the Lord Jesus Christ, your atonement for sin. Lay this foundation first, and then you will do all things well.

2 ... Neither must you say, "I cannot be accepted yet; I am not *good enough."* Who *is* good enough—who ever was, or ever will be—to merit acceptance with God? In fact, you are not good at all, and you never will be, until you believe in Jesus. Instead, you will find yourself worse and worse. There is no need to be worse; you are bad enough already! God knows it, and you know it! So, do not wait; all things are ready now! Arise, wash away your sins! God's fountain is open: Wash clean in the blood of the Lamb!

3 ... And do not say, "I am not contrite enough; I am not sensible enough of my sins." You are correct. I wish to God you were more sensible of your sin, and a thousand times more contrite. But do not worry about that now. It may be that God will make you so, not *before* you believe, but *by* believing. It may be that you will weep much, only when you love much; and you will love much only because you are forgiven much. Meanwhile, look to Jesus. Behold how he loves you! What more could he have done for you than he has done? Look closely at him, till his look of love breaks your hard heart; *then,* you may break into tears.

4 ... And do not say, "I must do something more before I come to Christ." Nothing more is required, but faith; besides, there may not be time to do more. The Lord may delay his coming, but he may

not. Perhaps he will appear before morning breaks. Do not try to guess; expect him *every* hour. He is near—at the door, even now!

5 ... And why would you wait to have more sincerity, before your sins are blotted out? To make you more worthy of God's grace? If so, you are still trying to gain your own righteousness. God will have mercy, not because you are worthy, but because his compassions fail not; not because you are righteous, but because Christ has atoned for your sins. Sincerity is certainly a good thing, but why would you expect it *before* you have faith? Faith is the only source for anything truly good and holy.

Above all, do not forget that whatever you do or whatever you have, *before* your sins are forgiven, count for nothing in procuring your forgiveness. Indeed, you must throw them all down, trample them under foot, and count them as nothing, or you will never find favor with God. Until then, guilty, lost sinners have nothing to plead, nothing to offer God, nothing but the merits of his beloved Son, "who loved you and gave himself for you."

6 ... To conclude: Whoever is under the sentence of death, whoever feels himself a condemned sinner, whoever has the wrath of God abiding on him—to him the Lord says, not, "Do this, and live," but instead, "Believe in the Lord Jesus, and you will be saved." Now, this very moment, just as you are, sinner that you are, believe the gospel. And God "will be merciful to your unrighteousness and remember your sins no more."

7

THE WAY TO THE KINGDOM

The kingdom of God is at hand: Repent, and believe the gospel.

—MARK 1:15

This text naturally leads us to consider: First, the nature of true religion, which Jesus calls "the kingdom of God." And second, the way to reach it, which Jesus describes as repentance and believing the gospel.

I / 1 ... So, according to Jesus, "the kingdom of God" is the essence of true religion. Paul, to the Romans, expands on that term, when he says, "The kingdom of God is not meat and drink; but righteousness, peace, and joy in the Holy Spirit."

2 ... "The kingdom of God is not meat and drink." We know that many of the early Jewish Christians, though they had faith in Christ, continued to be "zealous for the law," even the ceremonial laws of Moses. The ritual laws concerning meat and drink offerings, and the distinctions between clean and unclean meats, they not only observed themselves, but tried to impose on Gentile Christians. Some went so far as to say, "Unless you are circumcised, and keep the law (meaning the whole ritual law), you cannot be saved."

3 ... In opposition to these Jewish Christians, Paul declares, both here and in many other places, that true religion does not consist in "meat and drink"; in any other ritual observance, in any outward thing whatever, in anything exterior to the heart. Rather, its entire substance lies in "righteousness, peace, and joy in the Holy Spirit."

4 ... So, true religion does not consist of any outward thing, of even the most excellent practices or ceremonies. No matter how beautiful or meaningful they are, how expressive they are of inward things; no matter how helpful they may be to common men of limited religious understanding, or how fulfilling they may be to men of finer sensibilities; true religion does not consist in these. Not at all! Even those Jewish ceremonies, appointed by God himself, during the time of the old covenant, were not essential to true religion; much less is it true of rites and practices of human origin! The religion of Christ rises infinitely higher, and reaches infinitely deeper, than any of these. Such outward rites and ceremonies are fine in their place, insofar as they are subservient to true religion; it would be wrong to forbid them, as they are obviously helpful in lifting men's eyes to the divine. But let no man value them any higher than that. They have no intrinsic worth; true religion could exist without them. So, let us not make them more than they are; that would be an abomination!

5 ... True religion does not consist of religious ceremonies or forms of worship, or of any outward action at all. It is true that a man cannot have any religion, who is guilty of vicious, immoral actions; or who does to others what he would not wish done to him, under the same circumstances; or who "knows to do good, yet does not do it." It is further true that a man can abstain from all evil, and do much good, and still have no religion. In fact, two people may do the same outward works (such as feeding the hungry or clothing the naked); one may be truly religious, while the other has no

religion at all; one may act from the love of God, while the other acts from the love of praise. So, although true religion naturally leads to every good word and deed, its real nature lies deeper still, even in the "hiddenness of the heart."

6 ... I speak here of the *heart:* Religion does not consist of orthodoxy, or right opinions; for these are not of the heart, but of the understanding. A man may be orthodox in every point; he may hold right opinions, and zealously defend them against all opposition; he may correctly articulate the Incarnation and the holy Trinity, and every other scriptural doctrine; he may assent to the three orthodox creeds (Apostles', Nicene, and Athanasian) and still have no religion at all—no more than a Jew, a Moslem, or a pagan. He may be almost as orthodox as the devil himself, (who fully understands the truth, yet fully rejects it), but still be a stranger to the religion of the heart.

7 ... This alone is true religion; this alone is of infinite worth in God's sight. Paul sums it up in three words: "righteousness, peace, and joy in the Holy Spirit." The first of these is *righteousness:* We cannot go wrong, if we remember the words of Jesus describing the two great branches of Christian righteousness, the first of which is: "You shall *love the Lord* your God with all your heart, mind, soul, and strength." You shall delight yourself in the Lord, seeking and finding all your happiness in him. He shall be your "exceeding great reward," in time and eternity. Your soul shall cry, "Whom have I in heaven, but you, Lord? Whom on earth, but you?" Then you will hear him say, "My child, give me your heart." And having given him your heart, your inmost soul, to reign there without a rival, you may well cry out, "I love you, O Lord; you are my Rock, my Savior, my God, in whom I will trust; my shield, my refuge, my salvation."

8 ... The second great branch of Christian righteousness is closely

linked to the first: "You shall *love your neighbor* as yourself." To love is to reach out with tender good-will, cordial affection, and a passionate desire to prevent all evil and procure all good to the other. The neighbor is not only your friend, your kinsman, your acquaintance; not only the virtuous, the friendly, the one who loves you, and returns your kindness; but every man, every soul which God has made; even those you have never met, whose names you do not know; even those who are evil and unthankful, who despise and persecute you. All these you must love as yourself; with the same desire for their happiness, as for your own; with the same care to protect them from harm to soul or body.

9 ... This love is "the fulfilling of the law," the sum total of all Christian righteousness. First, it is *inward* righteousness—mercy, humility, gentleness, meekness, patience. And second, it is *outward* righteousness—doing no harm to the neighbor, in word or deed; doing good to all people, as opportunity arises.

10 ... But true religion, a heart right toward God and man, implies happiness as well as holiness. *Holiness* is the "righteousness" Paul spoke of; *happiness* is the "peace and joy in the Holy Spirit." What *peace* do we mean? The peace which only God can give, and the world cannot take away; the peace which "passes all understanding," which goes beyond the merely rational; a supernatural sensation, a divine taste, of "the powers of the world to come." The natural man cannot know this peace, however wise he may be in the things of the world; nor can he know it in his present state, for it is "spiritually discerned." It is a peace that banishes all doubt and uncertainty; it is the Spirit of God bearing witness with the Christian's spirit that he is a child of God. And it banishes fear: the fear of death, of wrath, of hell. The man who has this peace is even willing to die "and be with Christ," if it be God's will.

11 ... When a man has God's peace in his soul, he also has "*joy* in

the Holy Spirit." The blessed Spirit of God works in us that calm, humble rejoicing in God, through Christ, our atonement and our reconciliation with God; and that joy enables us to declare, with the psalmist, "Happy is the man whose unrighteousness is forgiven, whose sin is covered." The Spirit inspires the Christian's soul with that steady, solid joy which comes from knowing that he is a child of God; it inspires "joy unspeakable, in hope of God's glory." This is the hope of God's glorious image restored to him, now in part, but fully in eternity; and it is the hope of an unfading crown of glory, reserved in heaven for him.

12 ... This holiness and happiness, together, are sometimes referred to in scripture as the "kingdom of God," or the "kingdom of heaven." "The kingdom of *God*" refers to the immediate fruit of God's reigning in the soul. As soon as he sets up his mighty throne in our hearts, we are instantly filled with this "righteousness, peace, and joy." "The kingdom of *heaven*" refers to heaven already begun in the soul. Whoever experiences this can testify *'Everlasting life is won, Glory is on earth begun.'* Scripture everywhere bears record that God "has given us eternal life, and this life is in his Son." "This is life eternal, to know you, the only true God, and Jesus Christ whom you have sent." Believers may confidently say to God: *'For where your presence is, is heaven.'*

13 ... And "the kingdom of God," Jesus announced, "is *at hand!*" The time was then fulfilled, God being "made manifest in the flesh," when he would set up his kingdom among men, and reign in the hearts of his people. And is the time not now fulfilled? Yes, for "I am with you always, even to the end of the world." Wherever the gospel of Christ is preached, there the kingdom of God is at hand. It is not far from every one of you! You too may enter the kingdom, if you hearken to his voice, and "repent, and believe the gospel."

II / 1 ... This is the way; walk in it. First, *repent;* that is, know yourself—really know yourself! This is the first repentance, prior to faith; this is conviction or self-knowledge. Awake from your spiritual sleep. Know yourself to be a sinner, and what kind of sinner you are. Know the corruption of your inmost nature: You have fallen far from the original righteousness; your flesh is always contrary to the Spirit; your mind is in rebellion against God and the law of God; every aspect of your soul is off course. Your understanding is dark, so you cannot discern God or the things of God; the clouds of ignorance and error cover you with the shadow of death; you know neither God, the world, nor yourself, as you ought to know. Your will is not aligned with the will of God, but is utterly perverse and distorted, averse from the good which God loves, and prone to the evil which God hates. Your affections are alienated from God and focused on everything but God. All your desires and aversions, your joys and sorrows, your hopes and fears, are out of balance, either too strong or too weak, or focused on totally wrong things. So, there is no health in your soul, but, from top to bottom, only woundedness and decay.

2 ... Such is the inbred corruption of your heart, of your very inmost nature. And what kind of plant can grow from such a corrupt root? For one, unbelief: forever wandering from the living God; denying that God exists, or denying that God cares a whit for man or his worship. For another, independence: thinking oneself the equal of God. For another, pride: thinking oneself totally self-sufficient, needing nothing. From the evil source of pride flow the ugly streams of vanity, ambition, lust, and covetousness; anger, hatred, revenge, and envy; all the foolish and hurtful desires that, if not prevented, will drown the soul in an eternal abyss.

3 ... And what kind of fruit can grow on such a corrupt plant? Only, always, bad fruit! From pride comes contention, boasting,

seeking and receiving the praise of men, thus robbing God of the glory that alone is his. From the flesh comes gluttony and drunkenness, the love of luxury, and sexual immorality; all that defiles the body, which was designed as the temple of the Holy Spirit. From unbelief comes every evil word and deed; idle words which provoke and grieve the holy One; evil deeds, intrinsically evil, or at least not done to the glory of God. Man's sins are numberless, like sands of the sea or drops of rain.

4 ... Do you not realize that sin leads to death, death in time and eternity, the death of the body and the soul? Yes, "the soul that sins shall die," says the Lord. The death of the body is the first death, the death of the soul the second. This is God's sentence: to "be punished with everlasting destruction," banished from the Lord's presence and glory and power. Every sinner is under the sentence of hellfire, doomed already, even now being dragged to his execution. You are guilty of this eternal death; it is the just reward for your wickedness; it is right that the sentence now be carried out. Do you see this; do you feel this? Do you admit that you deserve God's wrath and damnation? Would God be wrong to carry out his judgment this very moment, to cast you now into the fiery pit? If you have truly repented, you have a deep sense that what I say is so; and that only God's mercy has spared you to this hour.

5 ... So, what will you do to appease the wrath of God, to atone for all your sins, and to escape the punishment you most justly deserve? Alas, you can do *nothing;* nothing that will make amends to God for even one evil thought, word, or deed. If, from this moment on, you could perform perfect, uninterrupted obedience, even this would not atone for past sins. Not increasing your debt would not eliminate your debt; it would still remain as great as ever. The present and future obedience of every man on earth and every angel in heaven would never make satisfaction to the justice of God for one

single sin. How vain, then, to think that *you* could atone for your own sins, by anything you could do. It costs more to redeem one soul than all mankind is able to pay. Were there no other help for the guilty sinner, he would certainly perish everlastingly.

6 ... But *imagine,* that by perfect obedience, from this time forward, you *were* able to atone for your past sins. Still, it would do you no good, for you are not capable of such obedience. Why not try it? Shake off just the *outward* sins that beset you. You cannot! How then can you transform yourself *inwardly* from all evil to all good? It is impossible, unless first your heart be changed. But are you able to change your heart, from sin to holiness; are you able to enliven a dead soul, dead in sin, dead to God, and alive only to the world? No, no more than you can resurrect a dead body from the grave! So, you can do nothing; you are utterly helpless! To be deeply sensible of your sin and guilt and helplessness is a major part of the repentance that leads to the kingdom of God.

7 ... To this strong conviction of sin, guilt, and helplessness, there needs to be added: remorse, shame, and self-condemnation; fear of the wrath of God hanging over your head; and an earnest desire to escape God's indignation, to cease from your evil, and learn to do good. Having thus repented, "you are not far from the kingdom of God." One step more and you shall enter in. So now, "believe the gospel."

8 ... The gospel (good news for guilty, helpless sinners) is the whole revelation made to men by Jesus Christ, all that our Lord did and suffered while he lived among us. The substance of the gospel is contained in these scriptures: "Jesus Christ came into the world to save sinners." "God so loved the world that he gave his only Son, that we might not perish, but have everlasting life." "He was bruised for our transgressions, wounded for our iniquities; and by his stripes we are healed."

9 ... Believe this, and the kingdom of God is yours! By faith you attain the promise. [Our church says], "God pardons and absolves all that truly repent, and unfeignedly believe his holy gospel." As soon as God speaks to your heart, "Your sins are forgiven you," his kingdom comes and reigns in you; you now have "righteousness, peace, and joy in the Holy Spirit."

10 ... Beware that you do not deceive yourself regarding the nature of this faith. It is not, as some have supposed, a mere assent to the truths of scripture or the creeds. The devils believe these truths, yet are devils still. But true faith goes beyond assent, to an inner trust in the mercy of God, through Jesus Christ. It is a confidence in a pardoning God. It is a conviction that "God was in Christ, reconciling the world to himself, not imputing [counting] their trespasses to them"; in particular, it is a conviction that the Son of God loved *me,* and gave himself for *me;* that *I, even I,* am now reconciled to God by the blood of the cross!

11 ... Do you believe this? Then the peace of God is in your heart, and the darkness flees. You no longer doubt the love of God; it is as bright as the noonday sun. You sing of the lovingkindness of the Lord; you speak his truths to all. You no longer fear the devil, death, or hell; nor do you cringingly fear God himself, but only fear to offend his fatherly heart. Are you a believer? Then your "soul magnifies the Lord" and your "spirit rejoices in God your Savior." You rejoice that you have "redemption through his blood"; "the Spirit of adoption"; a "hope full of immortality"; and "an earnest expectation of all the good things which God has prepared for them that love him."

12 ... Do you now believe? Then "the love of God is shed abroad in your heart." You love him, because he first loved us; and because you love God, you love your brother also. And being filled with "love, peace, and joy," you are also filled with all the fruits of the

Spirit, with whatever is holy or heavenly. And while you behold "the glory of the Lord," his glorious love, and the glorious image in which you were created, you are being "changed into the same image, from glory to glory, by the Spirit."

13 ... This repentance, this faith, this peace, joy, and love, this change from glory to glory, is what worldly wisdom judges to be religious fanaticism or utter insanity. Believer, pay no heed. You know in whom you have believed. Let no man steal your inheritance. Hold fast, continue on, till you obtain all the great and precious promises. If you are not yet a believer, do not let the critics shame you from the gospel of Christ. Do not be moved by those who speak evil of what they know not. God will soon turn your heaviness into joy. Do not be discouraged, for he will take away your fear, and give you a sound mind. He who justifies is near. So, who can condemn? Only Christ, but Christ died and rose and is making intercession for you, even now, at the right hand of God!

So, cast yourself and your many sins on the Lamb of God, and you shall make your entry "into the kingdom of our Lord and Savior, Jesus Christ!"

8

THE FIRST FRUITS OF THE SPIRIT

There is now no condemnation to those who are in Christ Jesus, who walk not after the flesh, but after the Spirit.

—ROMANS 8:1

1 ... By "those who are in Christ," Paul obviously means those who truly believe in him; those who, "being justified by faith, have peace with God, through our Lord Jesus Christ." Those who believe no longer "walk after the flesh," no longer follow their corrupt nature, but walk "after the Spirit," their thoughts, words, and deeds under the direction of the Spirit.

2 ... "There is now no condemnation" from God; for he has justified them "freely by his grace, through the redemption in Jesus." He has forgiven and blotted out all their sins. Likewise, there is no condemnation from within; for they "have received the Spirit of God, that they might know the things freely given them by God"; the Spirit which "bears witness with their spirits, that they are the children of God." And to all this is added the witness of their own conscience, "that in simplicity and godly sincerity, not with worldly wisdom, but by the grace of God, they live out their lives in this world."

3 ... The sermon text has often been misunderstood, and in ways that endanger the soul; many "unlearned and unstable men," men

who have not known godly truth, have interpreted it to their own destruction. Therefore, I propose to show, first, who those are "who are in Christ Jesus," who "walk not after the flesh, but after the Spirit." And, second, to show how they face no condemnation." I will then conclude with some practical inferences.

I / 1 ... Those who "are in Christ Jesus" are those who believe in his name, who are "found in him, not having their own righteousness, but the righteousness of God by faith." These, who "have redemption through his blood," are said to be "in Christ," for they dwell in Christ and Christ in them. They are joined to the Lord in one Spirit. They are grafted into him as branches into the vine; united to their Master in a way that words cannot express, or hearts conceive.

2 ... "Whoever abides in him does not sin," "does not walk after the flesh." The flesh, as Paul uses the word, is man's corrupt nature. Paul writes, in Galatians, "Walk in the Spirit, and you will not fulfill the desire of the flesh. For the flesh opposes the Spirit, and the Spirit opposes the flesh, so that you may not do the things that you would." (A literal translation from the Greek makes clear that the Christian *may not* do what the *flesh* desires; some have taken it to mean that the Christian *cannot* do what the *Spirit* desires. This latter understanding is just the reverse of what Paul is seeking to prove.)

3 ... Those who are in Christ, who abide in him, "have crucified the flesh with its affections and lusts." They abstain from *all* the works of the flesh: sexual immorality, drunkenness, and carousing; idolatry, sorcery, and heresy; envy, anger, hatred, strife, and murder—every thought, word, and deed which arises from a corrupt nature. Although they feel that deep-seated corruption

within, they are endued with power from on high to trample it continually under foot; and every fresh assault of the enemy, only gives them fresh occasions to praise: "Thanks be to God, who gives us the victory through Jesus Christ our Lord!"

4 ... They now "walk after the Spirit," both in their hearts and in their lives. They are taught by him to love God and neighbor; they are led by him into such a heavenly temperament, that every thought of the heart is "holiness to the Lord."

5 ... They who "walk after the Spirit" are also led by him into all outward holiness. Their conversation is always full of grace, reflecting both the love and fear of God; it never demeans, but always edifies. They exert themselves daily to do only what pleases God; they seek to follow in the steps of Jesus; they treat their neighbor according to justice, mercy, and truth; and "whatever they do, they do all to the glory of God."

6 ... These are they who "walk after the Spirit." Filled with faith and the Holy Spirit, they possess in their hearts and show forth in their lives, in word and deed, the genuine fruits of the Spirit (love, joy, peace, patience, gentleness, goodness, fidelity, meekness, and temperance), and everything else that is lovely and worthy of praise. "They adorn the gospel of God our Savior"; and give full proof to all mankind, that they are energized by the same Spirit "which raised Jesus from the dead."

II / 1 ... How is it, then, that "there is now no condemnation to them who are in Christ Jesus, who walk not after the flesh, but after the Spirit"? First, there is no condemnation on account of *past sins*. God does not condemn them for any of these; they are as though they had never been; like a stone cast into the depths of the sea, God remembers their sin no more. Having "sent forth his Son to be an atonement" for them, "through faith in his blood," God has declared them righteous, their past sins forgiven, their record clean.

2 ... And there is no condemnation within the believer; no sense of guilt, or dread of God's wrath. They "have the witness in themselves"; they are confident in their claim on the blood of Christ. "They have not received the spirit of bondage unto fear," unto doubt and racking uncertainty; rather they "have received the Spirit of adoption," crying out in their hearts, "Abba, Father!" Being justified by faith, they have the peace of God reigning in their hearts; they have a continual sense of his pardoning mercy, and "a good conscience toward God."

3 ... It has been said: "Sometimes a believer may lose sight of the mercy of God; darkness may descend upon him till he no longer sees the invisible God, till he no longer feels his connection to the atoning blood; he then begins to feel inwardly condemned, to feel "the sentence of death." My answer is: If all this be so, then he is no longer a believer. Faith implies the light of God shining on the soul. So far as a man loses this light, he, for the time, loses his faith. Even a true believer in Christ may possibly lose his faith, and may, for a time, fall again into condemnation. But this is not the case of those who are *now* in Christ, who now believe in his name. As long as they believe, and walk after the Spirit, neither God nor their own hearts condemn them.

4 ... Second, they are not condemned for any *present sins,* for now transgressing God's commandments. For they *do not* transgress them; they *do not* "walk after the flesh, but after the Spirit." This is the continual proof of their "love of God, that they keep his commandments." John states: "Whoever is born of God does not commit sin, for God's nature remains in him, and he cannot sin." He cannot sin, so long as God's nature (that loving, holy faith) remains in him. So long as he keeps the faith, the devil cannot

touch him. Obviously, then, he cannot be condemned for sins he does not commit.

Furthermore, those who are "led by the Spirit are not under the law," not under its curse or condemnation, for the law condemns only those who break it. For example, the laws against stealing or Sabbath-breaking condemn only those who steal or fail to keep the Sabbath holy. But against the fruits of the Spirit "there is no law." As Paul declares to Timothy, "The law is good, if a man use it lawfully, knowing that it is not directed against a righteous man"; it has no force against him, no power to condemn him; instead, it is directed against "the disobedient, the ungodly, and the profane (I Tim 1)."

5 ... Third, they are not condemned for *inward sin,* even though that still remains. The corruption of nature does still remain, even in those who are children of God by faith; they still have in them the seeds of pride, anger, lust, and sin of every kind. This is too plain to be denied, being a matter of daily experience. Paul spoke of the Corinthians as having been "called of God into the fellowship of his Son Jesus Christ"; and *yet* he declares that he could not speak to them as to spiritual men, but as to carnal men—"as to babes in Christ." So, we see that they were "in Christ," but only babes, only believers in a low degree. How much sin still remained in them! How much of that "carnal mind, which is not subject to the law of God (I Cor 3)!"

6 ... Yet for all this, they are not condemned. Although they *feel* the flesh, the evil nature within them; though they are sensible that their "heart is deceitful and desperately wicked"; *yet,* so long as they do not *yield* to it; so long as they do not give place to the devil; so long as they continue to fight with sin, so that the flesh does not gain dominion over them; just so long is there "no condemnation to those who are in Christ Jesus." God is well

pleased with their sincere, though imperfect, obedience; and they "have confidence toward God," knowing they are his, "by the Spirit he has given them."

7 ... Fourth, there is no condemnation from God or their own hearts: even though they are convinced that a *sinful nature* continues to adhere to all they do; even though they are conscious of not fulfilling the perfect law; even though they admit they do not *perfectly* love the Lord with all their being; even though they feel pride or self-will creeping in and mixing with their best efforts; and even though, in times of public and private worship, their thoughts wander, and their affections seem dull. As believers consider these many personal *defects,* they have an even deeper sense of their need to be sprinkled with the blood of Jesus, and of their need for an Advocate with the Father, "who lives forever to make intercession for them." These defects, far from driving the believer away from Christ, drive him closer still. And the more they feel their need of Christ, the more earnestly and diligently they desire to walk in his way.

8 ... Fifth, they are not condemned for *'sins of infirmity'* (so called). It might be best to simply call them infirmities, for they are not sins at all. Though I find the term to be ambiguous and dangerous, it is commonly used to refer to involuntary failings, such as saying something we believe is true, when it actually proves to be false; or inadvertently harming our neighbor when we intended to do him good. These are deviations from the holy, acceptable, and perfect will of God, yet they are not properly sins, and bring no guilt upon those in Christ Jesus. They do not separate believers from God; they are not inconsistent with their "walking after the Spirit."

9 ... Finally, there is no condemnation for anything which is *not* in their power to help: whether it be of an inward or outward nature, whether it be something done or left undone. For example, you fail

to partake of the Lord's supper, because you are ill. If you cannot help it, you are not condemned; there is no guilt, because there is no choice.

10 ... A believer may sometimes be grieved because he cannot do what his soul longs to do. For example, he may be detained from the public worship of God; and he cries out, "My soul thirsts for God, the living God! When shall I appear in his presence?" He may earnestly desire to "go with the multitude into the house of God," but if he cannot go, he feels no condemnation, no guilt, no sense of God's displeasure.

11 ... It is more difficult to determine concerning *'sins of surprise'* (so called), as when one who is normally patient, and in control of himself, suddenly, even explosively, speaks or acts in a manner not consistent with the commandment, "You shall love your neighbor as yourself." It is not easy to give a general rule concerning transgressions of this kind, but it seems that whenever a believer is taken by surprise, there is more or less condemnation, as there is more or less concurrence of his will. In proportion as a sinful desire, or word, or action, is more or less voluntary, so we may assume that God is more or less displeased, and there is more or less guilt upon the soul.

12 ... But there may be some sins of surprise which bring much guilt and condemnation. In some cases, our being surprised is owing to some willful and culpable neglect; or to a sleepiness of soul which might have been prevented or shaken off before temptation came. A man may have been previously warned by God or man, that trials or dangers were near, and yet did nothing. If a man falls into the snare which he might have avoided, he has no excuse; he might have foreseen and shunned the danger. Falling by surprise, in an instance like this, is, in effect, a willful sin; it exposes the sinner to condemnation from God and his own conscience.

13 ... On the other hand, there may be sudden assaults from the world, the devil, or (often) our own evil hearts, which we did not, and could not, foresee. By these, even a believer, still weak in faith, may occasionally be surprised, with hardly any concurrence of his will. In such a case, our fatherly God would surely show him that he had done foolishly. The believer would recognize that he had swerved from the perfect law, from the mind which was in Christ, and would therefore grieve with godly sorrow. But he would not be condemned. God would not lay his folly to his charge, but would have compassion on him. And the believer's own heart would not condemn him; even in his sorrow and shame he could still say, "The Lord is my strength, my song, and my salvation."

III / 1 ... What practical inferences can we draw from all this? First, if there be "no condemnation to them who are in Christ Jesus," then why are you fearful, you of little faith? Though your sins were once innumerable, what is that to you now, now that you are in Christ? "Who shall lay anything to the charge of God's elect?" All the sins which you committed, from your youth until the hour you first believed, are gone, lost, swallowed up, remembered no more. You are now "born of the Spirit"; how can you be troubled or afraid of what you did before you were reborn? Away with your fears! You are not called to fear, but to a "spirit of love and a sound mind." Own your calling! Rejoice in God your Savior and give thanks to God your Father through him!

2 ... But you may say, "I have committed sin again, since I was redeemed by his blood; I hate what I have done; I repent 'in dust and ashes.'" It is right that you should feel this way; it is God himself who inspires such godly sorrow. But, do you *now* believe? Has God enabled you to say, "I know that my Redeemer lives," "and the life I now live, I live by faith in the Son of God"? Then

that faith, once again, cancels all that is past, and there is no more condemnation. Whenever you truly believe in Jesus, all your sins, before that time, vanish like the dew. Now, "stand fast in the liberty" of Christ. Once more, he has made you free from the power of sin, as well as its guilt and punishment. "Be not entangled again with the yoke of bondage!"—neither the vile bondage of sin, the most grievous yoke this side of hell; nor the bondage of slavish, tormenting fear, of guilt and self-condemnation.

3 ... Second, if all who abide in Christ "walk not after the flesh, but after the Spirit," then we must conclude that whoever is now committing sin does *not* abide in Christ. He is even now condemned by his own heart. And if his own heart condemn him, and his own conscience bear witness to his guilt, surely God does; for God "is greater than our heart, and knows all things." So, we cannot deceive God, even if we can deceive ourselves. Do not try to excuse or comfort yourself by saying, "I was justified once; my sins were once forgiven me." I do not know that; I will not dispute whether that is true or not. At this point, it is next to impossible to know for sure, whether that was a true, genuine work of God in your soul, or whether you deceived yourself. But this I do know, with absolute certainty: "He that commits sin [now] is of the devil." It cannot be denied. Do not flatter yourself with vain hopes! Do not say to your soul, "Peace, peace," when there is no peace. Instead, cry out to God from the depths; hopefully, he will hear your voice. Come to him again, as you did before, wretched and poor, miserable, blind, and naked! Do not allow your soul to rest, till God's pardoning love be again revealed; till he "heal your backsliding," and fill you again with the "faith that works by love."

4 ... Third, there is no condemnation to those who "walk after the Spirit," even though the inward tendency toward sin still remains and adheres to all they do; no condemnation, so long as they do not

give in to it. Do not fret because of the ungodliness that remains in your all-too-human heart; or because you fall short of the glorious image of God; or because pride, self-will, and even unbelief cling to all your words and deeds. Do not be afraid to acknowledge your inclination toward evil, to know yourself honestly as you are known. Pray God that you may not think of yourself more highly than you ought to think. Let your continual prayer be, *'Show me, as my soul can bear, The depth of inbred sin; All the unbelief declare, The pride that lurks within.'* But when God hears your prayer, and clearly reveals to you what is in your heart, beware that your faith fail not. Yes, be humbled in the dust; see yourself as nothing, less than nothing. But still, "let not your heart be troubled, neither let it be afraid." Hold fast, for you "have an Advocate with the Father, Jesus Christ the righteous." His love is greater than your sins! He is your merciful Father; you are his beloved child. He will not withhold from you anything that is good. Is it good that the sin, which is now crucified in you, should be destroyed? It shall be done. Is it good that nothing should remain in your heart but the pure love of God alone? Be of good cheer. "You shall love the Lord your God with all your heart, mind, soul, and strength." "Faithful is he who has promised, who also will do it." For your part, patiently continue in the work of faith and love, in cheerful peace, in humble confidence, with a resigned yet earnest expectation, waiting for the zeal of the Lord to fulfill his promise [of entire sanctification].

5 ... Fourth, if they who are in Christ are not condemned for their infirmities, or their involuntary failings, or anything else they are not able to help, then beware that Satan not slip in here and gain an advantage over you. You are still foolish and weak, blind and ignorant, knowing nothing as you ought to know. Yet do not let your unavoidable weakness and folly shake your faith, your child-like trust in God, your peace and joy in the Lord. (It would be dangerous to apply this comforting rule to willful sin; it

applies only to the weakness and folly of a babe in Christ.) Have you fallen, man of God? Do not lie there fretting and bemoaning your weakness. Of course, you will fall, will fall every moment, unless the Lord upholds you. So, stand up and walk; "run the race that is set before you!"

6 ... Finally, if a believer should suddenly be overtaken in a fault, caught by surprise, thinking, saying, or doing what his soul hates (and it was not due to carelessness or neglect on his part), then he should grieve unto the Lord. Pour your heart out before him and tell him your troubles; pray mightily that he would establish, strengthen, and settle your soul, that you would fall no more. But remember: He does not condemn you. Why should you fear? You shall love him, who loves you, and that is enough. More love will bring more strength. And as soon as you love him with all your heart, you shall be "perfect and entire, lacking nothing." Wait in peace for that hour, when "the God of peace shall sanctify you wholly [entire sanctification], so that you may be preserved blameless until the coming of our Lord Jesus Christ!"

9

THE SPIRIT OF BONDAGE AND ADOPTION

You have not received the spirit of bondage unto fear; but you have received the Spirit of adoption, whereby we cry, 'Abba, Father.'

—ROMANS 8:15

1 ... Paul speaks here to those who are children of God by faith: "You have not received the spirit of bondage"; "because you are sons, God has sent the Spirit of his Son into your hearts"; "you have now received the Spirit of adoption."

2 ... The spirit of bondage and fear is widely distant from the loving Spirit of adoption. Those who still feel a slavish fear cannot be called *'sons* of God'; yet some of them may be called *'servants* of God,' and are "not far from the kingdom of God."

3 ... Unfortunately, most people (even so-called Christians) have not yet attained even the status of God's 'servants'; they remain far off. So, a few may be found who *love* God, a few more who *fear* him, but most have neither fear nor love for God in their hearts.

4 ... Perhaps most of you, by the mercy of God, remember when you were as they are now, under the same condemnation. At first you did not realize it, though you were wallowing daily in your sins. But then, you received the spirit of fear (yes, fear also is a gift of God); afterwards, that fear vanished, and the Spirit of love filled your hearts.

5 ... A person who neither fears nor loves God, scripture calls a 'natural man'; one who fears God is said to be 'under law' (although that expression usually designates one who is under the *Jewish* law). But the one who has exchanged the spirit of fear for the Spirit of love, is said to be 'under grace.'

Because it is so important to know what spirit we are of, I will try to point out clearly: (1) the state of a 'natural man'; (2) the state of a man 'under law'; (3) the state of a man 'under grace'.

I / 1 ... The *'natural man'* is a man asleep. His soul is in a deep sleep; his spiritual senses are not awake; he discerns neither spiritual good nor evil. The eyes of his understanding are sealed shut; he lives in clouds and darkness. Having no inlets of spiritual knowledge, he lives in a stupor of ignorance concerning what he most needs to know; he is ignorant of God and the law of God, as to its true and inward meaning. He has no conception of evangelical [scriptural] holiness, "without which no man shall see the Lord"; no conception of the happiness of those whose lives are "hid with Christ in God."

2 ... And because he is asleep, he is, in some sense, at rest; because he is blind, he is also secure. He scoffs at spiritual danger. The darkness which covers him, keeps him in a kind of peace, insofar as peace can consist with a godless perspective. He does not see that he stands on the edge of hell, so he does not fear it; he cannot tremble at the danger he does not know. He has no fear of God because he is totally ignorant of him. He may deny the existence of God [atheism]; he may claim that the Creator is totally aloof from his creation [deism]; or he may have a distorted sense of God's mercy [universalism]—an unconditional mercy that contradicts God's utter holiness and essential hatred of sin; a mercy that contradicts divine justice, wisdom, and truth, [as revealed in

scripture]. He does not dread God's vengeance, because he does not believe in it. He imagines that the main point of religion is to do this or that, and to be outwardly blameless; he does not realize that it involves the whole inner life of the heart. Or, he imagines that the obligation to obedience has ceased; that Christ came to "destroy the Law and the Prophets"; that God intends to save his people *in* their sins, not *from* their sins; to bring them to heaven *without* holiness. All this, despite Christ's words to the contrary: "Not one jot or tittle of the law shall pass away, till all things be fulfilled." "Not everyone who calls me Lord will enter the kingdom of heaven; but only he who does the will of my Father."

3 ... The natural man is secure because he is totally ignorant of himself. He may talk of repenting by and by, some time or other before he dies; he takes it for granted that he is quite in control of the matter. What could possibly keep him from doing exactly as he intends? Once he puts his mind to something, it is as good as done!

4 ... But this ignorance is never so evident as in those who are called 'men of learning.' If a natural man be one of these, he can lecture *ad nauseum* about man's rational faculties and the absolute necessity of man's free will, in order to demonstrate man's moral agency. He reads and argues and seeks to prove that every man may do as he wills; may turn his own heart toward evil or good, as he chooses. Thus, the devil doubly blinds the intellectual's heart, lest "the light of the glorious gospel of Christ should shine" upon him.

5 ... From that same ignorance of himself and God, the natural man may possess what the world calls 'joy,' as he congratulates himself on his own intelligence and goodness. He may have various pleasures, especially if he enjoys an affluent fortune, as he indulges his desire for luxury and status. And so long as he lives sumptuously, men will doubtless speak well of him, will think him a truly happy

man. For this is the sum total of worldly happiness [the leisurely life of the rich]: to dress and visit and talk; to eat and drink and play.

6 ... It is not surprising if such a man, drugged with the opiates of flattery and worldliness, should imagine that he is free of the common man's errors and prejudices. He imagines that his own educated viewpoints are superior, exactly nuanced. He considers himself free of the foolish superstition, the pious hypocrisy, and the religious fanaticism of weak and narrow souls; free of the bigotry of those who lack his liberal and generous way of thinking. Whatever he may think of his freedom, it is obvious that he *is* free: free of the wisdom from above, free of the way of holiness, free of the religion of the heart, free of the mind of Christ!

7 ... Despite his sophistication and reputation, he is still a servant of sin. He commits sin, more or less, every day; but he is not troubled by it; he feels no condemnation. Even if he professes to be a Christian, he excuses himself by arguing that man, by nature, is frail and weak; that every man has his little sins; that religious hypocrites only *pretend* to be better than others. If a serious spiritual thought ever occurs to him, he stifles it immediately, telling himself not to worry, since God exists to be merciful, since Christ died to save the imperfect. So, he remains a willing servant of sin, content to be enslaved by it; he is inwardly and outwardly sinful, but completely satisfied to remain so. Not only does he not conquer sin, he does not try to conquer it—particularly his own besetting sins.

8 ... Such is the natural man—whether he be an infamous, scandalous sinner; or a reputable, decent sinner, having the form but not the power of godliness. How can such a man come under conviction of sin? How is he brought to repentance, brought under the law? How does he receive the spirit of bondage unto fear, [the bondage that leads to adoption, the fear that leads to faith]? This is my next point.

II / 1 ... By some awesome providence, or by God's word powerfully applied by his Spirit, God touches the heart of him who slept in the darkness of sin and the shadow of death. He is frightfully shaken out of sleep and awakes to a consciousness of his danger. Perhaps in a moment, perhaps by degrees, his eyes are opened, and he discerns his spiritual state. Horrid light breaks in on his soul; an eerie light that gleams from the bottomless pit, from the lake of burning brimstone. Finally, he sees that the loving, merciful God is also "a consuming fire," a terrifying Judge. He now clearly perceives that the great and holy God is "of purer eyes than to behold iniquity"; that he is "an avenger of everyone who rebels against him"; that it is, indeed, "a fearful thing to fall into the hands of the living God."

2 ... The inward, spiritual meaning of the law of God now begins to glare upon him. He perceives that "the commandment is very broad," that it relates not just to outward obedience, but to the inner recesses of the soul. When the law says, "You shall not kill," the gospel thunders, "He that hates his brother is a murderer." When the law says, "You shall not commit adultery," the voice of God sounds in his ear, "He that looks on a woman with lust has committed adultery already in his heart." And thus, at every point, he feels the word of God, "quick and powerful, sharper than a two-edged sword." He is finally conscious of having "neglected so great a salvation," of having "trodden underfoot the Son of God," of having "counted the blood of the covenant a common," ordinary thing.

3 ... He now sees himself naked before God, stripped of all his fig leaves, all his pathetic pretenses to religion or virtue, all his wretched excuses for sinning against God. His heart is laid open before God; he sees that it is "deceitful and desperately wicked," corrupt and loathsome, full of unrighteousness and ungodliness, and continually evil.

4 ... He now sees and feels, by an emotion of his soul [born of the Spirit], that even if his *outward* life were perfect (which it is not and cannot be!), the corruption of his *inward* heart would still condemn him to hell. He feels that "the wages of sin (*his* sin!) is death," the second death, the eternal death and destruction of the soul in hell.

5 ... Here ends his pleasant dream, his soothing delusion, his false peace, his vain security. His joy vanishes; pleasures once loved, delight no more. What once was sweet, has become nauseous; the shadows of happiness slip away, and sink into oblivion. Stripped of everything, he wanders to and fro, seeking rest, but finding none.

6 ... His head beginning to clear, he feels the anguish of a wounded spirit. He finds that sin let loose upon the soul is perfect misery. He feels sorrow for all the blessings he has not been open to receive; sorrow for having destroyed himself, and having rejected God's mercies toward him. He feels overwhelming fear: The fear of God's wrath, of punishment richly deserved, hanging over his head; the fear of death--for him, the gate to hell; the fear of the devil—for him, the executioner of God's wrath; the fear of men, who, if they could kill his body, would immediately plunge his soul into hell; fears so great that this poor, sinful, guilty soul is terrified of everything! Sometimes it may border on insanity, being unable to think clearly, to remember, to function at all; sometimes it may approach despair, causing him to think of ending his life. Well may he cry out, "Who can bear a wounded spirit?"

7 ... Now he truly desires to break loose from sin and begins to struggle with it. But though he fights with all his might, sin is stronger still; he is helpless against it. He resolves not to sin, but sins on; he sees the snare, hates it, but runs into it. So much for his boasted reason and free will! His reason only enhances his guilt and increases his misery; his free will is only free to commit evil

and sin, only free to wander farther and farther from the living God, only free to despise the Spirit of grace.

8 ... The more he strives to be free, the more he feels his chains, the grievous chains of sin; he is Satan's prisoner, no matter how he agonizes and struggles. He is in bondage and fear, perhaps to some outward sin, to which he is peculiarly prone by reason of nature, custom, or circumstance; but always to some inward sin, some evil trait or unholy affection. And the more he frets against it, the more it prevails; he may bite, but cannot break his chains. Thus he continues, repenting and sinning, repenting and sinning, till finally he is at his wit's end, and can barely groan, "O wretched man that I am! Who shall deliver me from this body of death?"

9 ... The struggle of a man who is *"under law,"* under the "spirit of fear and bondage," is beautifully described by Paul in Romans 7, where the apostle speaks as a man awakened, [looking back on his experience of being under conviction of sin, but not yet justified by faith].

"Once I was alive without the law" (v 9a): [Before I came under conviction of sin], I blissfully thought that I was very much alive, full of wisdom, strength, and virtue. "But when the commandment came, sin revived, and I died" (v 9b): When the law, in its spiritual meaning, penetrated my heart by the power of God, my inbred sin was stirred up and inflamed, and all my so-called virtue died away.

"And the commandment which promised life proved deadly to me. For sin, finding opportunity in the commandment, deceived me and killed me" (vs 10-11): Sin, through the law, crept up on me unawares; it dashed all my hopes, and plainly showed me that, even in the midst of life, I was dead.

"The law is holy, and the commandment is good" (v 12): I cannot lay the blame on the law, but on the corruption of my own heart. "The law is spiritual, but I am carnal, sold out to sin" (v 14): I now see the spiritual nature of the law, and my own fleshly, devilish heart, totally enslaved by sin, totally at the disposal of my master—Satan.

"For I do not do what I want to do, but rather I do what I hate" (v 15): Such is the bondage under which I groan; such is the tyranny of my hard master! "I can will what is right, but I cannot do it. I do not do the good I want, but rather the evil I do not want" (vs 18-19). I experience an inner, constraining power, "that when I want to do good, evil lurks close at hand. I delight in (or consent to) the law of God in my inmost self," but I see another power also at work within me, "at war with that higher law, and making me captive to the law of sin" (vs 21-23), dragging me as a slave, behind the chariot of my conqueror, to do the very thing my soul abhors.

"O wretched man that I am! Who will deliver me from this body of death?" (v 24): Who will deliver me from this helpless, dying life, from this bondage of sin and misery? Till this is done, "I will serve the law of God with my mind, but the law of sin with my flesh" (v 25): My mind, my conscience, [my higher nature] is on God's side; but my flesh, my appetites, [my lower nature] is on the side of sin, being propelled by a force I do not understand and cannot resist.

10 ... What a vivid picture this is of a man under conviction, "under law"; who feels a burden he cannot shake off; who pants after freedom, power, and love; but is in fear and bondage still! This wretched man cries out, "Who, who will deliver me?" And the answer comes: "The grace of God, through Jesus Christ your Lord!"

III / 1 ... It is now that the miserable bondage ends, and the man is no more "under law, but *under grace.*" We now consider the state of the one who has found grace or favor in the sight of God the Father; and the grace or power of the Holy Spirit, reigning in his heart—the Spirit of adoption, that leads to the cry [of confession]: "Abba, Father!"

2 ... His eyes are now open in a new and different way, open to see a loving and gracious God. While he prays, "Show me your glory," he hears a voice in his inmost soul, "I will make all my goodness pass before you; I will be gracious to whom I am gracious, will show mercy to whom I show mercy." And soon, "the Lord descends in a cloud, and proclaims his great name." And the man sees, but not with physical eyes, "The Lord God, merciful and gracious, abundant in goodness and truth; merciful unto thousands, forgiving iniquities and sin."

3 ... Heavenly, healing light now breaks in on his soul. "God, who commanded light to shine, shines now in his heart." He sees the light of the glorious love of God, in the face of Jesus Christ. He has a divine insight into the "deep things of God," especially of God's pardoning love to them who believe in Jesus. Overwhelmed with the sight, his whole soul cries out, "My Lord and my God!" He beholds the Lamb of God taking away his sins; he clearly discerns that "God was in Christ reconciling the world to himself," and that he himself is reconciled to God by the blood of the covenant.

4 ... Here end both the guilt and power of sin. He can now say, "I am crucified with Christ. Nevertheless, I live; yet not I, but Christ lives in me. And the life I now live in the flesh, I live by faith in the Son of God, who loved me, and gave himself for me." Here end sorrow of heart and anguish of spirit; God wounded, and now God heals. Here ends also that bondage to fear. He fears no longer the wrath of God, for he knows it is now turned away from him;

he looks upon God no longer as an angry Judge, but as a loving Father. He has no fear of the devil, knowing that he has "no power, except it be given him"; no fear of hell, knowing that he is now an heir of heaven. Consequently, he has no fear of death, knowing that if this "earthly house [physical body] be dissolved, he has a building of God, not made with hands, eternal in the heavens." He groans to shake off this earthly house, that his mortality may be swallowed up by immortality, knowing that God "made him for this very thing, and gave him a claim [on eternity] by his Spirit."

5 ... And "where the Spirit of the Lord is, there is freedom"; freedom from guilt and fear; freedom from sin, the heaviest of all yokes, the basest of all bondage. His labor is no longer in vain. The snare is broken, and he has escaped. He not only strives, but prevails; not only fights, but conquers. Henceforth he is "dead to sin, and alive to God"; sin no longer reigns over him. "Being now made free from sin, he has become the servant of righteousness."

6 ... Thus, "having peace with God, through our Lord Jesus Christ," "rejoicing in hope of the glory of God," and having power over all sin, over every evil desire, every evil word and deed, he is a living witness of the "glorious liberty of the sons of God," all of whom "have received the Spirit of adoption, whereby we cry, Abba, Father!"

7 ... It is this Spirit which continually "works in them, both to will and to do" what pleases God. It is the Spirit who sheds the love of God and of all mankind abroad in their hearts, thereby purifying their hearts from the love of the world and the desires of the flesh. It is the Spirit who delivers them from anger, pride, and all vile affections. Thus, they are delivered from all unholiness of life, doing no wrong to any man, and being zealous of all good works.

8 ... To sum up: A *natural man* neither loves nor fears God; a *man under law* fears God; and a *man under grace* loves God. The first

has no light of God at all, but walks in utter darkness; the second sees only the dreadful light of hell; the third sees the joyous light of heaven. He who sleeps has a false peace; he who is awakened has no peace at all; he who believes has true peace, the peace of God filling and ruling his heart. The heathen (unbaptized or baptized) has an imagined freedom (which is actually depravity); the Jew (or anyone under law) is in abject slavery (to sin and fear); the Christian enjoys the glorious freedom of the sons of God. The unawakened child of the devil sins willingly; the awakened sins unwillingly; the child of God sins not at all. The natural man does not even fight sin; the man under law fights it, but never wins; the man under grace fights and wins—indeed, he is "more than conqueror, through him who loves us."

IV / 1 ... From this account of the three-fold state of man (the *natural,* the *legal,* the *evangelical),* it is readily apparent that it is not sufficient to divide mankind into sincere or insincere; a man may be sincere in any of these states. There may be sincere heathens, as well as sincere Jews and sincere Christians. Sincerity has nothing to do with acceptance by God!

Examine carefully, not whether you are sincere, but whether you have faith. What is the ruling principle in your soul? Is it the love of God, the fear of God, or neither? If the ruling principle is the love of the world (the love of pleasure, wealth, leisure, or status), then you are a *heathen* still. Stop your pretense! You are no Christian! Admit, in the presence of the awesome God, that you are not his son—not even his servant! However, if you cry out to God, overwhelmed with a sorrow for sin and a fear of hell, then you are a *man under law,* [a step closer to being a Christian]. Finally, if you have heaven in your heart, and the Spirit of adoption, then you are truly a *man under grace.*

Whoever you are: Do you commit sin, or not? If you do, is it willingly or unwillingly? Scripture says, "He who commits sin is of the devil." If you commit sin willingly, you are Satan's faithful servant; he will reward your labor. If you commit it unwillingly, you are still his servant, [but God is obviously working in your life]. May God deliver you out of Satan's hands!

Are you daily fighting against sin, and daily overcoming it? Then you are a child of God! Stand fast in that glorious liberty! Are you fighting, but not overcoming; striving to master sin, but falling short? Then you are not yet a child of God, a believer in Christ; but follow on, and you shall know the Lord! Are you not fighting sin at all, but leading an easy, indolent, fashionable life? How dare you call yourself a Christian! You are a disgrace to the name! Wake up, and call upon God, before hell opens up to receive you!

2 ... Perhaps one reason why so many think of themselves more highly than they ought to think, why they do not properly discern which state they are in, is because the several states are often mingled together in the same person. Experience shows that the *legal* state (the state of fear) is frequently mixed with the *natural;* few men are so fast asleep in sin that they do not sometimes wake a bit. Sometimes the Spirit of God *will* be heard [over the clamor]. He puts them in fear, so that, for a time at least, they feel the burden of sin, and earnestly desire to flee from the wrath to come. But not for long. They seldom allow the arrows of conviction to penetrate deep into their souls; but quickly stifle the grace of God and return to wallowing in the mire.

Likewise, the *evangelical* state (the state of love toward God) is frequently mixed with the *legal* state. Few men in that state of bondage and fear remain always without hope; our wise and gracious God rarely allows it. "He remembers that we are dust [human]," and desires that neither our flesh nor spirits will fail.

Therefore, as he wills, he gives a dawning of light to those who abide in darkness; he causes glimpses of his goodness to pass before their eyes. They can see the promise, though they see it afar off. And by this, they are encouraged to "run with patience the race which is set before them."

3 ... Another reason why many deceive themselves, is because they do not consider how far a man may go, and still be in a natural, or at best, a legal state. A man may have a compassionate and benevolent temperament; he may be courteous, friendly, and generous; he may have many of the moral virtues; and he may desire to be even better than he now is. He may abstain from much evil; he may do much good; he may attend public worship and engage in private devotion; and still be, for all this, a natural man, knowing neither himself nor God; a stranger to the spirit of fear and of love; having neither repented nor believed the gospel.

But suppose there were added to all this, a deep conviction of sin, with much fear of the wrath of God; strong desires to cast off sin and fulfill all righteousness; hints of hope and touches of love revealed to the soul. [These describe a man under law]—not yet a man under grace, not yet a man with true, living, Christian faith. The man under grace has, in addition, the Spirit of adoption abiding in his heart; he continually cries out, "Abba, Father!"

4 ... Beware, then, you who are called by Christ's name, that you do not fall short of your high calling. Do not rest in the natural or legal states with many who are considered good Christians, those who are content, in those lesser states, to live and die. No, God has better things for you! You are not meant to fear and tremble like devils, but to rejoice and love like angels! "You shall love the Lord your God" with every faculty of your soul. You shall rejoice always, pray without ceasing, and in all things give thanks. You shall do the will of God on earth, as it is done in heaven. Present

yourself "a living sacrifice, holy and acceptable to God." Hold fast to what you have already attained, but reach out to that which lies ahead, until "the God of peace make you perfect in every good work, working in you that which is well-pleasing in his sight, through Jesus Christ, to whom be glory forever and ever. Amen!"

10

THE WITNESS OF THE SPIRIT (I)

The Spirit itself bears witness with our spirit, that we are the children of God.

—ROMANS 8:16

1 ... How many vain men, not understanding what they affirmed, have twisted this scripture to the great loss, if not destruction, of their souls! How many have mistaken their own imagination for the witness of the Spirit, and presumed they were children of God, while continuing to do the works of the devil! These men are the real 'enthusiasts' [religious fanatics], [*not* the Methodists!] And how difficult it is to convince them otherwise, especially if they have drunk deep of that spirit of error! They will vehemently resist all efforts, believing that they are fighting for God, and "contending for the faith."

2 ... No wonder, then, that many reasonable men, seeing the dreadful effects of this delusion, lean to the opposite extreme. They are skeptical of any who claim to have the inner witness; they consider fanatical any who speak too much of the Spirit; they believe the witness of the Spirit to be an *extraordinary* gift, limited to the apostolic age, and not a gift for *ordinary* Christians in the centuries since.

3 ... But why must we run to either of these extremes? May we not

steer a middle course, keeping a sufficient distance from that spirit of error and enthusiasm, without denying the very real gift of God, which is the great privilege of all God's children, in every age? We certainly may. Therefore, let us consider: (1) What is the witness of our own spirit; what is the witness of God's Spirit; and how does his Spirit actually bear witness with our spirit? (2) How can this joint witness of God's Spirit with ours be clearly distinguished from the presumption of man's natural mind or the devil's delusion?

I / 1 ... First, what is the witness (testimony) of *our own spirit?* Some would so emphasize the rational testimony of the human spirit, that they dilute or obliterate the testimony of God's Spirit. But that does great injustice to the text: Paul is so far from speaking of the testimony of the human spirit *only,* that it could easily be argued that he is not speaking of it *at all*—that he is speaking here *only* of God's Spirit. And the Greek text *may* be understood this way. I personally take a middle position: Other scriptures and the experience of genuine Christians, convince me that there is, in every believer, both God's Spirit and his own spirit, both testifying that he is a child of God.

2 ... There are many scriptures which plainly describe the marks of the children of God; there are collections of these texts, compiled by ancient and modern writers. If you need further light on the subject, you can attend the preaching of God's word, or meditate on these texts yourself, or converse with mature believers who understand God's ways with man. And thus, by your own *God-given reason* or understanding—which religion was designed not to extinguish, but to perfect—you may measure yourself by those scriptural marks [traits; characteristics] and determine whether or not you are a child of God. For example, scripture tells us, infallibly, that "as many as are led by the Spirit of God (into holiness), are the sons of

God." We *know* that we are thus "led by the Spirit." We therefore *conclude* that we "are the sons of God."

3 ... There are numerous verses in I John that also speak to the witness of the human spirit: "We *know* that we know him, if we keep his commandments." We *"know* that everyone who does righteousness is born of him." "We *know* that we have passed from death to life, because we love the brethren." "We *know* that we are of the truth, because we love one another." "Hereby we *know* that he abides in us, by the Spirit which he has given us."

4 ... There were probably never any children of God, who were further advanced in the grace and knowledge of God through Christ, than the apostle John and those to whom he wrote. It is evident that they did not make light of those marks which pointed to their being the children of God; and that they applied them to their own souls for the confirmation of their faith. This is nothing other than rational evidence, the witness of *our own* spirit, *our own* reason or understanding. It boils down to this: Those who have these marks are children of God. If *we* have these marks, then *we* are children of God.

5 ... But how do we know that we have these marks? How do we know that we love God and neighbor, and that we keep God's commandments? The question is not how *others* know this, but how *we* know it. I would ask you this question: How do you know that you are alive, or that you are not in pain? You are immediately conscious of it. By the same immediate consciousness, you will know if your soul is alive to God; if you are saved from wrath and have a quiet and easy spirit. By the same means, you will know if you love, rejoice, and delight in God; if you love your neighbor as yourself, and have benevolence toward all mankind. As to that outward mark of God's children, which is the keeping of his commandments, you undoubtedly know in your own heart, if, by the grace of God,

you do keep them. Your conscience continually informs you, if you reverently honor the name of God; if you keep the Sabbath holy; if you honor father and mother; if you do to others as you would have them do to you; if you discipline your body in temperance and holiness; and if you do all to the glory of God.

6 ... So, this is the testimony of our own spirit, our own conscience, which God has given us to be holy of heart and outward behavior. It is a consciousness of having received, in and by the Spirit of adoption, the traits mentioned in scripture as belonging to his adopted children: a loving heart toward God and all mankind; a child-like trust in God our Father, desiring nothing but him, casting all our care on him, and embracing every man with earnest affection. It is a consciousness that we are inwardly conformed, by his Spirit, to the image of his Son; that we walk before him in justice, mercy, and truth, doing that which is pleasing in his sight.

7 ... And now, what is the testimony of *God's Spirit,* which is joined to the testimony of our spirit? How does he "bear witness with our spirit that we are the children of God"? It is hard to find words to explain "the deep things of God"; none will adequately express what the children of God experience. But one might say: The testimony of the Spirit is an inward impression on the soul, whereby the Spirit of God directly witnesses to my spirit, that I am a child of God; that Jesus Christ loved *me,* and gave himself for *me;* that all *my* sins are blotted out, and that *I, even I,* am reconciled to God.

8 ... The testimony of the Spirit must *precede* the testimony of our own spirit: We must *be* holy of heart and life, before we can be conscious that we are holy, before our own spirit can testify to our holiness. But we must love God, before we can be holy, love being the source of all holiness. And we cannot truly love God, till we know he loves us; after all, "we love him, because he first loved us." And we cannot know his pardoning love, till his Spirit witnesses

it to our spirit. Therefore, since the testimony of his Spirit must precede our love of God and all holiness, it must *precede* our inward consciousness of it, the testimony of our own spirit to it.

9 ... When God's Spirit bears witness with our spirit, that "God loved us, and gave his Son to be an atonement for our sins"; that "the Son of God loved us, and washed us from our sins in his blood"—then, and only then, can we truly love God who "first loved us"; and for his sake, we love our brother also. So now we *"know* the things that are freely given to us by God." We *know* that we love God and keep his commandments; from this, it is evident that we belong to God. This is the testimony of our own spirit, which, as long as we continue in love and obedience to God, continues joined to the testimony of God's Spirit, "that we are God's children."

10 ... Please understand that, in this discussion of our own spirit, I do not mean to exclude the operation of God's Spirit. Far from it. It is God's Spirit that works in us everything that is good; that shines on his own work, and clearly shows what he has done. According to Paul, one of the main results of receiving the Spirit is "that we may know the things which are freely given to us by God"; that he may strengthen the testimony of our conscience, and help us to more fully discern that we now do the things which please him.

11 ... Some may still ask how the Spirit bears witness with our spirit, to exclude all doubt, and to convince us of the reality of our sonship? The answer should be clear by now. First, *our* spirit: It as clearly perceives when it loves God, as when it loves anything on earth. And it can no more doubt whether it loves or not, as whether it exists or not.

So: (1) He who loves, delights, and rejoices in God is a child of God. (2) I love, delight, and rejoice in God. (3) Therefore, I am a child of God. A Christian cannot doubt being a child of God. He has full confidence in the first proposition, as it is based on scripture, that he who loves God is a child of God. He has an inward proof, nothing short of self-evident, in the second proposition, that he himself loves God. Thus, the testimony of his own spirit is manifested to his heart with such conviction, that he cannot doubt the logical conclusion, that he is indeed a child of God.

12 ... Second, *God's* Spirit: Exactly *how* his testimony is manifested to the heart, I cannot explain. Such knowledge is too high and wonderful for me! Like the wind blowing, I cannot tell where it comes from, or where it goes. As no one really knows what is in a man, but the man's own spirit; so, no one knows the things of God, but God's own Spirit. But this much we do know: The Spirit of God gives the believer such a testimony of his adoption, that while it is present in the soul, he can no more doubt the reality of his sonship, than he can doubt the shining of the sun, while standing in the full blaze of its glory.

II / 1 ... The next thing to be considered is how the *joint* testimony of God's Spirit and our spirit may be clearly distinguished from the presumption of a natural mind, and the delusion of the devil. It is highly important to all who desire salvation to carefully consider it, lest they deceive their own souls. An error in this can have the most fatal of consequences, because he who errs seldom discovers his mistake till it is too late to remedy it.

2 ... So, how is this testimony to be distinguished from the presumption of a natural mind? You may be sure that a man, who never acknowledged his own sin, is always ready to flatter himself, and to think of himself (in spiritual things) more highly than he ought. It

is not strange that such a man, vain and puffed up, when he hears of this privilege of true Christians (which he considers himself to be), persuades himself that he must *already* possess the testimony of the Spirit. Such instances now abound, as they always have. How then may the real testimony of the Spirit with our spirit, be distinguished from this dangerous presumption?

3 ... I answer: Scripture abounds with definite marks, whereby the one may be distinguished from the other. It plainly describes the circumstances which go before, accompany, and follow, the genuine testimony of the Spirit of God with the spirit of a believer. Whoever carefully weighs these, will not confuse darkness for light. He will perceive so wide a difference between the real and pretended witness of the Spirit, that there will be no possibility of confusing them.

4 ... By these marks, the one who vainly presumes on the gift of God can know for sure (if he really desires to know), that he has been "given up to a strong delusion," to believing a lie. A little reflection would soon convince him that these clear, obvious marks were never found in his soul. For instance, scripture describes repentance, or conviction of sin, as always going *before* the witness of the Spirit: "Repent and believe the gospel." "Repent and be baptized." "Repent and be converted." Likewise, the Church [of England] also places repentance *before* pardon, or the witness to it. "He pardons all those who truly repent and believe his holy gospel." "Almighty God has promised forgiveness of sins to all, who, with hearty repentance and true faith, turn to him." But the vain man is a stranger to this repentance; he has never known a broken and contrite heart; the remembrance of his sins was never "grievous unto him," nor "the burden of them intolerable." In praying these words, he never meant what he said; he was merely flattering God. And were it *only* from his lack of repentance, he

still has every reason to believe that he has been grasping at a mere shadow, and has never yet experienced the real privilege of the sons of God.

5 ... Again, scripture describes being born of God, which must *precede* the witness that we are his children, as a vast and mighty change; a change "from darkness to light," "from the power of Satan unto God," "from death to life," a resurrection from the dead. As Paul said, "When we were dead in sins, he brought us to life together with Christ, and raised us up to heavenly places." But the self-deluded man knows nothing of any such change as this; this is a reality with which he is totally unacquainted. He tells you that he has *always* been a Christian, that he has never *needed* such a change. This also proves that he is not born of the Spirit, that he has never really known God, but has mistaken the voice of nature for the voice of God.

6 ... But even forgetting what he has experienced in the *past*, we may easily distinguish a child of God from a presumptuous deceiver by *present* marks. Scripture describes that joy in the Lord which accompanies the witness of his Spirit, as a humble joy, a joy that abases, a joy that causes a pardoned sinner to cry out, "Now that my eye sees you, [holy Lord], I humble myself in dust and ashes." And wherever there is such lowliness, there is also meekness and gentleness; a soft, yielding spirit and a tenderness of soul. But do these fruits attend the *supposed* testimony of the Spirit in a presumptuous man? Just the opposite: The more confident he is of the favor of God, the more he exalts himself, and the haughtier his behavior; the more overbearing to all around him; the more incapable of receiving reproof; the more impatient with contradiction. Instead of being more teachable, more "swift to hear, and slow to speak," he is slower to hear, and swifter to speak; less ready to learn, more fiery of temper, more extreme in speech. There may be a kind of

fierceness in his manner, as if he were going to take the matter out of God's hands entirely and set the whole world straight on his own!

7 ... Scripture also teaches that keeping God's commandments is a sure mark of loving God. Jesus himself said, "He who keeps my commandments is he who loves me." Love rejoices to obey; to do everything to please the beloved. A true lover of God hastens to do his will on earth as it is done in heaven. But is this the character of the presumptuous pretender to the love of God? No, his 'love' gives him liberty to disobey, to break, not keep, the commandments of God. Perhaps, when he was in fear of God's wrath, he did labor to do his will. But now, looking on himself as "not under the law," he thinks he is no longer obliged to observe it. He is therefore less zealous of good works; less careful to abstain from evil; less watchful over his own heart and behavior; less earnest to deny himself and take up his cross daily. The whole tenor of his life has changed since he has imagined himself to be 'at liberty'. He no longer "exercises himself unto godliness"; no longer "wrestles with principalities and powers"; no longer endures hardships, or struggles "to enter at the narrow gate." No, he has found an easier way to heaven; a broad, smooth, flowery path; an easy, merry, self-indulgent road. Undeniably then, he has not the true testimony of his own spirit; he cannot be conscious of having those marks which he has not. Nor can God's Spirit bear witness to a lie, testifying to his spirit that he is a child of God, when, clearly, he is a child of the devil.

8 ... Search yourself, you poor self-deceiver! You are so confident of being a child of God, so insistent on having that inner witness. But, alas, you are weighed in God's balance and found lacking; the word of the Lord has tried your soul and proved you guilty. You are not lowly of heart; you are not gentle and meek; you do not keep his commandments. Therefore, you do not truly love God; you do not follow Jesus; you do not partake of the Holy Spirit. It

is as certain as scripture can make it, that his Spirit does *not* bear witness with your spirit that you are a child of God. Cry out to God, then, that he may remove your blindness; that you may know yourself as God knows you; that you may acknowledge that you are dead in sin. Only then will you hear the voice that raises the dead, saying, "Be of good cheer! Your sins are forgiven; your faith has made you whole."

9 ... "But how may one who has the *real* witness in himself distinguish it from presumption?" How, I ask, do you distinguish day from night, or the light of a star from the light of the noonday sun? Is there not an inherent, obvious, essential difference? Do you not immediately perceive that difference? Likewise, there is an essential difference between spiritual light and spiritual darkness; between the blazing light of the Sun of righteousness and the flickering light which arises from "sparks of our own kindling." This difference is immediately and directly perceived, if our spiritual senses are rightly ordered.

10 ... To require a more minute and philosophical explanation of *how* we know the voice of God is impossible, even to one with the deepest knowledge of God. Suppose Agrippa, the wise Roman, had said to Paul, "You talk of hearing the voice of the Son of God. How do you know it was his voice? By what criteria, what intrinsic marks, do you know it? Explain how you distinguish God's voice, from the voice of humans or angels." Can you imagine the apostle trying to answer such a demand? Yet, undoubtedly, the moment he heard that voice, he knew it was the voice of God. *How* he knew it, neither man nor angel can explain.

11 ... If God were now to speak to any soul, he would want to be sure that that soul would hear his voice; otherwise, he would speak in vain. God can do as he wishes; that soul will assuredly hear his voice. But one who hears his voice, who has that inner witness,

cannot explain it to one who has it not; nor should we expect it. Were there any natural method to explain the things of God to inexperienced men, then the natural man might know the things of the Spirit. But this is contrary to the teaching of Paul, that "he cannot know them, for they are spiritually discerned," by spiritual senses, which the natural man has not.

12 ... "But how can I know that my spiritual senses are intact and well-developed?" This question is vastly important, for if a man mistake in this, he may run on in endless error and delusion. "How can I be assured that I do not mistake the voice of the Spirit?" It is by the testimony of your own spirit; by the fruits which he has produced in you. This is how you will know that you have not deceived your own soul. The inner fruits of the Spirit, ruling in the heart, are "love, joy, peace, mercy, humility, meekness, gentleness, and endurance." And the outward fruits are doing good to all, doing no evil to any, and walking in the light—a zealous, continuous obedience to all the commandments of God.

13 ... By those same fruits shall you distinguish the voice of God from the delusion of the devil. That evil spirit would not humble you before God. He would not soften your heart, melting it first into repentance, and then into filial love. The Adversary would not enable you to love your neighbor, or to put on the whole armor of God. He does not work against himself, destroying sin. No, it is none but the Son of God who comes "to destroy the works of the devil." As surely as holiness is of God, and sin the work of the devil, so surely your inner witness is not from Satan, but from God.

14 ... Well then may you say, "Thanks be to God for his unspeakable gift!" Thanks be to God, who has "sent forth the Spirit of his Son into my heart," "bearing witness with my spirit that I am a child of God!" And see to it that, not only your lips, but your life, show forth his praise. He has claimed you for his own, so glorify him in body

and spirit. Beloved, as you ponder the Father's love for you, you must cleanse and purify yourself from all sin, "perfecting holiness in the fear of God." Let all your thoughts, words, and deeds be a spiritual sacrifice, holy and acceptable to God through Christ Jesus!

11

THE WITNESS OF THE SPIRIT (II)

The Spirit itself bears witness with our spirit, that we are the children of God.

—ROMANS 8:16

I / 1 ... None who believe the scriptures to be the word of God, can doubt the importance of this truth—a truth revealed not once only, not obscurely or incidentally, but frequently, expressly, and purposely, to point out one of the specific privileges of the children of God.

2 ... It is all the more necessary to explain and defend this truth, because there is danger on both sides. If we *deny* it, there is danger that our religion will degenerate into mere formality; that "having the form of godliness," we will neglect or "deny the power of it." If we *believe* it, but do not fully understand what we believe, we are liable to run into wild enthusiasm [religious fanaticism]. It is absolutely necessary to guard those who fear God from both these dangers, by a scriptural and rational illustration and confirmation of this momentous truth.

3 ... An explanation and defense of this truth is also necessary, because so little has been written on the subject with any clarity. Some have attempted to explain away the witness of the Spirit, undoubtedly in reaction to others, who tried to defend it, but in the crudest, most unscriptural, most irrational way.

4 ... It especially concerns the Methodists, to understand, explain, and defend this doctrine; because it is a great part of the testimony which God has given them to proclaim to the world. It is because of God's singular blessing on them, that in searching the scriptures, and in finding biblical truth confirmed by the experience of believers, this great evangelical truth has been recovered, which had been for many years nearly lost and forgotten.

II /1 ... But what is the witness of the Spirit? The Greek word *'marturia'* may be translated as 'witness,' 'testimony,' or 'record.' (John says, "This is the record," the testimony, the sum total of what God reveals in scripture, "that God has given us eternal life, life in his Son.") The testimony now under consideration is given by the Spirit of God to and with our spirit; God is the one testifying. What he testifies to us is, "that we are the children of God." The immediate result of this testimony is "the fruit of the Spirit": "love, joy, peace, endurance, gentleness, goodness." Without these, the testimony itself cannot continue; it is inevitably destroyed, not only by the commission of any outward sin, or the omission of any known duty, but by giving way to any inward sin—by whatever grieves the Holy Spirit.

2 ... I stated many years ago: "It is hard to find words of men, to explain the deep things of God. None can adequately express what the Spirit works in his children. But one might say that the testimony of the Spirit is an inward impression on the soul, whereby the Spirit of God *immediately* and *directly* witnesses to my spirit, that I am a child of God; that Jesus Christ loved *me*, and gave himself for *me;* that all *my* sins are blotted out, and *I, even I,* am reconciled to God."

3 ... After twenty years' reflection, I see no reason to retract or alter any part of it, in order to make it more intelligible. If any believer

can suggest other wording, which is clearer and more scriptural, I will gladly lay mine aside.

4 ... Meanwhile, please understand that I am *not* saying that the Spirit testifies by any outward voice, nor always by an inward voice, though he may do this sometimes; and he may not always apply to the heart specific verses of scripture. But he so works upon the soul by his immediate influence, in a strong, but inexplicable way, that stormy winds and troubled waves subside, and all is sweet calm; the heart now resting in the arms of Jesus; the sinner now satisfied that God is reconciled, that his sins are forgiven and forgotten.

5 ... So, what is the dispute concerning the witness of the Spirit? It is not that there *is* a testimony of God's Spirit, or that he testifies to *our* spirit, that we are the children of God. None can deny this without flatly contradicting scripture and charging God with a lie. All agree thus far.

6 ... Nor is it questioned whether there is an *indirect* witness or testimony that we are God's children. This is practically the same as having a clear conscience; it is the result of reason, or reflection on what we feel in our souls. It is a conclusion drawn partly from scripture, and partly from our own experience. Scripture teaches that everyone who has the fruit of the Spirit is a child of God; experience or inward consciousness tells me that *I* have the fruit of the Spirit; and so I rationally conclude that I am a child of God. There is no controversy concerning this.

7 ... Neither do we assert that there is any real testimony of the Spirit without the fruit of the Spirit. On the contrary, the fruit springs immediately from the testimony; but not always to the same degree. Neither love, nor joy, nor peace is always equally clear and strong; it can vary. And the same is true of the testimony itself.

8 ... So, the point in question is whether there is any *direct* testi-

mony of God's Spirit; whether there is any other testimony of the Spirit, than that which comes from our own consciousness of having the fruit.

III / 1 ... I believe there is! That is the plain, natural meaning of the text, "The Spirit itself bears witness with our spirit, that we are the children of God." Obviously, there are *two* witnesses mentioned, who together testify to the same thing—the Spirit of *God* and our *own* spirit. The late Bishop of London seems astonished that any would doubt this. He says, "The testimony of our *own* spirit is the consciousness of our own sincerity"; or, even better, the consciousness of the fruit of the Spirit. When our spirit is conscious of this, it easily infers that we are children of God.

2 ... The Bishop then affirms that the testimony of *God's* Spirit is "the consciousness of our own good works." [The Bishop is incorrect here]; the consciousness of our own good works and of our sincerity are virtually identical; both are included in the testimony of our *own* spirit. So, we still have only *one* witness, while the text speaks of *two*.

3 ... What then is the other witness? The text is perfectly clear. However, if you need further proof, examine the verse preceding it: "You have received, not the spirit of bondage, but the Spirit of adoption, whereby we cry, Abba, Father." So, "the *Spirit itself* bears witness with our spirit."

4 ... And in Galatians is a similar text: "Because you are sons, God has sent forth the Spirit of his Son into your hearts, crying, Abba, Father." This is something *immediate* and *direct*, not the result of our own reflection. God's Spirit cries, "Abba, Father" in our hearts, *before* we ever reflect on our sincerity, [or on the fruit of the Spirit within, or on our good works]; *before* we do any reasoning

whatsoever. All these texts plainly, naturally, obviously, describe a *direct* testimony of the Spirit.

5 ... And the testimony of God's Spirit must *precede* the testimony of our spirit. We must *be* holy in heart and life *before* we can be conscious that we are so. But we must love God *before* we can be holy at all, love being the root of all holiness. And we cannot love God, till we know that God loves us; and we cannot know God's love, till *his* Spirit witnesses it to *our* spirit. Only then can we believe it; only then can we say, "The life I now live, I live by faith in the Son of God, who loved me, and gave himself for me." *'Then, only then we feel Our interest in his blood, And cry, with joy unspeakable, Thou art my Lord, my God!'* Since the testimony of God's Spirit must precede the love of God and all holiness, it must obviously precede our consciousness of it.

6 ... This biblical doctrine is confirmed by the experience of the children of God; the experience, not of a few, but of a great multitude, in this and every age, "a cloud of witnesses." It is confirmed by your experience and mine. The Spirit itself bore witness to my spirit, that I was a child of God, gave me evidence thereof, and immediately I cried, "Abba, Father." I did this (and so did you), *before* I ever reflected on, or was conscious of, any fruit of the Spirit. It was from this testimony that all the fruit of the Spirit flowed. First, I heard, *'Thy sins are forgiven! Accepted thou art! I listened, and heaven sprung up in my heart.'*

7 ... Thousands of Christians can declare that they never knew themselves to be in God's favor till it was directly witnessed to them by his Spirit. *Till then,* they felt the wrath of God abiding on them; nothing less than a *direct* testimony from God could convince them! If you had tried to tell them that the way to know for sure that they were the children of God, was to consider rationally what God had already wrought in their hearts and lives,

they would have replied like this: "I *cannot* conclude that. I feel more like the child of the devil, my mind alienated from God. I have no joy in the Spirit; my soul is sorrowful. I have no peace; my soul is a troubled, stormy sea." So, how can these poor souls [under conviction of sin] possibly be comforted, but by a divine testimony, *not* that they are good, or sincere, or have the fruits, but *rather* that God justifies the ungodly? Till the very moment a man is justified, he *is* ungodly, void of all true holiness. He does nothing truly good, till he is conscious of being accepted by God, not for any "works of righteousness which he has done," but by the free mercy of God, based solely and wholly on what Christ has done for him. It cannot be otherwise if "a man is justified by faith, without the works of the law." How could he possibly be aware of any goodness, inward or outward, *before* his justification? Just the contrary: My overwhelming consciousness that "there dwells in me no good thing" is absolutely necessary prior to being "justified freely, through redemption in Jesus." Was any man, in all the world, ever justified, till he was brought to this point? *'I give up every plea beside–Lord, I am damned, but Thou hast died.'*

8 ... Therefore, whoever denies the existence of a direct testimony of the Spirit, in effect, denies justification by faith. Either he has never experienced justification (his "purification from former sins," as Peter terms it); or he has already forgotten God's great work in his soul.

9 ... Even the experience of non-believers helps explain that of believers: Some of these have a real desire to please God, but they consider it absurd to talk of *knowing* one's sins are forgiven; they do not even pretend to such a thing. Many of these are aware, to some degree, of their own sincerity, and even of their own uprightness; but this brings no awareness that they are forgiven, no knowledge that they are the children of God. In fact, the more sincere they

are, the more uneasy they are in *not* knowing it; which only proves that it cannot be known, satisfactorily, simply by the testimony of our own spirit, without God himself *directly* testifying that we are his children!

IV / 1 ... There are many objections to this doctrine, which we will now consider. First, it has been objected, "Experience is not sufficient to prove a doctrine which is not based on scripture." This is certainly true, but it does not speak to this case, for it has been shown that this doctrine *is* based on scripture, and that the experience of believers only confirms it.

2 ... "But madmen, French prophets, and enthusiasts of every kind have imagined that they experienced this witness." That is true, and perhaps a few of them did, for a while. But the fact that madmen have claimed it, does not prove that others have not truly experienced it; madmen can claim to be kings, but that does not prove that there are no real kings.

"But many who argue strongly for this doctrine have utterly rejected the Bible." Perhaps so; but thousands argue for it who have the highest regard for the Bible.

"And many have fatally deceived themselves because of this doctrine and cannot be reasoned with or rescued." Yes, but a scriptural doctrine is no less true, just because men abuse it to their own destruction.

3 ... "Undoubtedly, the *fruit* of the Spirit *is* the *witness* of the Spirit." Not so; thousands doubt it—and flatly deny it! But to continue this objection: "The witness of the fruit of the Spirit is sufficient, without any direct witness at all, except when the fruit is absent, or is not perceived. And to contend for the direct witness of the Spirit, while

not perceiving the fruit, is to contend for being in the favor of God, while not knowing it for sure." I answer: The fruit *is* absent when the direct witness is first given; [the fruit follows]. And before the fruit can be perceived, the *only* way to know that one is in the favor of God is by a direct witness of the Spirit. The direct witness may shine clear, while the indirect one is still under a cloud.

4 ... Second, this objection is made: "The purpose of the witness of the Spirit is to prove that our profession of faith is genuine; but it does *not* prove it." I answer: Proving this is *not* the purpose of the witness. The witness *precedes* any profession; our only profession prior to the witness is that we are guilty, helpless sinners. The purpose of the witness is to assure those to whom it is given that they are *now* the children of God, "justified freely by his grace, through redemption in Jesus." This does *not* suppose that their preceding thoughts, words, and deeds were conformable to scripture; quite the opposite; it supposed that they were sinners, from top to bottom, in heart and life. Otherwise, God would be justifying the *godly,* and their own *works* would be counted to them as righteousness. I fear that a belief in justification by works is at the root of all these objections; whoever sincerely believes that God *imputes* righteousness *without* works has no difficulty in understanding the witness of the Spirit preceding the fruit.

5 ... Third, "One gospel tells us that God will give the *Holy Spirit* to those who ask; another gospel says he will give *good gifts.* That shows that the Spirit's way of bearing witness is by giving good gifts." I answer: Neither text says anything about bearing witness. Till this argument can be better argued, I will simply pass it by.

6 ... Fourth, "Scripture says, 'The tree is known by its fruits. So, prove everything; try the spirits; *examine* yourselves.'" This is true. And I contend that every man who believes he has the witness within, should examine himself, should test his conviction. If the

fruit follows, it is of God; if not, it is not.

And further objections: "The direct witness of the Spirit is never referred to in the Bible." No, not as a single witness; it is always joined with the witness of our own spirit, testifying that we are the children of God. Who could argue otherwise?

"'Examine yourselves to determine whether you are in the faith.' Can you not determine yourselves whether Christ is in you?" I contend that when a man thus examines himself, the direct and indirect witnesses *together* lead him to conclude that he has faith in Christ; it is not one witness without the other, or one against the other. First, he has the inward witness of the Spirit, and then the outward fruit of the Spirit.

7 ... "But the testimony arising from the internal and external *change* [in a believer] is constantly referred to in the Bible." It is; and *we* constantly refer to it as well, as a means to *confirm* the witness of the Spirit.

"But all the marks *you* have given, to distinguish the work of God from delusion, refer to the *change* wrought in us and on us." Again, true; [but the marks *follow* the direct witness of the Spirit, and in no way disprove its reality or necessity.]

8 ... Fifth, "The direct witness of the Spirit does not guarantee us against delusion. Can we trust such an undependable witness?" I answer: To guarantee us against delusion is precisely *why* God gives us two joint witnesses that we are his children. Their testimony *can* be trusted; we need nothing further to prove it.

"But the direct witness only asserts, and does not prove, anything." By two witnesses shall every truth be established. When God's Spirit witnesses with our spirit, as God intends it should, that does prove that we are the children of God.

9 ... Sixth, "You claim that the change wrought within us is a sufficient testimony, except in extreme trials, like that of Christ on the cross; but none of us can face anything like that." Not so; any of us may face extreme trials, such that it would be impossible for us to keep our filial trust and confidence in God, without the direct witness of his Spirit.

10 ... Finally, "The greatest proponents for this doctrine are some of the proudest and most uncharitable of men." Perhaps some of the *hottest* proponents are such, but many of the *firmest* proponents are meek and lowly in heart, *'True followers of their lamb-like Lord.'*

The preceding objections are the ones I have heard most; they contain, I believe, the main points in the argument against the witness of God's Spirit. But if one calmly and impartially considers both the objections and the answers given, together, he will easily see that they do not weaken or destroy that great scriptural truth, that the Spirit of God, both directly and indirectly, witnesses that we are the children of God.

V / 1 ... To sum it all up: The testimony of the Spirit is an inward impression on the souls of believers, whereby the Spirit of God directly testifies to their spirit, that they are the children of God. The question is *not* whether there is a testimony of the Spirit, but whether there is a *direct* testimony; whether there is any witness except our own consciousness of the fruit of the Spirit within. We believe there is: Because this is the plain, natural meaning of the text, illustrated by its context and by the parallel passage from Galatians. Because, logically, the testimony must *precede* the fruit which springs from it. And because the plain meaning of this scripture is confirmed by the experience of innumerable believers; and by the experience of all who are under conviction of sin, and cannot rest till they have the direct witness; and even by the experience of non-believers who, not having the witness in themselves, can never know their sins forgiven.

2 ... Let me briefly repeat the common objections to the doctrine: (1) Experience is *not* sufficient to prove an *un*scriptural doctrine. (2) Madmen and fanatics have imagined such a witness. (3) The purpose of the witness is to prove our profession genuine, which it does not do. (4) Scripture tells us to examine ourselves, to prove that we exhibit the fruit of the Spirit. (5) A direct witness is never referred to in scripture. (6) Such a witness cannot keep us from delusion. (7) The change wrought in us is a sufficient testimony, except in extreme trials, like Christ on the cross.

And again, I briefly answer those objections: (1) Experience *is* sufficient to *confirm* a doctrine which *is* grounded in scripture. (2) Though many do imagine they experience what, in fact, they do *not*, that does not detract from the real experience. (3) The witness is to assure us that we are God's children, which, in fact, it does. (4) The direct witness of the Spirit is known by its fruit, which follows it. (5) The direct *and* the indirect witness are referred to in this verse, "Do you yourselves not *know* that Jesus Christ is in you?" (6) The Spirit of God, witnessing with our spirit, *does* keep us from delusion. (7) We are all subject to trials, in which the testimony of our own spirit is *not* sufficient; only God's Spirit can assure us that we are his children.

3 ... Two inferences may be drawn from this: First, no one should ever presume to rest in any supposed testimony of the Spirit which is separate from the fruit of it. If the Spirit really testifies that we are God's children, the immediate consequence will be the fruit of the Spirit—"love, joy, peace, patience, gentleness, goodness, fidelity, meekness, temperance." And however much this fruit may be clouded for a time, while the person is being strongly

tempted by Satan, still a substantial part remains, even under the thickest cloud. Joy in the Spirit may be withdrawn during a time of trial, and the soul may be exceedingly sorrowful, but even this is generally restored and increased, so that, in the end, we rejoice "with joy unspeakable."

4 ... Second, no one should ever rest in any supposed fruit of the Spirit without the witness. There may be real *foretastes* of joy, peace, and love from God, *before* we have the witness in ourselves; *before* the Spirit of God witnesses with our spirit that we have "redemption in the blood of Jesus, the forgiveness of sins." And there may be a *degree* of the other fruits, by the prevenient grace of God, *before* we are accepted in Christ, and have the testimony of acceptance. Nevertheless, it is not advisable to rest here; it is at the peril of our souls if we do. If we are wise, we will continually cry to God, until his Spirit cries in our heart, Abba, Father! This is the privilege of all the children of God, and without it we can never be assured that we are his children; without it we cannot maintain a steady peace, or avoid perplexing doubts and fears. But once we have received this Spirit of adoption, this "peace which passes all understanding," which expels all doubt and fear, our hearts and minds will be kept in Christ Jesus. And when this has brought forth its genuine fruit, all inward and outward holiness, it is undoubtedly God's will to give us *always* what he has *once* given; so that we should never be deprived of either God's Spirit or our own spirit, that [absolute] consciousness of walking in all righteousness and true holiness.

Preached at Newry, 1767

12

THE WITNESS OF OUR OWN SPIRIT

This is our rejoicing: the testimony of our own conscience, that in simplicity and godly sincerity, not with fleshly wisdom, but by the grace of God, we have lived our lives in the world.

—I CORINTHIANS 1:12

1 ... This is the voice of every true believer in Christ, so long as he abides in faith and love. He who follows Christ never walks in darkness, and while he has the light, he lives in joy. He who has received the Lord Jesus, walks in him; and as he walks in the Lord, he rejoices in him.

2 ... But in order not to build the house on sand (lest the rains and winds beat upon it, and it fall), I intend to show the nature and ground of a Christian's *joy*. In general, it is that happy peace, that calm satisfaction of spirit, which arises from the testimony of his conscience. But to understand the text more thoroughly, it will be necessary to consider all of Paul's words and phrases.

3 ... First, what do we mean by the common word *'conscience'*? One would think that it was an exceedingly difficult concept, considering how many volumes have been written on the subject, by scholars ancient and modern. And yet, from all their elaborate inquiries, we have learned little; in fact, the scholars have tended to complicate and obscure what should be plain and easy to understand. Set aside all their difficult words, and every man of honest heart will soon understand it.

4 ... God has made us thinking beings, capable of perceiving what is present, and reflecting on what is past. In particular, we are capable of perceiving whatever occurs in our own hearts and lives, knowing whatever we feel or do, present or past. This is what we mean when we say that man is a *conscious* being: he is conscious of himself, conscious of his inner life and outward behavior, both present and past. But *conscience* implies more than this. Conscience includes such consciousness, but its main purpose is [value judgment]: to excuse or accuse, to approve or disapprove, to acquit or condemn.

5 ... Some recent writers have given this a new name, calling it a 'moral sense.' But 'conscience' is still preferable, because it is more familiar, and thus more easily understood. For the Christian, it is doubly preferable, because it is the word used in scripture. And the meaning there, particularly in the epistles of Paul, is this: A faculty or power, implanted by God in *every* soul, of perceiving right or wrong in his own heart and life, in his feelings, thoughts, words, and actions.

6 ... So, what is the rule by which men are to judge of right and wrong, by which their conscience is to be directed? The rule for *heathens,* as Paul teaches in Romans, is "the law written in their hearts (by the finger of God). These, not having the (outward) law, are a law unto themselves, their conscience bearing witness" to whether they walk by this rule or not, "and their thoughts either accusing or excusing them," acquitting or defending them. But the *Christian* rule of right and wrong is the word of God, the writings of the Old and New Testament; that "scripture which was given by inspiration of God, and is profitable for doctrine (or teaching the whole will of God), for reproof (of what is contrary to it), for correction (of error), and for instruction (or training us up) in righteousness."

This is a lamp to a Christian's feet and a light to his paths. This alone he takes as his rule of right or wrong, of what is good or evil. He considers nothing good, but what scripture prescribes, either directly or by plain inference; he considers nothing evil, but what scripture prohibits; and whatever scripture neither prescribes nor prohibits, he considers neither good nor evil, but of an indifferent nature. This is the whole, sole outward rule by which his conscience is to be directed in all things.

7 ... If it is so directed, then he has "a good conscience toward God," "a conscience void of offense, toward God and men." To have such a conscience, several things are required: (1) A right understanding of God's word; for it is impossible to walk by a rule if we do not understand what it means. (2) A true knowledge of ourselves, a penetrating knowledge of our hearts and lives, of our inner feelings and outward behavior; for it is impossible, without such knowledge, to compare ourselves with our rule. (3) A conformity of our hearts and lives with the written word of God; for without it, we could have only a guilty conscience. (4) An inward perception of this conformity to the rule; this is what is meant by "a good conscience."

8 ... Whoever desires to have this conscience must lay the right foundation. "No other foundation can any man lay, than that which has been laid, even Jesus Christ." And no man can build on Christ [the foundation], except by a living faith; no man is joined to Christ, till he can testify that he lives his life "by faith in the Son of God (now *revealed* in my heart), who loved me and gave himself for me." (1) Faith alone is the evidence, the conviction, the demonstration of things invisible, by which our minds are opened, and flooded by divine light, that we may "see the wondrous things of God's law," the excellency and purity of every commandment contained in it. (2) It is by faith that, beholding "the

light of the glory of God in the face of Jesus Christ," we perceive all that is in ourselves. (3) And by faith alone can the blessed love of God be "shed abroad in our hearts," which enables us to love one another as Christ has loved us. (4) By faith is the gracious promise fulfilled: "I will put my laws in their minds and engrave them in their hearts." This produces in their souls a complete conformity with God's holy and perfect law and brings "into captivity every thought to the obedience of Christ." As a bad tree cannot bring forth good fruit, so a good tree cannot bring forth bad fruit. When a believer's heart is good, so is his life, thoroughly conformed to the rule of God's commandments. (5) As a result, the believer is conscious of that conformity and gives glory to God, proclaiming: "This is our rejoicing: the testimony of our own conscience, that in simplicity and godly sincerity, not with fleshly wisdom, but by the grace of God, we have lived our lives in the world."

9 ... When Paul says, in our text, that *"we have lived our lives,"* he is speaking broadly of our total conduct, of soul and body, in every circumstance of life. It includes our thoughts and feelings, our words and actions; the use of all our powers and abilities, with respect to God or man.

10 ... "We have lived our lives *in the world,*" in the world of the ungodly, among the children of the devil. What a world this is! As our God is good, and does good, so the god of this world, and all his children, are evil, and do evil to the children of God. Like their father, they are always lurking, or "walking about, seeking whom they may devour"; using fraud or force, secret cunning or open violence, they try to destroy those who are not of this world; continually at war against our souls, and using old weapons and new, they labor to bring us back into the snare of the devil, into the wide road that leads to destruction.

11 ... "We have lived our lives *in simplicity and godly sincerity.*" *Simplicity* is what Jesus called a 'single eye': "If your eye be single, your whole body shall be full of light." What the eye is to the body, the intention is to our words and actions; if our intention is pure, all our words and actions will be pure, full of heavenly light, full of love, peace, and joy in the Holy Spirit. So, we are simple of heart, when our mind is singly fixed on God; when in all things we aim at God alone, as our strength and happiness, as our exceeding great reward, as our all in all, in time and eternity. This is simplicity: when a single intention of promoting God's glory, of doing and suffering God's blessed will, runs through our soul and fills our heart, and is the spring of all our thoughts, desires, and purposes.

12 ... Godly *sincerity* differs from *simplicity* in this way: Simplicity has to do with the intention itself, sincerity with the execution of it; sincerity actually hits the mark, which simplicity only aims at. (Paul sometimes uses 'sincerity' in a more restricted sense, for speaking the truth without guile; but here it has a more extensive meaning.) In our text, sincerity implies that we do, in fact, speak and do all to the glory of God; that our whole life flows on in a steady stream, always subservient to God's glory; walking on in the highway of holiness, in the paths of justice, mercy, and truth.

13 ... This sincerity is called '*godly* sincerity,' to prevent any confusion with *heathen* sincerity (for even they valued a kind of sincerity). Godly sincerity has God himself as its focus and goal, God himself as its source and author, "from whom comes every good and perfect gift."

14 ... "We have lived our lives, *not with fleshly wisdom*": It is as if Paul had said, "We cannot live in this world, in simplicity and godly sincerity, relying on our own mental acuity or acquired wisdom. We cannot attain this simplicity or practice this sincerity, based on good sense, good nature, or good breeding. It exceeds our natural

courage and determination, the precepts of human philosophy, and the power of custom or education. So long as a man (even a highly accomplished man) is in the *flesh,* in his natural state, relying only on his own fleshly, natural wisdom, [he will fail in his quest for simplicity or sincerity].

But if any man *could* have succeeded, it would have been the apostle Paul. Who was more highly favored with all the gifts of nature and education, than he? Besides his extraordinary natural abilities, he had all the benefits of learning; he had received a classical education at Tarsus, and a Judaic education at the feet of the great Gamaliel [in Jerusalem]. He was raised a Pharisee, the strictest of all sects; he was "abundantly zealous" in seeking to please God, and "blameless in the righteousness of the law." But none of this availed in attaining this simplicity and godly sincerity; it was all labor lost. In deep and piercing desperation, he was forced to cry out, "The things which were gain to me, those I counted loss for Christ. Indeed, I count all things but loss, for the excellence of knowing Christ Jesus my Lord."

15 ... Paul could only attain it by the 'excellent knowledge of Jesus Christ,'—or 'by the grace of God,' an expression equally applicable. The grace of God is often to be understood as that unmerited love and mercy, by which a sinner, through the merits of Christ, is reconciled to God. But in this passage, it refers more to the power of God the Holy Spirit, which "works in us both to will and to do his good pleasure." When the grace of God in the former sense (pardoning love) is manifested to our soul, the grace of God in the latter sense (spiritual power) takes place there. Now we can perform, through God, what to man was impossible. Now we can order our entire lives properly. Now we can do all things in the light and power of that love, through Christ who strengthens us. We now have "the testimony of our conscience," which we could

never have had by fleshly wisdom, "that in simplicity and godly sincerity, we live our lives in the world."

16 ... This is the basis for a Christian's *rejoicing.* He who has this testimony can say [with Mary], "'My soul magnifies the Lord, and my spirit rejoices in God my Savior.' I rejoice in him who, of his own unmerited love and mercy, has called me to the salvation in which I now stand. I rejoice because his Spirit bears witness with my spirit, that I am bought with the blood of the Lamb, and that believing in him, 'I am a member of Christ, a child of God, and an heir of the kingdom of heaven.' I rejoice because the knowledge of God's love toward me, by the Spirit, causes me to love him, and to love every soul he has made. I rejoice because he allows me to feel in myself 'the mind that was in Christ.'"

[Of what does the mind of Christ consist?] *Simplicity:* the power always to fix the loving eye of my soul on him alone, "who loved me and gave himself for me"; to aim only at his glorious will, in all I think, or speak, or do. *Purity:* desiring nothing more than God; "crucifying the flesh"; "setting my affections on things above." *Holiness:* recovering the image of God; renewing the soul after his likeness. *Godly sincerity:* directing all my words and works to his glory.

"I rejoice because my conscience bears me witness that I 'walk worthy of my vocation'; that I 'abstain from all appearance of evil'; that, as I have opportunity, I do all possible good to all men; that I follow my Lord in all my steps, and do what is acceptable in his sight. I rejoice because I see and feel, through his inspiration, that it is he who works my works in me. I rejoice, through the light of God shining in my heart, that I have the power to walk in his ways, not turning to left or right."

17 ... From all this, we may infer that the joy of a mature Christian is not a *natural* joy; it does not arise from any natural cause.

Physical sensations may mimic joy *temporarily,* but the Christian knows real joy *continually.* This joy is not based on bodily health or ease, on physical strength or soundness of constitution; it is equally strong in sickness and pain, perhaps even stronger. Many a Christian has experienced the greatest joy imaginable when the body was well-nigh worn out with pain or consumed with deteriorating sickness. Least of all can this joy be ascribed to outward prosperity, or to the favor of men; for often, when their faith has been sorely tried, with all kinds of afflictions, the children of God have rejoiced in him with joy unspeakable. And never have any Christians rejoiced more than those who were treated as "the filth and refuse of the world"; who wandered about in hunger and cold and nakedness, ridiculed and imprisoned; who sacrificed all, "that they might finish their course with joy."

18 ... Furthermore, we may infer that Christian joy is not a *blind* joy; it does not arise from any blindness of conscience, from any inability to discern good from evil. Far from it. The Christian was an utter stranger to this joy, till the eyes of his understanding were opened, and he was given spiritual discernment. Never has he been so sharp-sighted as now, so quick to perceive the smallest things! As a mote is visible in the sunlight, so, to him who is walking in the light, every mote of sin is visible. Never does he close the eyes of his conscience; his soul is always wide awake. He is always standing on the ramparts, harkening to the voice of his Lord, and rejoicing in "him who is invisible."

19 ... Finally, Christian joy is not a *dull* joy; a false joy may arise in those whose heart is dull, unfeeling, and without spiritual understanding. These may even rejoice in sin, probably calling it 'Christian liberty,' while, in fact, it is nothing but drunkenness of soul, numbness of spirit, and the stupid insensibility of a seared conscience. On the contrary, a Christian has the most exquisite

sensibility; he has never had such a tender conscience, since the love of God has reigned in his heart. His daily prayer would be: *'O that my tender soul might flee The first approach of ill; Quick, as the apple of an eye, The touch of sin to feel.'*

20 ... To conclude: Christian joy is joy in obedience; joy in loving God and keeping his commandments. But *not* keeping them as if to fulfill the terms of the covenant of works; as if by any works of righteousness, we were to procure pardon and acceptance with God. No! We are already pardoned and accepted through the mercy of God in Christ. We have life, life from the death of sin, not by our own obedience, but through the grace of God. God "has brought us to life, who were dead in sins"; and now we are "alive to God through Jesus our Lord." And we rejoice to walk according to the covenant of grace, in holy love and happy obedience. We rejoice that we have "not received the grace of God in vain"; that God having reconciled us, we run in the way of his commandments. He has "girded us with strength," and we gladly "fight the good fight of faith," rejoicing to "lay hold of eternal life." This is our rejoicing, that, not by our own resources, but through the power of his Spirit, freely given in Christ, we can work the works of God. And may he work in us what is well-pleasing in his sight! To whom be praise forever and ever!

Note: The preceding sermon describes the experience of those who are strong in faith. It may cause those who are weak to be discouraged. To prevent this, the following sermon may be of use.

13

ON SIN IN BELIEVERS

If any man be in Christ, he is a new creature.
—II CORINTHIANS 5:17

I / 1 ... Is there any sin in him who is in Christ? Does any sin *remain* in those who are born of God, or are they wholly delivered from it? This is not a question of mere curiosity, or of little importance. Rather, it is of the utmost importance to every serious Christian; it concerns his present and eternal happiness.

2 ... There was no controversy in the early Church concerning this, as all were agreed. The Church fathers, whose writings we possess, declare with one voice that even believers in Christ, till they become "strong in the Lord and in his mighty power," need to "wrestle with flesh and blood," with their own evil nature, as well as "with principalities and powers."

3 ... The Church of England follows the early Church, when it declares in Article IX: "Original sin is the corrupt nature of every man, which is inclined to evil, and is contrary to the Spirit. This infection remains even in those who are regenerated, whose fleshly desires continue to be at odds with the law of God. Although there is no condemnation for them who now believe, still this desire must be considered sinful."

4 ... This same doctrine is held by all other churches, Greek, Roman, or Reformed. Indeed, some of these seem to carry the thing *too* far: They describe the remaining corruption in the believer's heart in such a way as to *minimize* any dominion over it, and to *maximize* their continuing bondage to it, leaving hardly any distinction between a believer and an unbeliever.

5 ... To avoid this extreme, many well-meaning men, particularly the Moravians, ran to the *other* extreme, affirming that "all true believers are not only saved from the *dominion* of sin, but from the very *existence* of sin, so that it no longer dwells in them at all." Twenty years ago, many Englishmen, influenced by the Moravians, began preaching the same thing.

6 ... To be fair, when the Moravians themselves were pressed on the matter, many admitted that, though "sin might still remain in the *flesh* of a believer, it did not remain in his *heart.*" When the absurdity of this was shown, they compromised a bit more, saying that perhaps sin did still *remain* in the believer, but it did not *reign* in him.

7 ... But the Englishmen, who had received the teaching from them, were not so easily persuaded to part with a favorite opinion. And even when shown that it was indefensible, they refused to give it up, but maintain it to this day.

II / 1 ... For the sake of those who fear God and seek truth, I want to consider this point calmly and impartially. I will use the terms *'regenerate' [born-again], 'justified,'* and *'believers'* indiscriminately; though they have not precisely the same meaning, they end up at the same place, since everyone who believes is both justified and born of God.

2 ... By sin, I mean *inward* sin; any sinful inclination or affection or desire; such as pride, self-will, or love of the world; such as lust, anger, or peevishness; any inward disposition which is contrary to the mind of Christ.

3 ... So, the question is not about *outward* sin; whether a believer *commits* sin. We all agree that he who commits sin is of the devil. Neither is the question about whether inward sin will *always* remain in the children of God, or whether a believer may *relapse* into inward or outward sin. [We can discuss these at another time.] No, the question is simply this: Is a justified, regenerate believer freed from *all* sin the moment he is justified? Is there then no sin in his heart, and none thereafter, unless he fall from grace?

4 ... We gladly admit that the state of a justified person is inexpressibly great and glorious: He is born again, not "of the will of man, but of God." He is a child of God, a member of Christ, an heir of heaven. "The peace of God keeps his heart and mind in Christ Jesus." His body is a "temple of the Holy Spirit." He is "created anew in Christ"; he is washed and sanctified. His heart is purified by faith; he is cleansed from worldly corruption. "The love of God is shed abroad in his heart"; and so long as he "walks in love," which he may always do, he worships God in spirit and in truth. He keeps God's commandments and does what is pleasing in God's sight, having *power* over both inward and outward sin, from the very moment he is justified.

III / 1 ... "But was he not then freed from *all* sin, so that *none* remains in his heart?" No, I do not believe this; nor does the apostle Paul. In describing the state of believers in general, he says in Galatians, "The flesh opposes the Spirit, and the Spirit the flesh; they are contradictory." Nothing can be clearer. Paul here directly states that the flesh, the evil nature, even in believers, opposes the Spirit; and that even in the regenerate there are two opposing principles.

2 ... Again, when Paul writes to Corinth, he says, "Brothers, I could not speak to you as to spiritual men, but as to carnal men, as to babes in Christ, for you are still carnal." Paul is speaking to those who were unquestionably believers, his brothers in Christ, but he also calls them 'carnal,' 'of the flesh.' He also refers to strife among them, but never hints that they had lost their faith. He speaks of them being carnal, and being babes in Christ, at the same time; plainly showing that every believer is (to some degree) carnal, while he is still a babe in Christ.

3 ... Indeed, this important point, that there are two contrary principles in believers—nature and grace, flesh and Spirit—runs all through Paul's writings, and all through scripture in general. Almost all the directions and exhortations in scripture are based on this idea, pointing to wrong feelings or practices in believers; they are continually exhorted to fight against and overcome these, by the power of faith within.

4 ... In Revelation, the church at Ephesus was told: "I know your works; for my name's sake you have labored and not fainted. Nevertheless, I have something against you, because you have left your first love." These Ephesians were certainly believers, yet there was sin in their hearts, from which they were told to repent.

5 ... The church at Pergamum was also told to repent, which implies sin, though Christ acknowledged that they had "held fast, and not denied my faith." The church at Sardis was told to "strengthen the things that remain, that are ready to die." The good which remained was ready to die, but was not yet dead; there was still a spark of faith which needed to be strengthened.

6 ... Again, when Paul exhorts the Corinthian believers to "cleanse themselves from all filthiness of flesh and spirit," he is plainly teaching that those believers were not yet fully cleansed.

You may remark, "Whoever abstains from all *appearance* of evil, thereby 'cleanses himself from all filthiness.'" Not so! For instance, someone reviles me; I feel resentment, which is filthiness of spirit; but I say nothing. I have abstained from all appearance of evil, but this does not cleanse me from filthiness, as I learn to my sorrow.

7 ... This position (that there is *no* sin in a believer, no carnal mind, no inclination to backsliding) is not only contrary to the word of God, but also to the experience of believers. Believers continually feel a heart inclined toward backsliding, a natural tendency toward evil, a proneness to depart from God and to cling to things of the world. They are continually aware of sin remaining in their hearts (pride, self-will, unbelief); and of sin clinging to all they say and do, even their best actions and holiest duties. Yet, at the same time, they "know that they are of God," not doubting it for a minute. They feel his Spirit witnessing to their spirit that they are his children. They rejoice in Christ's atonement. So, they are equally assured that sin is in them, but that Christ, their hope of glory, is *also* in them.

8 ... "But can Christ be in the same heart where sin is?" Undoubtedly, he can; where sickness is, there is the Physician, *'Carrying on his work within, Striving till he cast out sin.'* It is true that Christ cannot *reign,* where sin reigns; neither will he *dwell* where sin is allowed. But Christ *is* and *dwells* in the heart of every believer, who is fighting against all sin, though not yet purified.

9 ... The opposite doctrine, that there is *no* sin in believers, is quite new to the Church, never taught till recently, when it was

'discovered' by Count Zinzendorf [the Moravian leader]. I do not think I have ever seen it in any of the ancient or modern writers, unless in some of the wild, ranting antinomians. And even these may admit that there is sin in their *flesh,* but not in their *heart.* But *new* doctrine must be wrong; while *old* doctrine is the only true one; no doctrine can be right, unless it is the same "which was from the beginning."

10 ... One further argument against this new, unscriptural doctrine may be drawn from the dreadful consequences of it. If a believer admits he felt anger, must I tell him that, obviously, he has no faith? If another says that his will is averse to my good advice, must I tell him that he is an unbeliever, under the wrath and curse of God? What would be the consequence of this? His soul would not only be grieved and wounded, but perhaps destroyed. And having cast away his shield, how shall he "quench the fiery arrows of the wicked one"? How shall he overcome the world? He stands disarmed amid his enemies, open to all their assaults. No wonder, then, if he be overthrown; if they take him captive at will; if he fall from one wickedness to another, and never see good anymore. Therefore, I cannot believe that there is no sin in a believer from the moment he is justified. Why? Because it is contrary to God's word; it is contrary to the experience of believers; it is a brand-new doctrine, never heard of till recently; and it is attended by the most fatal consequences, not only grieving those whom God has not grieved, but perhaps dragging them to everlasting destruction.

IV / 1 ... Nevertheless, we should fairly consider the chief arguments of those who attempt to support this [Moravian] position. First, they try to prove their point from scripture. They contend that every believer is born of God; is clean, holy, and sanctified; has a new pure heart; is a temple of the Holy Spirit. Since "that which is born of flesh is flesh (altogether evil), and "that which is born of the Spirit is spirit (altogether good, they claim), how can a believer be clean, sanctified, and holy, and at the same time unclean, unsanctified, and unholy? How can he be pure and impure, or have a new and an old heart, all at the same time? How can he be unholy while he is a temple of the Holy Spirit?

I have made their case as strongly as possible, so that its full weight may be understood. Now, let me answer it: It is true that "that which is born of the Spirit is spirit." But the text does not conclude that he is "altogether good"; that is *their* conclusion. The text simply affirms that the believer is a *spiritual* man, yet not, necessarily, *altogether* spiritual. The Christians at Corinth were spiritual; otherwise, they would not have been Christians. But they were certainly not altogether spiritual; they were still partly carnal. They had not fallen from grace; they were simply babes in Christ. So, yes, a believer may be clean and unclean, holy and unholy, at the same time. The Corinthians were. Paul says that they were sanctified, cleansed from all *outward* sin; yet at the same time, in another sense, they were unsanctified, not cleansed from all *inward* sin. They, indeed, had a new heart and an old heart simultaneously; their hearts were *truly,* but not *entirely* renewed. Their carnal mind was nailed to the cross, but not wholly destroyed. They were temples of the Holy Spirit, but still, to some degree, carnal.

2 ... But they have yet another scripture that they feel clinches their argument: "If any man be in Christ, he is a new creature. Old things have passed away; behold, all things are new." A believer, they argue, cannot be an old creature and a new creature at once. Actually, I argue, he can. He may be *partially* renewed, like the Corinthians; they were still babes in Christ and did not yet have the *whole* mind of Christ. When Paul said that old things were gone and all was now new, he meant that our old understanding

of justification, holiness, and happiness, of the things of God in general, was now gone; that our old desires, designs, affections, and outlook on life were gone. All had become new, greatly changed from what they were; and yet, though they were new, they were not *wholly* new. Still the Christian feels, to his sorrow and shame, remains of his old self, taints of his old nature; though, so long as he remains spiritually alert, they will not overcome him.

3 ... It is further argued that "if he is clean, he is clean; if he is holy, he is holy—period." This is a play on words; it is the fallacy of arguing from the particular to the general. What they really mean is that "if he is holy *at all,* he is holy *altogether."* That does not follow: Every babe in Christ *is* holy, but not *altogether* so; sin still *remains,* but it does not *reign.* If you think it does not remain, then you have not considered the full extent of the law of God (even the law of love), and that every deviation from that law is sin. All must admit that [at least] a new Christian, a babe in Christ, often deviates from the law of God. (What may be the case in a mature believer is a matter for further discussion.)

4 ... An article in Mr. Dodd's magazine, which I am very surprised he published, argues in a similar vein: "that there is *no* sin in a believer." Some of the article's points are added here, with my responses. The article claims "that since believers 'walk after the Spirit,' and the Spirit dwells in them, that they are thereby delivered from the *guilt,* the *power,* the very *existence* of sin." These three terms are not the same: Believers *are* delivered from the guilt and power of sin, but *not* from the existence of sin. A man may indeed walk after the Spirit; the Spirit may indeed dwell in him; but still he may feel his flesh opposing the Spirit.

5 ... The article claims "that since 'the Church is the body of

Christ,' any hint of sin in a member of that body would imply that Christ and Satan can co-exist." That those who are part of Christ's mystical body still feel the tug of the flesh against the Spirit, does *not* mean that Christ has fellowship with Satan, or with the sin that he enables believers to resist and overcome.

6 ... It claims "that since Christians have 'come to the heavenly Jerusalem where nothing defiled can enter,' it follows that they must be without defiling sin." It is true that they are holy and undefiled, while they "walk after the Spirit," yet still they are sensible that there is another principle within, a principle contrary to the Spirit.

7 ... The article claims "that since Christians are reconciled to God, nothing carnal can remain; that reconciliation cannot occur without the total destruction of the flesh." It is true that we are "reconciled to God through the blood of the cross." And in that moment, the corruption of our nature, which is opposed to God, has no more *dominion* over us. But it still *exists,* struggling against God's Spirit.

8 ... It claims "that since Christians 'have crucified the flesh,' they have no fleshly affections." It is true that their flesh has been crucified, but still it *remains* within, struggling to break free from the cross. (A hundred similar texts may be cited; each has a similar answer.) It also cites this scripture: "Christ gave himself for the Church, that it might be holy and without blemish." And so it will be in the end. But it never has been yet, from the beginning to this day!

9 ... It claims "that Christian experience shows that all who are justified, find *immediate, absolute* freedom from all sin." I do not believe that! If they did experience an immediate freedom from sin, it would not last; and if it did not last, it would not matter.

10 ... The article asks "how a believer can still have pride in him,

and not *be* proud; or have anger, and not *be* angry?" I believe a man may have a bit of pride in him, may think of himself, in some way, above what he ought to think, but still not be proud in his general character. He may have anger in him, even a propensity to furious anger, without giving way to it. "Can anger and pride be in a heart where *only* meekness and humility are felt?" No. But *some* pride and anger may be in a heart where there is also *much* humility and meekness.

It denies the distinction between sin *remaining* and sin *reigning;* it insists that sin, in any kind or degree, is sin reigning; that it cannot exist in a man without reigning there. I find that to be a strange idea, contrary to all experience, all scripture, and all common sense. For example, resentment of an affront is sin, inconsistent with the law of love. This has existed in me a thousand times. Yet it did not, and does not, reign. If the resentment I feel is not yielded to, there is no guilt, no condemnation from God; and therefore, it has no power; though it is in opposition to the Spirit, it does not prevail. So, once again, there *is* sin, but *without* the guilt or the power.

11 ... The article claims "that allowing for the existence of *any* sin in a believer is a dangerous and discouraging proposition; it implies that an evil power is still in control of our soul, usurping God's place in the heart, and waging war against our Redeemer." I say that the usurper has been dethroned; yes, he still remains where once he reigned, but he remains in chains. He attempts to continue his warfare, but he grows weaker and weaker; while the believer goes from strength to strength.

12 ... The article claims "that if a believer has *any* sin in him, then he is a *slave* to sin. How can a man be justified and still be a slave to sin, still have pride, anger, and unbelief within? No wonder there are so many proud, angry, unbelieving believers!"

I do *not* believe that a justified man is a *slave* to sin; but I do believe that sin remains (at least for a time) in all believers.

It continues the argument: "If *any* sin remains, then the man is a sinner: if any pride, he is proud; if any self-will, he is self-willed. How then does he differ from the unregenerate unbeliever?" I do not deny that a believer may have *some* pride or self-will in his heart, but he is not proud and self-willed in the same way that the unbeliever is—that is, *governed* by it. The unregenerate *obey* sin; he does not. The flesh plagues them both; the unregenerate "walk after the flesh," while the believer "walks after the Spirit."

It asks "how there can be unbelief in a believer." Well, the word has two meanings: either *no* faith, or *little* faith; either the *absence* of faith, or the *weakness* of it. In one sense, there is unbelief in the believer; in the other sense, there is not; so that faith can be mixed with fear and doubt. Jesus said, "Why are you fearful, you of little faith?" He is referring to unbelief in [new or weak] believers.

13 ... Finally, the article claims "that to admit there can be sin in believers is to encourage sin in believers." This does not follow: A man may be in God's favor, even if he still *feels* residual sin, but not if he *yields* to it. Having inward sin does not forfeit the favor of God; giving in to sin does. Your flesh may oppose the Spirit, and still you may be a child of God; but if you "walk after the flesh," you are a child of the devil. So, our teaching does not encourage obedience to sin, but resistance to it.

V / 1 ... To sum up: There are two contrary principles in every man, even after he is justified: nature and grace, the flesh and the Spirit. Even though babes in Christ are sanctified, it is only in part; to a degree, they are spiritual; to a degree, carnal. That is why believers are continually exhorted, in scripture, to guard against the flesh. This agrees with their experience as well: While they feel the witness of the Spirit within, they still feel a will not wholly resigned to the will of God. They know they are in Christ; yet they also sense a heart ready to depart from Christ, a proneness to evil, and a lukewarmness to good. The contrary doctrine [which I have been refuting] is brand new; it was never heard of in the Church, till the time of Zinzendorf; and it leads to the most fatal consequences. It causes us to relax our guard against our evil nature, against the 'Delilah' who still lurks in our lives. It removes the shield from weak believers, depriving them of their faith, and leaving them exposed to all the assaults of the world, the flesh, and the devil.

2 ... Let us, therefore, hold fast to the sound doctrine "once delivered to the saints," and delivered by them to succeeding generations: That, though we are renewed, cleansed, and purified, the moment we truly believe in Christ, we are not then renewed, cleansed, and purified *altogether.* The flesh, our evil nature, remains (though subdued) and fights against the Spirit. So let us more earnestly "watch and pray" against the enemy within; let us more carefully "put on the whole armor of God," that we may "wrestle with flesh and blood, with principalities and powers"; let us more diligently "fight the good fight of faith," "that we may be able to withstand in the evil day, and having done all, to stand."

14

ON REPENTANCE IN BELIEVERS

Repent and believe the gospel.

—MARK 1:15

1 ... It is generally supposed that repentance and faith are only the gate of religion, only necessary at the beginning of our Christian life, as we are first setting out on the way to the kingdom. And this *seems* to be confirmed by Hebrews, where Christians are exhorted to "go on to perfection, *leaving* "these first principles of Christian doctrine," "not laying again the foundation of repentance from dead works, and of faith in God." That means that we must *comparatively* leave these behind, which at first took up all our thoughts, in order to "press on toward the prize of our high calling."

2 ... It is certainly true that there is a repentance and a faith which are especially necessary at the beginning: A repentance, which is a conviction of our utter sinfulness, guiltiness, and helplessness, and which precedes our receiving the kingdom of God within; and a faith, whereby we receive that kingdom, which is "righteousness, peace, and joy in the Holy Spirit."

3 ... But there is also a repentance and a faith (taking the words in another sense, not quite the same, but not entirely different), which are required *after* we have believed the gospel; indeed, required at

every stage of our Christian life, without which we cannot "run the race set before us." And this *second* repentance and faith are just as necessary to our *continuing* and *growing* in grace, as the *first* repentance and faith were in [*receiving* grace and] *entering* the kingdom of God.

So, in what sense are we to repent and believe *after* we are justified? It is an important question, worthy of consideration.

I / 1 ... First, in what sense are we to repent? Repentance often means an inward change, a change of mind from sin to holiness. But we are now speaking of it in a different sense, as a kind of honest Christian self-knowledge; knowing ourselves to be sinners, even as we know ourselves to be children of God.

2 ... When we first knew ourselves to be sinners, and first found redemption in the blood of Jesus; when we first experienced the love of God in our hearts, and his kingdom established there; it was easy to imagine that we were no longer sinners at all, that all our sins were not only covered [by the blood], but radically destroyed. Since we felt no evil in our hearts, we readily imagined that none was there. In fact, some well-meaning men [Moravians] have taught that when they were *justified,* they were, at the same time, entirely *sanctified,* never to know sin again. They taught this, despite scripture, reason, and experience. I certainly acknowledge that "he who is born of God does not *commit* sin," but I cannot agree that the Christian does not *feel* it within. Sin definitely does not *reign* [in a believer], but it does *remain*. And a conviction of the sin which *remains* in our hearts is the core of the repentance which we now consider.

3 ... It is seldom long before the man who imagined that all sin was gone, begins to feel that there is still *pride* in his heart. He

realizes that he has thought more highly of himself than he ought to think, or has taken credit for something which he received from another, and gloried in it as if he had earned it; and yet he still knows that he is in God's favor. He cannot and ought not "cast away his confidence," for the Spirit still "witnesses with his spirit, that he is a child of God."

4 ... Nor is it long before he feels *self-will* in his heart, a will contrary to the will of God. This will is an essential part of human nature, inevitably present in every intelligent being. Jesus himself had a human will, without which he would not have been fully man. But his human will was totally surrendered to the will of God. At all times, and on all occasions, even in his deepest affliction, he could say, "Not as I will, but as you will." But this is not always the case with us who believe in Christ. We often find our will exalting itself against the will of God; we will things that are pleasing to nature, but not to God; we avoid things that are pleasing to God, but not to nature. Indeed, a man of faith fights against his self-will with all his might—which proves that it really does exist and that he is painfully conscious of it.

5 ... Self-will and pride are both a kind of idolatry, both contrary to the love of God. The same may be said of the *love of the world*. Even true believers feel this in themselves, more or less, sooner or later, in one way or another. When a believer first "passes from death to life," he desires nothing but God. "Lord, there is none on earth I desire but you!" But this does not last; in time, he begins to feel again "the desire of the flesh, the desire of the eye, and the pride of life." If he does not continually watch and pray, he finds that the *desire of the flesh* (lust, inordinate affection) is reviving and assaulting him. He has a strong urge to "love the creature more than the Creator," whether it be his child, his parent, his mate, or his friend. He may feel, in a thousand different ways, a desire for

earthly things or pleasures. In the same proportion, he will forget God, not seeking all his happiness in him, but being a "lover of pleasure more than a lover of God."

6 ... If he does not guard himself every moment, he will again feel the *desire of the eye,* by which I understand gratifying oneself with that which is great or beautiful or exotic. This desire assaults the soul with the poorest of trifles, such as dress or furniture, things that were never intended to satisfy an immortal spirit. Yet, how natural it is, even after we have "tasted of the powers of the world to come," to sink again into these foolish desires for things that perish in the using! How hard it is, even for believers, to overcome just this one example of the desire of the eye: *novelty,* desiring something simply because it is new.

7 ... And how hard it is, even for children of God, to completely conquer the *pride of life,* what the world calls the 'sense of honor.' This is nothing else but a desire and love for the praise of man, and an equal fear of man's displeasure; it is being ashamed of what we ought to glory in. Even among those who seem to be strong in faith, one can detect these weaknesses. So, it plainly appears that even these are but partly "crucified to the world"; an evil root [below the surface] still remains in the heart.

8 ... These sinful inclinations are all contrary to the full love of *God.* Are there not also other inclinations that are just as contrary to the full love of *neighbor?* Do we never find (in ourselves) jealousy, unkind thoughts, groundless suspicions, all of which are contrary to brotherly love? There may be no outright malice, or hatred, or bitterness in believers, but what about *envy* toward those who enjoy some real or supposed good, which we desire but cannot attain? What about *resentment,* when we are injured, insulted, or betrayed, especially by those whom we have loved or labored to assist? Does injustice or ingratitude never excite in us a degree of

revenge, a desire to return evil for evil, instead of "overcoming evil with good"? This also shows how much is still in our heart, which is contrary to the love of neighbor.

9 ... *Covetousness* is another concern for the Christian. It may be the love of money, "the root of all evil"; or it may the insatiable desire to always have more. How few, even of the real children of God, are free from this! (Luther once said that covetousness was one sin he had never struggled with; but, if that is so, he was the only man who ever lived who did not!) Every believer will struggle with some degree of covetousness, at some time or other. It is irrefutably true that covetousness, along with pride, self-will, and anger, remain in the hearts even of the justified.

10 ... Having experienced this *remaining* sin within, many serious thinkers have understood the famous passage from Romans 7 to refer, not to those "under the law," under conviction of sin (which is undoubtedly the meaning of Paul), but of them "under grace," who are "justified freely through the redemption that is in Christ." And there is some reason for their misunderstanding: There does still *remain,* even in those who are justified, a mind somewhat carnal; a heart inclined to backsliding, ever ready to "depart from the living God"; a predisposition to pride, self-will, anger, revenge, love of the world, and all other evil; a root of bitterness, which, if the restraint were removed for even a moment, would instantly spring up; yes, such a depth of corruption as we could not possibly imagine, without the clear light of God. An inner conviction of all this sin remaining in their hearts is part of the repentance which belongs to those who are justified.

11 ... As sin remains in our *hearts,* so it clings to all our *words.* Sadly, many of our words are more than *mixed* with sin; they are *altogether* sinful. For example: Unkind conversation, which does not spring from brotherly love, which is inconsistent with that

golden rule, "What you would have others do to you, do likewise to them." Back-biting, tale-bearing, evil-speaking, discussing the faults of those who are absent—how few there are, even among believers, who are totally innocent of this; who follow the good old rule, "Of the dead and the absent, speak only good!" Frivolous, useless conversation, which "grieves the Holy Spirit"—truly, "for every idle word that men speak, they shall give an account in the day of judgment."

12 ... But even if believers continually "watch and pray"; even if they constantly guard their lips; even if they earnestly try to make their conversation "minister grace to the hearers"; yet do they not daily drift into useless discourse, notwithstanding all their caution? And even when they endeavor to speak for God, are their words and intentions absolutely pure? Do they speak only to please God, and not partly to please themselves; to do only the will of God, and not partly to do their own will? Even if they begin with their eye fixed on Jesus, do they keep that focus as they converse with their neighbors? When reproving sin, do they feel no anger or resentment to the sinner; when instructing the ignorant, do they feel no pride or superiority? When comforting the afflicted or encouraging the slacker, do they never congratulate themselves on their fine words, or crave the commendation of others? We can see how much sin clings even to the best conversation of believers! An inner conviction of this sin is another part of the repentance which belongs to those who are justified.

13 ... As sin clings to our *words,* so it clings to all our *actions.* Are there not many of a believer's actions which the world would never condemn, but which would never be commended, or even excused, if we judge by the word of God? Are there not many which they themselves know are not done to the glory of God; in which they never even aimed at it? And if they did aim at his glory, did they

keep their eye fixed only on God; or did they not begin to do their own will as much as his; or to please themselves as much as to please him? While endeavoring to do good to their neighbors (works of *mercy*), do they not detect mixed motives and wrong attitudes within? And is the same not true of their works of *piety?* Even while hearing the word which is able to save their souls, or offering up their prayers to God in public or private, do they not frequently think such thoughts as make them fear God's displeasure? And while at the Lord's table, are their hearts sometimes wandering to the ends of the earth, filled with such frivolous thoughts as make them fear that their worship has become an abomination? So that they are now more ashamed of their best duties, than they once were of their worst sins?

14 ... And how many *sins of omission* are they guilty of! Paul said, "To him who knows to do good, and does it not, to him it is sin." Are there not a thousand instances where they might have done good, to enemies, strangers, even their own brethren, and they did it not? And how many omissions have they been guilty of, in their duty toward God? How many opportunities have they neglected, of communing, of hearing the word, of praying? Even that holy man, Archbishop Usher, with his dying breath, cried out, "Lord, forgive my *sins* of omission!"

15 ... In addition, how many *inward defects* may they find! They have not the love, the fear, the confidence toward God they ought to have. They have not the love which is due to their neighbor; nor that which is due to other children of God. They are slack in inward holiness, and defective in all things—so much so that they would cry out with [French Catholic Gaston] DeRenty, "I am a ground all overrun with thorns!" or with Job, "I abhor myself; I repent in dust and ashes!"

16 ... A conviction of their *guiltiness* is another aspect of the repen-

tance which belongs to the children of God. But this is to be cautiously understood, and in a particular sense. It is certain that "there is no condemnation to them who are in Christ Jesus," who believe in him, and, in the power of that faith, "walk not after the flesh, but after the Spirit." Yet they can no more bear the *strict* justice of God now, than before they believed; they are still *worthy* of death! And it would absolutely condemn them, were it not for the atoning blood! So, they are thoroughly convinced that they still deserve punishment, even though [through Christ] it is turned aside. But here there are extremes on either side, and few steer clear of them. Some Christians think themselves condemned when they are not; others think themselves too righteous to be condemned. The truth lies between: They still strictly *deserve* the damnation of hell. But what they deserve does not happen to them, because they "have an Advocate with the Father," whose life, death, and intercession stand between them and condemnation!

17 ... A conviction of their utter *helplessness* is yet another aspect of this repentance. First, they are no more able now, *of themselves,* to think one good thought, to form one good desire, to speak one good word, or do one good work, than before they were justified. They have no strength of their own; no power to do good, or resist evil; no ability to overcome, or even withstand, the world, the devil, or even their own evil nature. They can certainly do all these things, but not in their own strength. They have power to overcome all these enemies, but it is not from nature; it is the gift of God. Nor is it given all at once, as if they had a stockpile of grace, but only moment by moment.

18 ... Second, this helplessness also shows itself in an absolute inability to deliver ourselves from a sense of guilt or a consciousness of deserving punishment. We are unable to remove (even with all the grace we have), either the pride, self-will, love of the world, anger,

or general proneness to depart from God, which we know (from personal experience) to remain even in the regenerate heart; or to remove the evil which clings to all our words and actions, despite our best efforts. Add to this, an utter inability to avoid uncharitable or unprofitable conversation, to avoid sins of omission, or to correct our many defects, especially the lack of love toward God and man.

19 ... If any man believes that whoever is justified is thereby rendered capable of removing all these sins from his heart and life, let him try an experiment. Let him prove to himself that, by the grace he has already received, he can expel pride, self-will, and inbred sin in general. Let him see if he can cleanse his words and actions from all mixture of evil; if he can avoid all uncharitable and unprofitable conversation, all sins of omission, and correct all the defects which remain within. Let him repeat the experiment again and again; and the longer he tries, the more deeply will he be convinced of his utter helplessness.

20 ... This is all so evident, that nearly all the children of God, wherever they are, and however much they differ in other points, generally agree in this: Although we may, by the Spirit, resist and overcome and weaken both outward and inward sin, we cannot totally drive it out. Even by all the grace given at justification, we cannot annihilate it. Though we watch and pray ever so much, we cannot wholly cleanse either our hearts or hands. Only if it please the Lord to speak to our hearts a *second* time ("Be clean!") will the leprosy be cleansed, will the evil root, the carnal mind, all inbred sin be destroyed. [A second work of grace? Entire sanctification?] But if there be no second change, no instantaneous deliverance *after* justification; if there be none but a *gradual* work of God (which none can deny there will be), then we must be content to deal with residual sin till death, still guilty (strictly speaking), still worthy of punishment. So long as all this sin remains in our heart,

and clings to our words and actions, our guilt and worthiness of punishment remain. Applying strict and rigorous justice to our situation, [devoid of God's grace], all that we think, speak, or do [even as believers] merely adds to this guilt.

II / 1 ... It is in this sense that we are to repent, *after* we are justified. And till we do so, we can go no further. Till we are aware of our disease, we cannot be cured. But once we have repented, we are then called to "believe the gospel."

2 ... This also is to be understood in a particular sense, different from that when we believed unto justification. Believe the good tidings of a great salvation! Believe that he who is "the brightness of the Father's glory, the express image of his person," is "able to save to the *uttermost* all who come to God through him." He can save you from all the sin that still remains in your heart, from all the sin that clings to your words and actions, from all your sins of omission, and to supply whatever is lacking in you. This is impossible with man, but with the God-Man all things are possible. What can be too hard for him who has "all power in heaven and earth"? His bare power to accomplish this is one thing; his willingness to do so is another. But he has promised it over and over, in the strongest terms; he has given us "exceeding great and precious promises," both in the Old and New Testaments. We read in the ancient Law, "The Lord will circumcise your heart, to love God with *all* your heart and soul." In the Psalms, "He shall redeem Israel (the Israel of God) from all his sins." In the Prophets, "From all your filthiness will I cleanse you. I will put my Spirit within you, and you shall keep my commandments and do them." In the New Testament, "Blessed be the Lord, for he has visited and redeemed his people, that we should serve him in holiness and righteousness all the days of our life."

3 ... So, you have very good reason to believe that he is both *able* and *willing* to cleanse you from all filthiness of flesh and spirit. This is what you now long for; this is the faith you now need—that the Great Physician, the lover of my soul, is perfectly able to cleanse and heal me. But is he willing to do it only in the future, or now, today? Let him answer for himself: *"Today,* if you will hear my voice, harden not your hearts." If you put it off till tomorrow, you are hardening your heart, refusing to hear his voice. So, believe that he is willing to save you today, *now!* "Now is the accepted time." Only believe, and you will find that all things are possible.

4 ... Continue to believe in him who loved you and gave himself for you; who bore all your sins in his own body on the cross; who saves you from all condemnation, by his blood continually applied. This is how we continue in a justified state.

But when we go on "from faith to faith," when we have faith to be cleansed from indwelling sin, from all our uncleanness, we are likewise saved from all the guilt and deserved punishment, which we felt before. By faith in Christ's life, death, and intercession for us, renewed moment by moment, we are perfectly clean; there is not only no condemnation, but no reason for condemnation as before, the Lord cleansing both our hearts and lives. [Entire sanctification in this life?]

5 ... By that same faith, we feel the power of Christ every moment resting on us, which alone makes us what we are; by which we are enabled to continue a truly spiritual life, and without which our present holiness would immediately vanish. But so long as we retain this faith in him, leaning on Christ who dwells in our hearts, who also intercedes for us with God, he helps us to think, speak, and act in ways acceptable to him. Thus, does he go before them that believe, with his continual help, so that all their thoughts, words, and deeds are "begun, continued, and ended in him." Thus, does

he "cleanse the thoughts of their hearts, that they may perfectly love him and worthily magnify his holy name."

6 ... Thus it is, that in the children of God, repentance and faith exactly answer each other. By repentance, we feel the sin remaining in our hearts, and clinging to our words and actions; by faith, we receive the power of God in Christ, purifying us inwardly, and cleansing us outwardly. By repentance, we acknowledge that we deserve punishment for all that we think, say, and do; by faith, we are conscious that our Advocate is continually pleading for us, turning aside all condemnation and punishment. By repentance, we have a constant conviction that there is no help in us; by faith, we receive mercy, and "grace to help in every time of need." Repentance despairs of any other help; faith gratefully accepts all the help we need, from him who has all power in heaven and earth. Repentance says, "Without him, I can do nothing"; faith says, "I can do all things through Christ who strengthens me." Through him, I can overcome and expel all the enemies of my soul. Through him, I can love the Lord with all that is in me, and "walk in holiness and righteousness before him all the days of my life."

III / 1 ... And so we see, first, how troublesome is the opinion that believers are *wholly* sanctified at the time they are justified, that their hearts are then cleansed of *all* sin. It is true that we are then delivered from the dominion of outward sin; and, at the same time, the power of inward sin is so broken, that we need no longer be led by it. But it is by no means totally destroyed; the root of pride, self-will, anger, love of the world remains within [waiting to spring up, if we are unguarded]; the carnal mind and the heart bent to backsliding are not entirely eradicated. To suppose the contrary is not a harmless mistake; indeed, it does immense harm. It entirely blocks the way to further change. Only the sick need a Physician;

those who believe themselves to be healthy will not seek further healing. We should expect no further deliverance for these, whether gradual or instantaneous.

2 ... On the contrary, a deep conviction that we are not yet whole; that our hearts are not yet purified; that there is yet within us a carnal mind opposed to God; that a whole body of sin remains in our heart, *weakened* but *not destroyed;* shows, beyond doubt, the absolute necessity of further change. It is true, that at the very moment of justification, we are *born again:* In that instant we experience the inward change from "darkness into marvelous light"; from the image of the devilish brute into the image of the holy God; from the corrupt mind to the mind which was in Christ. But are we then entirely changed, wholly transformed into the image of him who created us? Far from it! We still retain a depth of sin; and it is a consciousness of this which constrains us to groan for full deliverance, to him who is mighty to save. So, those believers who are not deeply convinced of the deep corruption of their hearts, or but slightly convinced, have little concern about *entire sanctification.* They may possibly hold the opinion that such a thing will occur at death, or maybe sometime prior to death. But they are not really uneasy about their lack of it, and do not hunger or thirst after it. They simply cannot, until they know themselves better, until they experience believer's repentance, until God reveals the monstrous face of inbred sin, and shows them the real state of their souls. Only then, when they feel the burden, will they groan for deliverance. Only then will they cry out, in the agony of their soul, *"Break off the yoke of inbred sin, And set my spirit free! I cannot rest till pure within, Till wholly lost in thee."*

3 ... We see, also, that a deep conviction of our demerit, *after* we believe and are accepted, is absolutely necessary, in order to see the true value of the atoning blood; in order to feel that we need it

as much, after we are justified, as ever we did *before*. Without this conviction, we cannot help but count the blood of the covenant a common thing, something which we really need no longer, now that our past sins are blotted out. But if, in fact, our hearts and lives are still unclean, there is a kind of present guilt which we are contracting every moment. And thus the need for repentance and faith even in believers: *"I sin in every breath I draw, Nor do thy will, nor keep thy law, On earth as angels do above: But still the fountain open stands Washes my feet, my heart, my hands, Till perfected in love."*

4 ... We see, finally, that a deep conviction of our utter helplessness, of our total inability to retain anything we have received, or to deliver ourselves from the iniquity remaining within, teaches us truly to live upon Christ by faith, not only as our Savior, but as our Lord. Thus, are we brought to "magnify him" indeed; to "give him all the glory of his grace"; to "make him a whole Christ, an entire Savior; and truly set the crown upon his head." These words are fulfilled in a strong sense when we go out of ourselves, in order to be swallowed up in him; when we sink into nothing, that he may be all in all. Then, his almighty grace having abolished "every high thing which exalts itself against him, is brought to obedience to Christ."

Preached at Londonderry, 1767

15

THE GREAT ASSIZE

We shall all stand before the judgment seat of Christ.

—ROMANS 14:10

1 ... How many factors converge to dramatize the awe and seriousness of these present proceedings: The vast assembly of *people* of every age, sex, rank, and condition, gathered from the neighborhood and from distant places; *criminals,* speedily to be brought to trial, having no way to escape; *officers,* waiting at their posts, ready to execute the orders soon to be given; and the *representative [judge]* of our gracious king [George II], whom we so highly reverence and honor. The occasion of this assembly adds to its solemnity: To hear and determine matters of life and death—death that reveals the face of eternity! It was to increase the sense of awe and seriousness in the minds and hearts of the people, that our ancestors adorned these proceedings with ceremonial trumpets, staffs, and robes.

2 ... But as awesome as *this* solemnity is, one far more awesome is at hand! For soon, "we shall all stand before the judgment seat of Christ." "Every knee shall bow, and every tongue confess." And "everyone shall give account of himself to God."

3 ... If all men had a deep sense of this, how beneficially would it impact society! What a strong motive to the practice of genuine

morality and solid virtue would this be! What could confirm us in all goodness, and deter us from all evil, like the strong conviction that "the Judge stands [even now] at the door," and we are soon to stand before him?

4 ... It would be appropriate at this time to consider: (1) the circumstances which will precede our standing before the judgment seat of Christ; (2) the judgment itself; and (3) the circumstances which will follow it.

I / 1 ... First, what are the circumstances which will precede the judgment? God will show "signs in the earth beneath": "The earth will reel to and fro like a drunkard"; "there shall be earthquakes in all places"; islands and mountains will disappear. All the oceans will feel the violence of the earth's contortions, the "waves roaring" with agitation, as never before. The air will be all storm and tempest, full of dark vapors and pillars of smoke, resounding with thunder from pole to pole, and pierced with myriad flashes of lightning. Above the air, the very powers of heaven also shall be shaken: "The sun shall be turned to darkness, and the moon to blood"; "the stars shall fall from heaven," being thrown from their orbits. And then shall be heard the universal shout, from all the hosts of heaven, followed by "the voice of the archangel," heralding the Son of God and Man; and the trumpet of God sounding an alarm to all that sleep in the dust. Then the graves shall open, and the bodies of men arise—each distinctive, but each changed beyond our comprehension. So, all who ever lived and died, since God created man, shall be raised incorruptible and immortal.

2 ... At the same time, "the Son of Man shall send forth his angels" over the earth, and they shall "gather his elect from the four winds." And the Lord himself shall come with clouds, in his own glory,

and the glory of the Father, with myriad saints and angels, and shall sit upon his glorious throne. And he shall gather all nations before him, and separate the sheep from the goats, the good from the wicked. Concerning this great assembly, John of Revelation says, "I saw the dead stand before God; the books were opened (a figurative expression that mortals can relate to); and the dead were judged according to their works, as written in the books."

II / 1 ... We consider, second, the judgment itself, so far as God has been pleased to reveal it. The person by whom God will judge the world is his everlasting, only-begotten Son, "who is God over all, blessed forever." To him, "being the outbeaming of the Father's glory, the express image of his person," the Father has committed all judgment. Though he was "in the form of God, and equal with God, yet he emptied himself, taking upon him the form of a servant, being made in the likeness of men"; and going yet further, "he humbled himself and became obedient unto death, even death on the cross. Wherefore God has highly exalted him" and designated him "to be the Judge of the living and the dead," both those who are alive at his coming, and those who had previously died.

2 ... The prophets spoke of the great and terrible day of the Lord. From the time of man's creation to the end of all things is 'the day of the *sons of men'*; when this is ended, 'the day of the *Lord'* will begin. But who can say how long it will continue? "With the Lord, one day is as a thousand years, and a thousand years as one day." And from this passage, some of the ancient fathers of the Church inferred that the day of judgment would last a literal thousand years. Certainly, it will last at least that long; but considering the number of persons to be judged, and the weighty matters to be inquired into, it may well last several thousand years. But God will reveal this in time.

3 ... Scripture does not explicitly say where mankind will be judged. Some have supposed it will be on earth, where the works were done. But perhaps it is closer to our Lord's own account of his coming in the clouds, to suppose that it will be above the earth. And Paul writes, "The dead in Christ shall rise first. Then we who remain alive, shall be caught up with them, in the clouds, to meet the Lord in the air (I Thes 4)." So, it seems probable that the great white throne will be high exalted above the earth.

4 ... The persons to be judged will be as numerous as the sands of the sea; all nations, peoples, and tongues; all of Adam's race throughout time! If there are four hundred million souls living upon earth at any given time (the common supposition), how many must there have been over the past seven thousand years! Every one of those people will hear the voice of the Son of God, and come to life, and appear before him—all, without exception, of every age, sex, and status. For long before judgment day, the fantasy of human greatness had disappeared, and sunk into oblivion. Indeed, most of it vanishes the moment of death. So, who is rich or great in the grave?

5 ... And every man shall "give an account of his own works"; a full and true account of all he ever did, whether good or evil. O what a scene that will be, in the sight of angels and men! It will not be their actions alone that will be brought into view, but also their words; seeing that for "every idle word which men speak, they shall give account in the day of judgment"; so that by word and deed they will be justified or condemned. And God will bring to light every circumstance that accompanied each word and deed, which lessened or increased its good or evil. How easy this is for the Judge, since "the darkness is no darkness to him, but the night shines as the day!"

6 ... Yes, he will bring to light not just the hidden works of darkness,

but the very thoughts and intents of the heart; for "all things are naked and open to the eyes of him with whom we have to do." "Hell and destruction are before him without a covering. How much more the hearts of men!"

7 ... In that dread day shall be discovered every inward working of every human soul; every inclination, affection, and passion; every combination of them, that constitute the whole complex character of each individual. And so, it shall clearly and infallibly be determined who was righteous and who was not; and to what degree each thought, word, or action was good or evil.

8 ... "Then the King will say to those on his right, Come, ye blessed of my Father!" All the good they did on earth will be proclaimed before men and angels, whatever they did, in word or deed, for the sake of the Lord Jesus. All their good desires and intentions, all their holy dispositions, will be remembered; and though they were unknown or forgotten among men, yet God took note of them. All their sufferings for Jesus and conscience will be displayed to their praise by the righteous Judge, and to their honor before men and angels, and to their "exceeding and eternal glory!"

9 ... But will their evil deeds also be remembered on the day of judgment, and proclaimed to the great assembly? (For, remember, even the most righteous of men have sinned.) Many believe those evil deeds will *not* be remembered and proclaimed. They argue: This would imply that believers' sufferings were not at an end when life ended; they would still have sorrow, shame, and embarrassment to face. Remember, God declared through Ezekiel, "If the wicked will turn from their sins, and do what is right, all their transgressions shall not once be mentioned against them." He declared through Jeremiah, "I will forgive their iniquities, and remember their sin no more." And he declared in Hebrews, "I will be merciful to their unrighteousness, and their sins I will remember no more."

10 ... [I see it differently: Even the evil deeds of believers will be exposed on that day.] It is absolutely necessary for the full display of the glory of God; for the perfect manifestation of his wisdom, justice, power, and mercy, toward the heirs of salvation; that *all* the circumstances of their life should be placed in open view. Otherwise, how could it be demonstrated out of what a depth of sin and misery the grace of God had delivered them? If the whole lives of all men were not revealed, the whole amazing context of divine providence could not be manifested; nor should we yet be able "to justify the ways of God to man." Jesus himself said plainly, "There is nothing covered that shall not be revealed." Without exposing hidden things, God's providential actions would still appear incomprehensible. But when God has brought to light all the hidden things of darkness, it will be clearly seen that all his ways were good and wise; that he saw through the thick clouds, and governed all things by his wise counsel; that nothing was left to chance or the caprice of men, but that God did all things strongly and sweetly, working one connected chain of justice, mercy, and truth.

11 ... And when, at last, the righteous fully understand God's perfect providence, they will rejoice with joy unspeakable; they will *not* feel painful sorrow or shame for any past transgressions, long since washed away by the blood of the Lamb. It will be abundantly sufficient for them that all their transgressions shall not once be mentioned *against* them, nor remembered to their condemnation. This is the plain meaning of the gospel promise; all the children of God shall find it to be true to their everlasting comfort.

12 ... After the righteous are judged, the King will turn to those on his left hand; they too shall be judged, every man according to his works. Not only will their outward works be brought to account, but all their evil words, and all the evil desires and designs of their

hearts. The joyful sentence of acquittal will be pronounced on those on the right; and the dreadful sentence of condemnation on those on the left; both of which will remain eternally fixed and irrevocable.

III / 1 ... We come now to a few circumstances which will follow the judgment. First, is the execution of the sentence pronounced on the evil and the good: "These shall go away into eternal punishment, but the righteous into life eternal." The meaning is grammatically clear: The punishment and the reward are everlasting. "Then shall the righteous shine forth in the kingdom of their Father," "and drink of the rivers of pleasure at God's right hand forever." But here all description falls short; all human language fails! Only one who is caught up into the third heaven [Paul] can even imagine it; but even he cannot express what he has seen; these things it is not possible for man to utter.

The wicked, all the people that forget God, will be cast into hell. They will be "punished with everlasting destruction from the presence of the Lord, and from his glory." They will be "cast into the lake of fire, prepared for the devil and his angels"; they will writhe in anguish and pain, as they look upward to curse God. The 'dogs of hell'—pride, malice, revenge, rage, horror, despair—will continually devour them; they will "have no rest, day or night"; the fire of their torment will never be quenched!

2 ... Then the heavens will shrivel to nothing and implode with a loud noise. Peter speaks of this when he says, "The heavens, being on fire, shall be dissolved." The whole beautiful fabric of the universe will be engulfed in raging fire, and every atom torn asunder from the others. The great works of nature, mountains that have defied the rage of time, unmoved for thousands of years, will sink in fiery ruin. How much less will the works of man—triumphal arches,

castles, pyramids—be able to withstand the flaming conqueror! All, all will die, perish, vanish away!

3 ... It has been imagined by some great and good men, that as it requires the same almighty power to annihilate things as to create them; to destroy into nothingness as to create out of nothingness; so no atom in the universe will be totally or finally destroyed. Rather, they suppose, the last consuming fire will reduce into glass what, by smaller force, it had reduced to ashes. So, in the final day, the whole earth, if not the material heavens also, will undergo this change, after which the fire can have no further power over them. This may explain, they say, "the sea of glass, like crystal" described in Revelation. I cannot affirm or deny this; but we will know hereafter.

4 ... Scoffers and philosophers will ask, "How can these things be? Where should such an immense quantity of fire come from, as would consume the starry heavens and the planet earth?" We would remind them that this difficulty is not peculiar to Christian thinking. The same idea was almost universally espoused by the classical philosophers. The celebrated Ovid wrote: *"Rememb'ring a time when fire Should to the heaven aspire; And all the world above should burn, And all the globe to cinders turn."*

But even from my own limited and superficial understanding of natural things, I can point to abundant stores of fire ready and able to be used on the day of the Lord. How soon may a comet, commissioned by the Lord, travel own from the most remote part of the universe! Were it to hit the earth, a thousand times hotter than a red-hot cannonball, what would be the consequence? Or might not lightning, if commanded by the Lord of nature, bring ruin and utter destruction? And who knows what huge reservoirs of liquid fire are contained deep within the earth itself? What are

Etna, Vesuvius, and other volcanoes, which belch out flames and fiery coals, but so many mouths of those subterranean furnaces; so many proofs that God has in readiness all he needs to fulfill his word? Indeed, it is scientifically certain that we ourselves, our very bodies, are full of a type of fire, as is everything around us. Admittedly, it is not easy to make this ethereal fire visible to the eye, or to produce the same effect on combustible material as with ordinary fire. Nevertheless, if God were to unleash this irresistible agent, which lies quiescent in every particle of matter, how soon would it tear the universe to pieces and involve all in common ruin!

5 ... One further circumstance, which follows upon the judgment, deserves our serious consideration: Peter wrote, "We look for new heavens and a new earth, wherein dwells righteousness." This reflects the prophecy of Isaiah, who wrote, "Behold, I create new heavens and a new earth; and the old shall not be remembered," so great shall be the glory of the new! John wrote, "I saw a new heaven and a new earth, for the first heaven and earth were passed away." "Behold, the dwelling of God is with men; God himself shall be with them and be their God!" "God shall wipe away all tears, and there shall be no more death, neither sorrow, nor crying, nor pain"; meaning, they will all be happy. "They shall see God's face"; meaning, they shall have the nearest access to God, and the nearest resemblance to him. "His name shall be on their foreheads"; meaning, they shall be acknowledged as God's own, and his glory shall shine forth in them. "And there shall be no night there; for the Lord God gives them light; and they shall reign forever and ever."

IV ... This present court session naturally points us to that day when the Lord will judge the world in righteousness. By reminding us of that awesome future event, it may provide us with many instructive insights. Let me mention just a few and may God himself write them on our hearts.

1 ... First, how worthy are those [royal judges], who are sent by the wise and gracious providence of God, to execute justice here on earth, to defend the injured, and punish the wrongdoer. Are they not truly the ministers of God for our good; the great supporters of public tranquility; the patrons of innocence and virtue; the security of all our temporal blessings? Do they not represent the universal Judge, "King of kings and Lord of lords," as well as our national sovereign? Would that all these esteemed judges be holy as our great Judge is holy, and wise with his wisdom; showing no partiality as God shows none, but rendering to every man according to his works; strictly and inflexibly just, but tenderly merciful as well. So shall they inspire fear in evildoers; so shall the laws of our land be upheld and honored; and so shall the throne of our king be established in righteousness.

2 ... You honored public servants, whom both God and the king have commissioned, in a lower degree, to administer justice—may you not be compared to the angelic spirits who will attend our Judge, when he comes in clouds of glory? May you, like them, burn with love for God and man! May you all serve, in your various capacities, the needs of man, to the glory of God! May you be establishers of peace, blessings to your country, protectors of the land, and guardian angels to all around you!

3 ... You whose job it is to carry out the judge's sentence—are you not like those who stand before the Son of Man, who do his pleasure and hearken to his voice? It is important that you be as incorrupt as they, doing justice and loving mercy, doing to others what you would have them do to you, thus showing yourselves the servants of God. So shall the great Judge say to you: "Well done, good and faithful servants: Enter into the joy of your Lord!"

4 ... Now let me speak a few words to you who are here as interested onlookers: Should you not constantly bear in mind that a greater and more awesome day than this is coming? Today's is indeed a large assembly; but how can it compare to the approaching day, when every person who has ever lived on earth will be gathered for judgment? Today, only a few will stand before the judge; they await their trial even now, in prison, perhaps in chains, until they appear for judgment and sentencing. But a day is coming, when all of us standing here will "stand at the judgment seat of Christ." We are even now awaiting that trial, perhaps bound in chains of darkness, in this prison of flesh and blood, until we are ordered to be brought forth. Today, men will be questioned on one or two acts which they are supposed to have committed. But on that day, all of us will give an account of all our works, from cradle to grave; of all our words; of all our thoughts, desires, and intentions; of all the use which we have made of our various talents, whether of mind, body, or fortune. In today's court, it is possible that some of the guilty will escape, for lack of evidence. But on that day, there will be no lack of evidence. All men with whom you had secret dealings, who were privy to your inmost thoughts and schemes, are ready to testify against you. So are the spirits of darkness, who inspired you to evil, and assisted you in putting it into action. So are the angels of God, who watched over your soul, and labored for your good, so far as you would permit. So is your own conscience, a thousand witnesses in one, no longer capable of being blinded or silenced, but constrained to see and speak the naked truth, concerning all your thoughts, words, and deeds. And, above all, so is the great God, our Savior Jesus Christ, who knows you infinitely better than your own conscience!

Behold, he comes! He comes on the clouds; he rides on the winds; a devouring fire goes before him! He sits on his throne, clothed in light, arrayed with majesty and honor! His eyes are a flame of fire; his voice the sound of mighty waters!

How will you escape? Can you call on the mountains to fall on you, to cover you from his sight? Alas, the mountains themselves, the earth and the heavens, are ready to flee from his wrath! Can you prevent his righteous sentence, even with all your silver and gold? Blind wretch! Naked you came from the womb; naked you enter eternity. Hear the Lord, the Judge: "Come, ye blessed of my Father, inherit the kingdom prepared for you!" What a joyful sound, and how different from the other sentence which resounds throughout the universe: "Depart, you cursed, into everlasting fire!" And who can prevent or postpone the full execution of either sentence? Vain hope! Lo, hell is moved to receive those who are ripe for destruction! And the gates of heaven are lifted up, that the heirs of glory may come in!

5 ... What kind of people ought we to be, in all holiness and godliness! It cannot be long before the Lord will descend, with the voice of the archangel and the sound of the trumpet; and every one of us shall appear before him to give account of ourselves. Since you know he will come and not tarry, "be diligent, that you may be found in him, without spot and blameless." Why should any of you be found on his left hand on that day? The Lord does not will that any should perish, but that all should come to repentance; and through repentance, to faith in a bleeding Savior; and through faith, to a spotless love, to the full image of God renewed in the heart, producing all holiness. How can you doubt this, when you remember that the Judge of all is the Savior of all? Has he not bought you with his own blood, that you might not perish, but have everlasting life? O make proof of his mercy, rather than his justice; of his gracious love, rather than his thunderous power! He is near to every one of us; he has come, not to condemn, but to save the world. Sinner, is he not, even now, knocking at the door

of your heart? O that you may know his salvation; that you may give yourself to him, who gave himself for you, in humble faith, in holy, active love! So shall you rejoice with exceeding joy, when he comes on the clouds of heaven!

Preached when the Assize Court met in Bedfordshire, 1758; Sir Edward Clive, Judge; published at the request of the High Sheriff of the county, and others.

16

THE MEANS OF GRACE

You have gone away from my ordinances and have not kept them.

—MALACHI 3:7

I / 1 ... But are there any ordinances now, since life and immortality were brought to light by the gospel? Are there, in Christianity, any means ordained of God as the usual channels of his grace? This question would never have arisen in the early Church, for all Christians were agreed that there were, indeed, certain outward means for conveying Christ's grace into the souls of men. The constant practice of the early believers makes this clear: They were all together and "continued steadfastly in the teaching of the apostles, in the breaking of bread, and in prayers."

2 ... But in time, when "the love of many grew cold," some began to mistake the *means* for the *end,* and to make their religion a matter of doing outward works, rather than a heart renewed after the image of God. They forgot that the goal of every commandment is a heart full of love and faith; loving God with all their heart, and their neighbor as themselves; and being purified from pride, anger, and evil desire, by a God-inspired faith. Others realized that, though religion did *not* consist primarily in these outward means, still there was something about them that pleased God; something that would make the users acceptable in his sight, even

though they were a bit slack about "the weightier matters of the law"—justice, mercy, and love of God.

3 ... Obviously, in those who thus abused them, the means of grace did *not* lead toward the goal for which they were ordained. Instead of leading to spiritual health and blessing, the means became an occasion of falling and drew down a curse on their heads; instead of growing more heavenly in heart and life, they became twice the children of hell they were before. Others, observing that the means did *not* seem to convey God's grace to the children of the devil, understandably concluded that the means did not, could not, convey grace to any.

4 ... The number of those who *abused* the means was far greater than those who flatly *rejected* them, *until* certain men [Moravians especially] arose in the Church, men of great understanding, men of love, men experientially acquainted with true, inward religion; men who were shining lights, famous in their generations, who stood in the gap against ungodliness.

These holy and esteemed men surely intended no more, at first, than to show that outward religion is worth nothing without inward religion, the religion of the heart; that "God is a Spirit, and they who worship him must worship in spirit and truth"; that external worship is labor lost without a heart devoted to God; that outward ordinances profit much when they advance inward holiness, but when they do not, they are shallow and worthless; indeed, when they are used as a substitute for heart religion, they become an abomination to the Lord.

5 ... Not surprisingly, some of these men, being strongly convinced of the shocking and widespread misuse of God's ordinances, which had nearly driven true religion out of the Church; and being zealous for the glory of God, and the rescue of souls from that fatal

delusion; began to speak as if outward religion were absolutely nothing, as if it had no place at all in Christianity. They did not always express themselves with sufficient caution, and simple hearers believed that they were condemning *all* outward means as unprofitable, as *not* designed by God to be the usual channels of conveying his grace into men's souls.

Possibly, some of these good men did finally fall into that very opinion, particularly those who were cut off from all these ordinances through extraordinary circumstances. And experiencing the grace of God in themselves, without any outward means, they might well infer that the same grace was available to those who purposely shunned them.

6 ... How easily this notion spreads and insinuates itself into men's minds, especially those who have been awakened from spiritual sleep and are under heavy conviction of sin! These awakened sinners are usually impatient with their present state, and open to any new proposal that offers a way of escape and a sense of ease. They have undoubtedly tried the outward means and found no immediate relief; they have found only more frustration, more hopelessness, more condemnation. It is easy, therefore, to convince them that it is better for them to abstain from these means altogether [advice given by some Moravians]. They already seem to be striving in vain; they are naturally glad for any excuse to cast aside what gives their soul no pleasure, to cease their spiritual striving, and to rest in quiet inactivity.

II / 1 ... I now propose to examine whether there are any means of grace. By "means of grace" I understand outward signs, words, or actions, ordained by God, and appointed to be the ordinary channels of conveying grace to men—prevenient, justifying, and sanctifying grace. I use this expression, 'means of grace,' because I know none better; and because it has been generally used in the Church for many ages; and especially by our own Church [of England], which teaches us that a sacrament is "an outward sign of an inward grace, and a means whereby we receive that grace."

The chief means of grace are prayer (private or congregational); searching the scriptures (reading, hearing, or meditating thereon); and the Lord's Supper (receiving bread and wine in remembrance of Christ's death). These we believe to be ordained of God, as the ordinary channels of conveying grace to the soul.

2 ... But we contend that the whole value of the *means* depends on their serving the *ends* of religion; when the means are separate from the ends, they are less than nothing. If they do not lead to the knowledge and love of God, they are not acceptable in God's sight; rather they are an abomination to him and a stench in his nostrils. If the means are used as a substitute for the religion they were designed to promote, it would be very foolish and wicked; it would keep Christianity *out* of the heart by the very means ordained for bringing it *in*.

3 ... We agree that all outward means of grace, if separate from the Spirit of God, cannot profit at all, cannot lead to the knowledge or love of God. It is God alone who, by his almighty power, works in us whatever is pleasing in his sight; and all outward things, unless he works through them, are simply empty forms. Whoever should imagine that there is any intrinsic power in the means themselves knows neither the scriptures nor the power of God. There is no inherent power in the words of prayer, in the letter of scripture, or in the material elements of the sacrament. God alone is the giver of every good gift, the author of all grace; his alone is the power to convey grace to our souls. He is perfectly capable of giving

that same grace, were there no ordained means whatsoever on earth; he can do whatever pleases him through *any* means, or by *no* means at all.

4 ... We also agree that even the continual use of all the means of grace will never atone for one sin; that it is the blood of Christ alone that reconciles sinners to God. Every believer in Christ is deeply convinced that there is no merit but in Christ; that there is no merit in any of his own works—not in uttering prayers, not in reading or hearing scripture, and not in communing on bread and wine. In this sense, it is true that "Christ himself is the only means of grace," the only meritorious cause of it.

5 ... Sadly, a large proportion of those who call themselves Christians abuse the means of grace to the destruction of their own souls. This is certainly true of those who are satisfied with the *form* of godliness, without the *power.* They fondly presume that they are Christians already, because they do thus and such, even though Christ has never yet been revealed in their hearts, nor the love of God shed abroad therein. Or they suppose that they will be Christians by and by, because they use the means of grace; idly dreaming that there is some power in the means that makes men holy, or some merit in using them that moves God to grant the users holiness, or to accept them without it.

6 ... These people obviously do not understand the great foundation of the Christian faith: "By grace are you saved." You are saved from the guilt and power of your sins, and restored to the favor and image of God, not because of any works, merits, or deserving on your part, but strictly by the free grace and mercy of God, through the merits of his Son. You are saved, not by any power or wisdom that is in you, or in anything else, but *only* through the grace and power of the Holy Spirit, who works all in all.

7 ... But the main question remains: "We know that salvation is the gift and work of God, but *how* do I attain it? I know I must believe, but how shall I believe? I know I must wait upon God, but how am I to wait? Am I to wait for the grace of God that brings salvation, *using* the means of grace, or *not using* them [as some Moravians advised]?"

8 ... It is not possible that the word of God is silent on such an important point; or that the Son of God, "who came down from heaven for us men and for our salvation," should leave us with questions about a matter which so closely concerns our salvation. We have only to consult the word of God, to inquire what is written there; and if we follow its direction, no doubt will remain.

III / 1 ... According to scripture, all who desire the grace of God are to wait for it in the means which God himself ordained; by *using* the means, not by laying them aside.

First, all who desire the grace of God should wait for it in the way of *prayer*. This is the express direction of Jesus himself; in his Sermon on the Mount, he instructs, "Ask, and it shall be given you; seek, and you shall find; knock, and it shall be opened to you." He tells us plainly that in asking, seeking, and knocking, we will find the grace of God and enter his kingdom.

2 ... Our Lord makes this point again when he says, "If you, being evil, know how to give good gifts to your children, how much more shall your Father give good things to those who ask him?" Or, on another occasion, "How much more shall your heavenly Father give the Holy Spirit to them who ask him?" The persons addressed had not yet received the Spirit; nevertheless, Jesus directs them to use this means of grace (prayer) and promises that it will be effective; if they ask for the Spirit in prayer, they will receive.

3 ... The absolute necessity of using this means, if we would receive any gift from God, becomes even clearer, when Jesus tells the parable of the man who comes to his friend at midnight seeking bread. The friend tells him to go away, despite their friendship. But because the man is doggedly persistent, the friend finally rises and gives him what he asks. And Jesus concluded, "Ask and it will be given you (Luke 11)." Jesus is plainly saying that when we pray persistently, we will receive from God what otherwise we would not receive at all.

4 ... Jesus tells a similar parable: A poor widow kept coming to a judge, seeking justice against an adversary. The judge, who was neither righteous nor compassionate, finally heard the widow's case, simply because she wore him down with her persistence. If the hard-hearted judge was willing to help the widow, simply because of her persistence, how much more will a loving Father help his children, when they cry to him day and night? And Jesus concluded: "Men ought always to pray and not grow weary (Luke 18)."

5 ... Jesus expressly directs us to wait for God's blessing in private prayer, promising that we shall obtain our request: "Enter your room and pray to your Father in secret; and your Father shall reward you openly."

6 ... No direction can be clearer than that which God gave us through James, with regard to prayer of every kind, public and private: "If any of you lack wisdom, let him ask of God, who gives to all men liberally, without scolding, and it will be given him."

Some may object that this is *not* a direction to unbelievers, to those who do not know the pardoning grace of God, because James adds, "But let him ask in *faith*"; otherwise, "let him not think that he will receive anything of the Lord." I answer this objection by suggesting that James does not use the word 'faith' here as Paul typically does. James amplifies his meaning by stating, "Let him ask in faith, nothing doubting"; not doubting that God hears his prayer and will fulfill the desire of his heart.

It is absurd to think that 'faith' is used in this passage in its full Christian [Pauline] meaning: That would mean that men without saving faith are to ask God for it, with the promise that it will be given; but then be told that it will *not* be given unless they already have it before they ask! It is obvious from this passage, and those cited above, that *all* who desire the grace of God [believers *and* unbelievers] are to wait for it through that means of grace called *prayer*.

7 ... Second, all who desire the grace of God are to wait for it through searching the *scriptures*. Our Lord's teaching, on this point, is clear. "Search the scriptures," he said to the unbelieving Jews, "for they testify of me." It was for this very reason that he directed them to study the scriptures, that they might believe in him. Some may object that this was not a command of Jesus, but only his observation that the Jews *did* search the scriptures. How shamelessly false! An outright command cannot be more clearly expressed than Greek grammar expresses it here.

And what a blessing from God attends those who use this means of grace. The Bereans, after hearing Paul preach, "searched the scriptures daily, so that many of them believed (Acts 17)." They found the grace of God by the means which God had ordained for this purpose. Probably, in some of those who "received the word with all readiness of mind," "faith came by hearing," and was only confirmed by studying the scriptures. But this means of grace includes hearing, reading, and meditating upon the scriptures.

8 ... The scriptures are a primary means of grace by which God not only gives, but also confirms and increases, true wisdom in

mankind. Paul wrote to Timothy: "The holy scriptures are able to make you wise unto salvation through faith in Jesus Christ." "All scripture is given by inspiration of God (and thus infallibly true), and is profitable for doctrine, for correction, and for instruction in righteousness, that the man of God may be complete, thoroughly prepared for all good works (II Tim 3)."

9 ... It should be noted that this is spoken primarily and directly of the scriptures which Timothy had known from childhood; namely, the Old Testament, since the New had not yet been written. The great apostle Paul was obviously very far indeed from making light of the Old Testament! Note this, you who make so little of the first half of the oracles of God—that which scripture declares to be "profitable for doctrine, correction, and instruction in righteousness."

10 ... Nor is scripture profitable only for men of God, for those who walk already in his light; but also for those who walk in darkness, seeking him whom they know not yet. Peter says, "We have the prophetic word (holy scripture) more surely, being eyewitnesses of his majesty, and hearing the voice which came from the heavenly glory. Take heed, as to a light that shines in a dark place, until the day dawns and the Daystar rises in your hearts (II Pet 1)." Let all who desire that day to dawn in their hearts, wait for it in searching the scriptures.

11 ... Third, all who desire an increase of the grace of God are to wait for it in partaking of *the Lord's supper.* "The same night Jesus was betrayed, he took bread, broke it, and said, Take, eat; this is my body (the sacred sign of my body); do this in remembrance of me. Likewise, he took the cup, saying, This cup is the new covenant in my blood (the sacred sign of that covenant); do this in remembrance of me." "As often as you eat this bread and drink from this cup, you show forth the Lord's death until he comes (I Cor 11)." You openly exhibit his death, by these visible

signs, before God, angels, and men; you manifest your solemn remembrance of his death, until he comes from heaven.

But let a man first examine himself, whether he truly understands the nature of this holy sacrament, and whether he really desires to be made conformable to the death of Christ; and then, not hesitating, let him eat and drink.

The words of Jesus are echoed by Paul, when he says, "Let him eat and drink," both words in the imperative mood; not implying permission only, but a clear command; a command to all those who are already filled with faith, but also to those who can truly say, "Our sins are grievous unto us, their burden intolerable," [those under conviction of sin, who are seeking a Savior].

12 ... That this is a usual, ordinary, stated means of grace is evident from these words of Paul: "The cup which we bless, is it not the communion of the blood of Christ? The bread which we break, is it not a communion of the body of Christ (I Cor 10)?" Is the eating of that bread, and the drinking of that cup, not the outward, visible means, whereby God conveys into our souls all that spiritual grace, all that righteousness, peace, and joy in the Holy Spirit, which were purchased by the body of Christ broken and the blood of Christ shed for us? Let all who truly desire the grace of God, partake of the bread and wine.

IV / 1 ... But as plainly as God has pointed the way in which he should be sought, many are the objections which men, wise in their own eyes, have raised against it. We need to consider a few of these, not because they have real substance, but because they have been so often used, especially in recent years, to confuse the weak; to trouble and subvert even those who once ran well, till Satan appeared as an angel of light.

The first and main objection is this: "You cannot use these means without *trusting* in them." Where do you find that idea? I expect you to show me plain scripture for your assertions. Otherwise, I dare not receive them, since I am not convinced that you are wiser than God. But if you were right about the danger of trusting in the means of grace, surely Christ would have been aware of it, and would have warned us. But since he did not, I am convinced that your assertion is false.

"Maybe you should at least avoid the means of grace for a short time, to see whether you trust in them or not." What? Am I to disobey God in order to know whether I trust in what he has provided for my good? Do you really teach men to "do evil, that good may come?" God will surely judge and damn such teachers!

"If you are troubled when you avoid the means of grace, it means that you must have been trusting in them." Not at all! If I am troubled when I willfully disobey God [by *not* using the means], it is plain that his Spirit is still striving with me; but if I am not troubled, it is plain that I am given up to a degenerate mind.

I ask: What do you mean by *trusting* in the means of grace? Do you mean looking for God's blessing by using them? Or believing that, by using them, you will attain what otherwise you would not? Yes, that is exactly what I believe, and what I will continue to believe to the end! I will *trust* in the means of grace, believing that what God has promised, he is faithful to perform. Since he has promised to bless me in this way, I trust he will do it.

2 ... A second objection is this: "Using the means of grace is seeking salvation by works." Do you understand this biblical expression? In Paul's writings, it means seeking to be saved by observing the rituals of the Mosaic law; or expecting salvation for the sake of your own good works, by the merit of your own righteousness. But how are

either of these implied in my waiting for salvation in the way God has ordained, and expecting that he will meet me there, because he has promised to do so? I do expect God will fulfill his word, that he will meet me and bless me in this way. Not for the sake of my good works, nor for the merits of my righteousness; but only through the atoning work and righteousness of his beloved Son.

3 ... A third objection is that "Christ himself is the only means of grace." This is a mere play on words. When *we* say that prayer is a means of grace, we mean that prayer is a channel through which the grace of God is conveyed. When *you* say that Christ is the means of grace, you mean that Christ is the one and only source of grace, the only way to the Father. I totally agree, but that does not negate the means of grace, [the channels through which Christ's grace normally flows].

4 ... A fourth objection is this: "Scripture directs us to *wait* for salvation. David said, 'My soul waits on God, for from him comes my salvation.' And Isaiah said, 'O Lord, we have waited for you.'" I agree. Since salvation is the gift of God, we should wait on him to give it. But if God has appointed a *way* to wait, can anyone find a better way? Isaiah makes it plain: "In the way of your judgments (ordinances), O Lord, have we waited for you." And David also: "I have waited for your salvation, O Lord, and have kept your law."

5 ... "Yes," some say, "but God has appointed *another* way [the Moravian 'stillness' teaching]. It is based on this verse from Exodus: 'Stand *still* and see the salvation of God.'" Let us examine that verse in context: The Israelites were fleeing Egypt, and they were afraid as they saw the forces of Pharaoh pursuing them. Moses told them, "Fear not; stand still and see the salvation of God." The Lord told Moses to have the people go forward, while he stretched out his hand over the sea, to divide it. This was the salvation of God, which they *stood still* to see, by *marching forward* with all their might!

The other passage where this expression occurs is in II Chronicles. In the time of Jehoshaphat, there came against Judah a mighty army from the east. The king and his people fasted and prayed, seeking the Lord's help. A prophet spoke for the Lord, and told the people not to fear, but to confidently face the enemy. "But," he said, "you will not need to fight the battle. Stand still and see the salvation of the Lord." The next day, as Judah watched, the Lord sent confusion on the invaders, and they destroyed each other. Such was the salvation that the people of Judah saw. But how does any of this prove that we ought not to wait for the grace of God by the means which he has ordained?

6 ... There is one final objection that I hesitate even to mention: "Does Paul not say, 'If you are dead in Christ, why are you subject to ordinances?' That means that a Christian need not use the ordinances anymore."

Do you hear what you are saying? "If I am a Christian, I am no longer subject to the ordinances of Christ!" Surely you see the absurdity of such a statement! Obviously, what is meant here are the old Jewish ordinances, to which Christians are no longer subject. Paul makes this clear when he continues, "Touch not, taste not, handle not"—undoubtedly referring to the Jewish law. This objection is the weakest of all.

So, despite all the objections put forth, this great truth remains unshaken: All who desire the grace of God, must wait for it, by using the means of grace, which God himself has ordained!

V / 1 ... It having been established that all who desire the grace of God should use the ordained means of grace, we now consider how the means should be used, and in what order.

There is a kind of order which God is generally pleased to use in bringing a sinner to salvation: A dull, insensitive wretch is drifting along in life, giving God not a second thought, when suddenly God confronts him, perhaps by an awakening sermon or conversation, perhaps by some providential circumstance, or perhaps by an immediate stroke of his convicting Spirit, without any outward means at all. Having now a desire to flee from the wrath to come, he purposely goes to hear how it may be done. If he finds a preacher who speaks to the heart, he is amazed at the message, and begins searching the scriptures to find out if it can really be true. The more he hears and reads, the more convinced he is, and the more he meditates on it. Perhaps he finds some books which explain and enforce what he has read in scripture. And by all these means, the arrows of conviction sink deeper into his soul. He begins to talk of the things of God, which are uppermost in his thoughts; and to talk with God, to pray to him; though, through fear and shame, he hardly knows what to say. He cannot do anything but pray, even though it may only be in "groans which are not intelligible." Being in doubt that "the high and lofty One" will consider a sinner such as he, he feels drawn to pray with those who know God, with the faithful in church. Here he observes others going to the table of the Lord. He thinks to himself, "Christ has invited us to his table. Why do I not go? Because I am too great a sinner; I am not worthy." After struggling awhile with these doubts, there is a breakthrough. And so the man continues in God's way, by hearing, reading, meditating, praying, and communing, till God finally speaks to his heart, "Your faith has saved you. Go in peace."

2 ... By noting this order, we may learn what means to recommend to any particular soul. If any means of grace will reach an insensitive, careless sinner, it is probably evangelical preaching or Christian conversation. We would recommend these to any man

with any thought toward salvation. To one who begins to feel the weight of his sins, reading the word of God, or other Christian literature, may bring deeper conviction. We would recommend that he meditate on what he reads, that it may have its full force on his heart; and that he speak unashamedly with those who walk the same path. When his soul is heavy with conviction, we would earnestly exhort him to pray, to pour out his soul before God; and when he feels the worthlessness of his own prayers, we would remind him to go up to the house of the Lord, and pray with those who fear God. There he will hear the invitation of the dying Lord to his table; we would encourage him to avail himself of that means of grace. And thus, we would lead him, step by step, through all the means which God has ordained; not according to our will, but just as providence and the Spirit go before and open the way.

3 ... Admittedly, we find no command in scripture for any particular order to be followed; neither do providence or the Spirit follow the same invariable order. Different men are led, and find the blessing of God, in a thousand different ways. Wisdom dictates that we follow the leadings of providence and the Spirit, giving us the opportunity to use sometimes one means, sometimes another. Meanwhile, the sure and general rule for all who seek salvation is this: Whenever opportunity allows, use *all* the means of grace which God has ordained. Who knows in which of these God will meet you with the grace that brings salvation?

4 ... As to the manner of using the means of grace, remember, first, that God is far above the means themselves. Be careful that you do not try to limit the Almighty! He does whatever he pleases, whenever it pleases him. He can convey his grace through the ordinary means or outside the means. "Who has known the mind of the Lord, or who has been his counsellor?" Look every moment for him to break through to your soul, whether diligently following all

the means of grace, or being totally hindered from them. God is never hindered; he is always ready, able, and willing to save. "He is the Lord. Let him do what seems good to him!"

And second, before you use any means of grace, let it be deeply impressed on your soul that there is no intrinsic power in the means itself. In itself, it is a poor, dead, empty thing; separate from God, it is nothing. Neither is there any merit in my using it; nothing intrinsically pleasing to God; nothing by which I gain his favor. But because God has ordained the means, I use them; because he directs me to wait for him in this way, I wait for his free mercy, from which comes my salvation.

Remember also that the mere work done [scripture duly read, prayer duly prayed, communion duly partaken] profits nothing.; there is no power to save, but in the Spirit of God; no merit, but in the blood of Christ; even the means which God has ordained convey no grace to the soul, if you do not trust in him alone. On the other hand, he who truly trusts in him, cannot fall short of the grace of God, even though he were forever cut off from every usual means of grace.

Third, in using the means, seek God alone. In and through every outward thing, look only to the power of his Spirit, and the merits of his Son. Beware that you do not get stuck in the thing itself; if you do, it is all labor lost. Nothing short of God himself can satisfy your soul. Therefore, concentrate on him in all the means, through all the means, and above all the means.

Remember to use all the means of grace as means; as ordained, not for their own sake, but to bring renewal to your soul, in righteousness and holiness. If the means lead to this, well and good; if not, they are less than worthless.

Finally, take care how you value yourself after using the means of grace. Do not congratulate yourself, as if you had done some great thing. That would undo any good that had been done through the means; it would turn the means into a blasphemous farce. If God was truly there [when using the means], if his love flowed into your heart, you would forget about the outward work; you would remember only that God was all in all. You would sink into nothingness before him and give him all praise. "Let God in all things be glorified through Christ Jesus!" Your inmost soul would cry out, "My song shall always be of the lovingkindness of the Lord."

17

THE CIRCUMCISION OF THE HEART

Circumcision is of the heart, in the spirit, not in the letter.

—Romans 2:29

1 ... A respected man has sadly concluded that he who now preaches the most basic Christianity, runs the risk of being considered, by most people, "a proclaimer of new doctrines." Most men, while proclaiming to be Christians, have drifted so far from the essentials, that the minute someone sets forth a truth which clearly contrasts the Spirit of Christ from the spirit of the world, they cry out, "You bring strange things to our ears; we want to know what these things mean." The truth is, he is only preaching "Jesus and the resurrection," with what directly follows from that: If Christ be risen, you ought to die to the world and live wholly to God.

2 ... This is a hard concept for the natural man, who is alive to the world and dead to God; he will not be persuaded by God's truth, unless it be so watered down as to have lost its substance and significance. He cannot accept the word of God in its plain and obvious meaning; it is "foolishness to him." He cannot fathom it because it is "spiritually discerned." Since it can only be perceived by a spiritual sense, which has never been awakened in him, he rejects, as the foolishness of men, what is actually the wisdom and power of God.

3 ... An important truth, which can only be spiritually discerned, is this: The "circumcision of the heart," the distinguishing mark of a true Christian, is neither physical circumcision, nor ritual baptism, nor any outward thing, but a right state of soul, a mind and spirit renewed after the image of the Creator. Paul advises the Christian to expect his praise, "not of men, but of God." It is as if he had said, "If you follow the great Master, do not expect the world, the ones who follow him not, to approve or praise you. Understand that the circumcision of the heart, the mark of your calling, is foolishness with the world. Be content to wait till the day of Christ's coming. Then you shall have God's praise, in the great assembly of men and angels."

I intend now to consider what circumcision of the heart is, and then to reflect on some things that follow from it.

I / 1 ... First, I ask in what circumcision of the heart consists, which receives the praise of God. In general, it is the habitual disposition of soul which scripture calls 'holiness.' This implies being cleansed from sin, "from all filthiness of flesh and spirit," and then being endued with those virtues which were in Christ Jesus; being so "renewed in mind" as to be "perfect as our Father in heaven is perfect." To be more specific: Circumcision of the heart implies humility, faith, hope, and love.

2 ... *Humility,* a right judgment of ourselves, clears our minds from those high conceits of our own perfections, from that exaggerated opinion of our own abilities and attainments, which arise from our corrupt nature. This eliminates the vain thought that "I am rich and wise, and need nothing," and convinces us that we are instead "wretched, poor, miserable, blind, and naked." It convinces us that, even at our best, we are all sin and vanity; that confusion, ignorance,

and error dominate our thinking; that irrational, earthly, animal, devilish passions usurp authority over our will; that there is no wholesomeness in our soul, that our very foundations are askew.

3 ... We are further convinced that we are not able, of ourselves, to help ourselves; that without the Spirit of God, we can do nothing but compound our sins; that it is he alone, working powerfully within, who is responsible for any good we do; that it is as impossible for us to even think a good thought, without his supernatural assistance, as it is to create ourselves, or to completely renew our souls in righteousness and holiness.

4 ... A sure sign of our having formed this right judgment of our sinfulness and helplessness is our disregard of the "honor which comes from man," which is usually paid to some supposed excellency in us. He who really knows himself neither desires nor values undeserved praise; he cares little about man's opinion of him. By comparing what they say, either for or against him, with what he feels in his own heart, he realizes that the world, and the god of this world, was "a liar from the beginning." When it comes to his fellow Christians, he would earnestly hope that they would affirm his faithfulness to the Lord, so that he might be of help to them. But though he wishes for their approval on this account, he does not require it; he knows that whatever God wills to do, he never lacks those to accomplish it, since he is able, even of these stones, to raise up servants to do his pleasure.

5 ... Humility is that lowliness of mind, learned of Christ, of those who follow his example and tread in his steps. This self-knowledge, which fully exposes their pride and vanity, helps them embrace, with a willing mind, the second thing implied in circumcision of the heart: *Faith*, which alone can make them whole; faith, the one medicine under heaven to heal their spiritual sickness.

6 ... The best guide of the blind, the surest light for them in darkness, the most perfect teacher of the foolish, is faith. But it must be such a faith as is "mighty through God, to the pulling down of strongholds"; overturning all the prejudices of corrupt reason, all the false maxims revered among men, all evil customs and habits, all that "wisdom of the world which is foolishness with God." It is a faith that "casts down every high thing that exalts itself against the knowledge of God, and brings into captivity every thought to the obedience of Christ."

7 ... "All things are possible to him who believes," who has a faith like this. "The eyes of his understanding being enlightened," he sees that his calling is to glorify God, who has bought him with so high a price, so that he is now God's own, both by creation and redemption. He feels "the exceeding greatness of God's power," who raised Christ from the dead, and is able to raise us from the death of sin, "by his Spirit who dwells in us." "This is the victory that overcomes the world, even our faith." This faith is not only a firm assent to all that God has revealed in scripture—especially those important evangelical truths concerning Christ, his cross, and his atonement for sinners, but also Christ revealed in our hearts, a divine conviction of his love—his free, unmerited love for me a sinner; a sure confidence in his pardoning mercy, wrought in us by the Holy Spirit. Every true believer can confidently affirm: I have "an Advocate with the Father, Jesus Christ the righteous." He "loved me and gave himself for me." I have "redemption through his blood, even the forgiveness of sins."

8 ... Such a faith cannot fail to show evidence of the power of God who inspires it, by freeing his children from the bonds of sin and "dead works"; by strengthening them so that they are no longer constrained to obey sin, but instead of yielding themselves to unrighteousness, they now yield

themselves entirely "unto God, as those who are alive from the dead."

9 ... Those who are born of God by faith have also a strong consolation through *hope*. This is the third thing implied in circumcision of the heart—even the testimony of their own spirit with God's indwelling Spirit that they are the children of God. That same Spirit works in them a cheerful confidence that their heart is right toward God; a firm assurance that they now do, through grace, what is acceptable in God's sight; that they are now in the path that leads to life, and shall, by God's mercy, endure to the end. It is the Spirit who gives them a living expectation of receiving all good things at God's hand; a joyous prospect of that glorious crown reserved in heaven for them. By this anchor [hope], a Christian is kept steady amid the waves of this troubled world, and kept from striking either of those fatal rocks—presumption, on the one hand; despair, on the other. He does not despair over an exaggerated sense of God's severity, nor does he cavalierly presume on God's grace. He does not expect the difficulties of the race set before him to be greater than he can possibly overcome, nor to be so slight as not to require his best efforts. His experience in Christian warfare thus far, assures him that his "labor is not in vain," if he gives it his all; on the other hand, it forbids him the vain thought that he can gain any advantage, show forth any virtue, or attain any praise, by faint heart or feeble hands. The Christian must follow in the steps of Paul, who said, "I run, not uncertainly; I fight, not as one who beats the air; I keep my body under subjection, lest, having preached to others, I myself should be shipwrecked."

10 ... Every good soldier of Christ is to discipline himself to endure hardship, just as the great apostle did. Confirmed and strengthened by this, he will be able to renounce the works of darkness, every appetite and affection which is not subject to the law of God. John

says that "everyone who has this hope purifies himself as God is pure." It is his constant care, by the grace of God in Christ, and through the blood of the covenant, to cleanse the inmost recesses of his soul from the lusts that once possessed and defiled it; from impurity, envy, malice, and wrath; from every fleshly passion that springs from and cherishes his natural corruption. He knows full well that his body is the very temple of God, and that he ought not admit into it anything common or impure; that holiness should pervade that temple where the Spirit of holiness is pleased to dwell.

11 ... If a man has a deep humility, a steadfast faith, and a lively hope, he has largely cleansed his heart from its inbred pollution. If he would be perfect, he must add to these—*love*. These four comprise the circumcision of the heart. "Love is the fulfilling of the law, the goal of the commandment." Excellent things are spoken of love; it is the essence, the spirit, the life of all virtue. It is not only the first and great commandment, but all the commandments in one. "Whatever things are just, pure, and honorable, if there be any virtue, any praise," they are all included in the one word—love. In love is all perfection, glory, and happiness. The royal law of earth and heaven is this: "You shall love the Lord your God with all your heart, soul, mind, and strength."

12 ... This law does not forbid us to love anything besides God; in fact, it implies that we must love our brother also. Nor does it forbid us to take pleasure in anything but God, as some have strangely imagined. To suppose this, is to suppose that the source of all holiness is also the author of sin; since God has most made pleasurable to man those very things necessary to the sustaining of life. So, this can never be the meaning of the various scriptural commands to love God. The real meaning, as our Lord and his apostles make abundantly clear, is this: The one perfect Good shall be your one ultimate goal. One thing only shall you desire for its

own sake—the intimate knowledge of him who is all in all. The one happiness of your soul is a union with him who created you; having "fellowship with the Father and the Son"; being joined to the Lord in one Spirit. Your one design is the enjoyment of God in time and eternity. You may also desire other things, but only so long as they tend toward this. Love the creation and the creature only as they lead you to the Creator. At every step, let this be the glorious point to which you aspire. Let every affection, thought, word, and deed be subordinate to this. Whatever you desire or fear, whatever you seek or shun, whatever you think or say or do, let it enhance your happiness in God, who is the source and goal of your being.

13 ... Have no goal, no ultimate goal, but God. Thus said our Lord: "One thing is needful," and if you are solely focused on this one thing, "your whole being shall be full of light." Thus said Paul: "This one thing I do; I press toward the mark, for the prize of the high calling in Christ Jesus." Thus said James: "Cleanse your hands, you sinners; purify your hearts, you vacillating ones." Thus said John: "Love not the world, nor the things in the world, for all that is in the world is not of the Father." Seeking happiness in what gratifies the "desire of the flesh," through the outward senses; or the "desire of the eye," through novelty, greatness, or beauty; or the "pride of life," through pomp, grandeur, or power, by admiration or applause; "is not of the Father," does not come from the Father, nor is it approved by him. Rather it is "of the world," the distinguishing mark of those who refuse to have God reign over them.

II / 1 ... Having considered what the circumcision of the heart is, I will now reflect on some things that naturally follow, as a way for every man to judge himself, whether he be of the world or of God.

First, it is clear that no man has title to the praise of God, unless his heart is circumcised by *humility;* unless he is little, low, and contemptible in his own eyes; unless he is deeply convinced of that inbred "corruption of his nature," which is "far gone from original righteousness," prone to all evil and resistant to all good, a carnal mind which continually opposes God and his law; unless he continually feels in his inmost being, that without the Spirit of God within, he cannot think, desire, speak, or act anything good and well-pleasing in God's sight.

No man, I say, has title to the praise of God, till he feels his lack of God; till he seeks the honor which can only come from God; and neither desires nor pursues the praise of men.

2 ... Second, no man shall receive the honor that comes from God, unless his heart be circumcised by *faith,* a faith inwardly wrought by God; unless he refuses any longer to be led by his own senses, appetites, and passions, or by that blind leader of the blind, so idolized by the world, natural reason, but lives and walks by faith; unless he directs every step toward the invisible God, looking "not at things which are seen and temporal, but at things which are unseen and eternal"; unless he governs all his desires and designs, all his actions and conversations, as one who has entered another realm, where Jesus sits enthroned at the right hand of God.

3 ... I wish that they were better acquainted with *this* faith, those [philosophers, theologians] who spend their time and energy laying *another* foundation. They seek to ground religion on the eternal *fitness* of things, on the intrinsic *excellence* of virtue and the *beauty* of virtuous acts, on the *reasons* for good and evil, and the *relation* of beings to one another. Either their accounts of Christianity coincide with scripture, or they do not. If they do coincide, why are well-meaning men perplexed, and drawn away from the basics, by a cloud of terms which obscure the simple truths? If they do not,

then we need to consider who is the author of this new doctrine. The one who preaches another gospel, not the gospel of Christ, has already been cursed by God.

4 ... Our gospel knows no other foundation of good works but faith, no other foundation of faith but Christ. So, clearly, we are not his disciples if we deny him to be the source, or his Spirit to be the inspirer and perfecter, of both our faith and our works. "If any man have not the Spirit of Christ, he is none of his." Christ alone can enliven those who are dead to God, can breathe into them the breath of Christian life, can precede, accompany, and follow them with his grace, all designed to bring their good desires to a good result. "As many as are led by the Spirit of God, they are the sons of God." This is God's short and plain account of true religion and virtue; no other foundation can any man lay!

5 ... Third, no man is truly "led by the Spirit," unless the "Spirit bear witness with his spirit, that he is a child of God"; unless he see the prize and crown before him, and "rejoice in *hope* of the glory of God." Those have erred greatly who have taught that, in serving God, we ought not to have a view to our own happiness. No, we have been expressly taught in scripture to consider the divine reward; to balance the earthly toil with the "joy set before us," to balance these "light afflictions" with the "exceeding weight of glory." We are "aliens to the covenant of promise," "without God in the world," until the merciful God brings us to new birth, "to a living hope of an inheritance incorruptible, undefiled, and unfading."

6 ... It is high time for honest soul-searching in those who are so far from finding this joyful assurance that they have fulfilled the terms, and shall obtain the promises, of that covenant, that they quarrel with the covenant itself; that they complain that the terms are too severe, that no man ever can or ever will live up to them. This is nothing but reproaching God as a hard taskmaster, requiring of

his servants more than he enables them to perform; as if God had mocked his creatures, by demanding impossibilities; by commanding them to overcome, where neither their own strength nor his grace was sufficient for them.

7 ... On the other extreme, are those who imagine themselves guiltless and hope to fulfill God's commands without taking any effort at all. Vain hope, that a child of Adam should ever expect to see the kingdom of Christ without striving, without agonizing "to enter in at the narrow gate." Vain hope, that one who "was conceived in sin" should ever think of being pure "as his Lord is pure," unless he follow in his steps and "take up his cross daily." Vain hope, that he should ever dream of shaking off his old opinions and passions, of being "thoroughly sanctified in spirit, soul, and body," without a constant regimen of self-denial.

8 ... Paul's story illustrates this well: Though "signs, wonders, and mighty deeds" attended his ministry, though ecstatically "caught up into the third heaven," still he lived with "infirmity, reproach, persecution, and distress" for Christ's sake. Some have suggested that all his virtues would have been insecure, and even his salvation in danger, without this constant self-denial. He himself states, "I run, not uncertainly; I fight, not as one beating the air." His plain meaning is that he who does not run or fight with disciplined determination, who does not deny himself daily, runs or fights to no avail.

9 ... Finally, no man can fight "the fight of faith" with any hope of claiming an eternal crown, unless his heart has been circumcised by *love*. Love, which casts off all sinful distractions and engages the whole man (body, soul, and spirit) in its ardent pursuit, is essential to a child of God; without such love, he is dead within. "If I have not love, I am as sounding brass or tinkling cymbal; if I have faith to remove mountains, and have not love, I am noth-

ing; if I give all my riches to feed the poor, and have not love, it profits me nothing."

10 ... So, this is the totality of the perfect law; this is the true circumcision of the heart. Let man's spirit return to God who gave it, like streams flowing back to the spring from which they came. Other sacrifices from us God has not chosen—only the sacrifice of the heart. Let love be continually offered up to God through Christ in flames of holy love. Let nothing be allowed to share that love with him; for he is a jealous God. His throne he will not share with another; his reign will be without rival. Let no desire or design be admitted, but what has God as its ultimate object. This is the way that saints of old once lived, who, being dead, still speak to us: "Desire not to live, except to praise his name; let all your thoughts, words, and works tend to his glory. Set your heart firmly on him, and on other things only as they are in or from him. Let your soul be so filled with love for him, that you may love nothing else, except for his sake." "Have a steadfast regard to his glory in all your actions." "Focus on the blessed hope of your calling and make all things of the world subservient to it." For then, and only then, is that "mind in us which was also in Christ Jesus"; when, in all things, we "pursue nothing but in relation to him, and in subordination to his pleasure"; when we neither think, speak, nor act to fulfill our "own will, but the will of him who sent us"; when, "whatever we do, we do all to the glory of God."

Preached at St. Mary's, Oxford University, January 1733

18

THE MARKS OF THE NEW BIRTH

So is everyone who is born of the Spirit.

—JOHN 3:8

1 ... What is meant by being born again, being born of God, or being born of the Spirit? What is implied in being a child of God or having the Spirit of adoption? We know that these privileges, by the free mercy of God, are generally attached to baptism, which Jesus described as being "born of water and the Spirit." But what exactly are these privileges? What is the new birth?

2 ... Perhaps it is not necessary to provide a definition, since scripture does not provide one. But since this question is of the deepest concern to every man; since, "except a man be born again, he cannot see the kingdom of God"; I want to describe its marks in a plain and scriptural manner.

I / 1 ... The first of these marks, the foundation of all the rest, is *faith*. Paul states, "You are all the children of God by faith in Jesus Christ." John states, "To them he gave power (the right or privilege) to become the sons of God, even to them who believe on his name; who were born (when they believed), not of blood, nor of the will of the flesh (not by natural means), nor of the will of man (like children adopted by men, in whom there is no inward change), but of God."

2 ... This is not a merely theoretical or speculative faith which is spoken of by the apostles. It is not a mere assent to the proposition that Jesus is the Christ; nor to *all* the propositions contained in scripture and the creeds. It is not an assent to any of these beliefs, as beliefs. If that were the case, the devils would be "born of God," since they have that kind of faith. They believe (and tremble!) that Jesus is the Christ, and that all scripture is inspired of God. They do not merely assent to divine truths, based on the testimony of scripture; the devils actually heard these truths from the lips of Jesus, whom even they admit is a faithful witness and true. They could not but receive his testimony, both of himself and of his Father; they saw his mighty works and were convinced that he "came forth from God." Yet notwithstanding this 'faith,' the devils are still "reserved in chains of darkness," awaiting the final judgment.

3 ... The devils' faith is no more than a dead faith. The true, living, Christian faith of the born-again is not only an assent, an act of understanding and agreement. It is *also* a disposition which God has wrought in the heart; "a sure trust and confidence in God, that through the merits of Christ, his sins are forgiven, and he is reconciled to the favor of God." This implies that a man must first renounce himself; that, in order to be "found in Christ," to be accepted through him, he must totally reject all "confidence in the flesh"; and "having nothing to plead," having no trust in his own works or righteousness, he comes to God as a lost, miserable, self-destroyed, self-condemned, ruined, helpless sinner; he comes as one without excuse, altogether "guilty before God." An abject sense of sin (often referred to as despair, by those who do not understand its necessity), together with a deep conviction that only Christ can save us from sin, and an earnest desire for that

salvation, must precede that living faith, that trust in Christ who "paid our ransom by his death, and fulfilled the law in his life." This faith, by which we are born of God, is "not only a belief in all the articles of our faith, but *also* a true confidence in the mercy of God, through our Lord Jesus Christ."

4 ... An immediate and constant fruit of this born-again faith, a fruit which cannot be separated from it, is *power over sin.* This means power over *outward* sin of every kind, over every evil word and deed, for wherever the blood of Christ is applied, it cleanses; it also means power over *inward* sin, purifying the heart from unholy desires and temperament. Paul describes this fruit of faith in Romans 6: "How shall we, who (by faith) are dead to sin, live any longer in it?" "Our old self is crucified with Christ, that the body of sin might be destroyed." "Reckon yourselves to be dead to sin, but alive to God through Christ. Let not sin reign in your mortal bodies, but yield yourselves to God, as those who are alive from the dead." "Sin shall not have dominion over you." Thank God that you, who were the servants of sin, have "become the servants of righteousness."

5 ... The same invaluable privilege of the children of God is just as strongly asserted in I John 3, especially the power over outward sin. John begins by crying out, as one astonished at the depth and richness of the goodness of God: "Behold, what love the Father has bestowed on us, that we should be called the sons of God! We know that when he appears, we shall be like him; we shall see him as he is." He then adds: "Whoever is born of God does not commit sin; for God's nature remains in him." Some men will say, "True, whoever is born of God does not commit sin *habitually.*" Habitually? Where did that come from? That is not written in scripture. God plainly said that those who are born of God do not commit sin, period. And you are bold to add 'habitually'? Who are you to mend

the oracles of God, to "add to the words of this book"? Beware, lest God curse you, especially when the comment you add to scripture quite emasculates the text. By this artful means of deceiving, the precious promise is utterly lost; by this manipulation of men, the word of God becomes meaningless. Beware, lest, taking away the whole meaning and spirit of scripture, leaving only a dead form, God take away your part in his eternal kingdom!

6 ... Let John interpret his own words by the whole tenor of his discourse. He had said, "You know that he (Christ) was revealed to take away our sins; and in him is no sin." What does he infer from this? "Whoever abides in him sins not; whoever sins has not seen or known him." He adds this word of caution, "Let no man deceive you"; for many will try to persuade you that you may continue to be unrighteous, that you may continue to commit sin, and *still* be children of God! Not so! "He who commits sin is of the devil. Whoever is born of God does not commit sin; for God's nature remains in him." By this plain mark (committing or not committing sin) are the children of the devil distinguished from the children of God. "He who is born of God keeps himself, and the wicked one does not harm him."

7 ... Another fruit of living faith is *peace*. "Being justified by faith, we have peace with God, through our Lord Jesus Christ." The night before his death, Jesus himself bequeathed this to all his followers: "Peace I leave with you; my peace I give you. Let not your heart be troubled, neither let it be afraid." This is that "peace of God that passes all understanding," that unimaginable serenity of soul, which the natural man cannot know, and the spiritual man cannot adequately express. It is a peace which all the powers of earth and hell cannot take from him; waves and storms beat upon it, but cannot shake it, for it is founded on a rock. This peace keeps the hearts and minds of the children of God, always and everywhere.

Whether in ease or pain, in sickness or health, in abundance or poverty, they are happy in God. In every situation they have learned to be content, being convinced that "whatever is, is best," being God's will for them. In all the changes of life "their heart stands fast, believing in the Lord."

II / 1 ... A second scriptural mark of those who are born of God is *hope*. Peter expressed it like this: "Blessed be the God and Father of our Lord Jesus Christ, who by his abundant mercy, has begotten us again to a living hope." He speaks of a living hope, because there is also a dead hope, just as there is a dead faith. A dead hope is not from God, but from the devil; it can be identified by its fruits; since it springs from pride, it produces evil words and deeds. However, every man who has the living hope is "holy, as he who calls him is holy."

2 ... This hope implies, first, the testimony of our own spirit (conscience) that we walk "in simplicity and godly sincerity." And, second, the testimony of God's Spirit, "bearing witness with (to) our spirit that we are the children of God, heirs of God and joint-heirs with Christ (Rom 8)."

3 ... Let us pay attention to what is taught here by God himself, concerning the glorious privilege of his children: Who is said to bear witness? Not only our own spirit, but the Spirit of God. And what does he bear witness of? "That we are the children of God, heirs of God and joint-heirs with Christ—*if* we suffer with him," if we deny ourselves, if we take up our cross daily, if we cheerfully endure persecution or reproach for his sake. And in whom does the Spirit bear this witness? In *all* who are the children of God. "As many as are led by the Spirit of God, are sons of God. *You* have received the Spirit of adoption, whereby *we* cry, Abba, Father!"

4 ... Note the variation in the verse above: *You,* by virtue of your sonship, have received the Spirit of adoption; *we,* your apostles and teachers, through whom you have believed, we "stewards of the mysteries of God," cry Abba, Father! Since we and you have one Lord, so we have one faith and one hope. We and you are sealed with one Spirit, who is the promise and first evidence of our future inheritance; the same Spirit bears witness with our spirits and your spirits that we are both the children of God.

5 ... The witness of the Spirit in the children of God is the fulfillment of this saying of Jesus: "Blessed are they who mourn, for they shall be comforted." Sorrow *may* (indeed *must)* precede this witness of God's Spirit, while we groan under conviction, fearing the wrath of God upon us; but as soon as a man experiences this witness, his "sorrow is turned to joy." Whatever his pain may have been, once that "hour is come, he remembers the anguish no more, for joy" that he is born of God.

It may be that many of you now have this sorrow, because you are apart from God's people, conscious that you have not the Spirit, "without hope and without God in the world." But when the Comforter has come, "your heart will rejoice" with a "joy that no one can take from you." You will cry out, "We rejoice in God, through our Lord Jesus Christ, by whom we have now received the atonement"; "by whom we have access to this grace (this favor and reconciliation with God) in which we stand, and rejoice in hope of the glory of God." You, whom God has "begotten again to a living hope, are kept by the power of God unto salvation. In this you greatly rejoice, though now for a time, if need be, you are in distress through many trials." But at the coming of Christ, you will "rejoice with joy unspeakable and full of glory!" Unspeakable indeed! It is not for the tongue of man to describe this joy in the Holy Spirit. It is "the hidden manna, which no man knows, except him who receives it." But this we know, it not only remains, but overflows, in the depth of affliction. When sufferings most abound, the consolations of God's Spirit do much more abound; so that the children of God "laugh at destruction when it comes"; at privation and pain, hell and death, knowing the One who will overcome and destroy them. "Behold, God will dwell with men, and they shall be his people. And there shall be no more death, neither sorrow, nor crying, nor pain; for the former things are passed away."

III / 1 ... A third scriptural mark of those who are born of God, and the greatest of all, is *love*. "Because they are sons, God has sent forth the Spirit of his Son into their hearts, crying, Abba, Father!" By this Spirit, continually looking to God as their reconciled and loving Father, they cry to him for their daily bread, for all things needful for soul or body. They continually pour out their hearts before him, knowing "they have the petitions which they ask of him." They delight in him; he is the joy of their hearts, their "very great reward." He is the desire of their souls; they hunger and thirst to do his will and are abundantly satisfied in doing it.

2 ... Likewise, "everyone who loves the Father loves his Son." His spirit rejoices in God his Savior. He "loves the Lord Jesus Christ in all sincerity," and is so joined to him as to be one spirit. He knows, he feels the meaning of these scriptures [as pointing to Jesus]: "My Beloved is mine, and I am his." "You are fairer than all the children of men; full of grace, because God has anointed you forever!"

3 ... The necessary consequence of this love of God is the love of neighbor; of every soul which God has made, even our enemies, those who "despitefully use and persecute us." We must love every man as we love ourselves. Indeed, Jesus put it even more strongly: "Love one another as I have loved you." "Herein we perceive the

love of God, that he laid down his life for us." Therefore, "we ought to lay down our lives for our brothers." If we feel ready to do this, then we truly love our neighbor. And loving our neighbor, "we know we have passed from death to life"; we know "that we are born of God"; that we "dwell in him and he in us." For "love is of God; and everyone who loves is born of God and knows God."

4 ... Some may possibly argue that the love of God is simply obeying his commandments. After all, does John not say, "This is the love of God, that we keep his commandments"? Yes, and it is just as true that the love of neighbor involves the keeping of God's commands. But surely you cannot argue that keeping outward commandments is *all* that is implied in loving God with all your heart, and in loving your neighbor as yourself. Surely the love of God and neighbor is more than outward service; surely it is an affection of the soul, a disposition of the heart. To argue otherwise results in a wild interpretation of John's words. His plain, indisputable meaning is that keeping the first and great commandment, and all the rest as well, is the outward sign or proof of our love of God. True love, once shed abroad in our heart, will constrain us to obedience; since, whoever loves God with all his heart, cannot but serve him with all his strength.

5 ... Another consequence of the love of God, then, is total obedience to him we love, and conformity to his will; obedience to all his commands (internal and external); obedience of heart and life, of disposition and conversation. One thing most obviously implied is being "zealous of good works," hungering and thirsting to do all possible good to all men, rejoicing to "spend and be spent for them," not looking for reward in this world, but only at the resurrection of the just.

IV / 1 ... I have here explained the marks of the new birth, as laid down in scripture. In this way God himself answers that crucial question: What does it mean to be born of God? It means so to *believe* in God, through Christ, as "not to commit sin," and to continually enjoy "the peace of God that passes all understanding." It means so to *hope* in God, as to have not only the "testimony of a good conscience," but also the Spirit of God "bearing witness with your spirit, that you are a child of God," which inevitably results in rejoicing. It means so to *love* God, who first loved you, more than any person or any thing. This love of God constrains you to love all men as yourself, with a loving heart flaming forth in loving deeds, making your whole life one "labor of love," one continued obedience to the commands to be merciful and holy as God is, to "be perfect, as your Father in heaven is perfect."

2 ... Who are you, then, who are born of God? You well know whether you are a child of God or not. (Answer to God, not to man!) The question is not what you were made at baptism, but what you are *now*. (Do not evade the question, but search your heart!) I ask not whether you were born of water and the Spirit at baptism, but whether you are *now* the temple of the Holy Spirit who dwells in you. I agree that you were "circumcised with the circumcision of Christ" when you were baptized, but does his Spirit and glory *now* rest upon you? If not, your baptism has become void.

3 ... Say not in your heart, "I was *once* baptized; therefore, I am *now* a child of God." That consequence does not follow. How many are the baptized gluttons and drunkards, the baptized liars and swearers, the baptized whores and thieves and slanderers! Are these now the children of God? No, they are the children of the devil, whose works they do. To all baptized sinners, who crucify Christ again [with their sins], I issue this warning which

was issued to their circumcised predecessors, "You snakes, how can you escape the damnation of hell?"

4 ... How, indeed, except you be born again! For you are now dead in your sins. To say that you cannot be born again, that there is no new birth but baptism, is to consign yourself to damnation and hell, without help and without hope. Some [religious zealots] may think this is appropriate punishment for sinners, that they rightly deserve it. And truly they do deserve damnation and hell. But, so do I! So do you! It is only God's mercy, free and undeserved, that keeps us all, at this very moment, from the fire of hell! You [respectable folk] may argue that you were baptized, and thus born again "of water and the Spirit." I would remind you that most of these sinners were baptized too. Baptism does not guarantee that you will not become as they are. You, who are "highly esteemed by men," may well be "an abomination in the sight of God." So, who will cast the first stone at these sinful wretches, at these harlots, adulterers, and murderers? Remember, "He that hates his brother is a murderer." "He that looks on a woman with lust, has already committed adultery with her in his heart." [Despite your religion and respectability, are you not such a sinner?]

5 ... "Truly I say to you, you (also) must be born again." "Except you be born again, you cannot see the kingdom of God." Lean no more on that flimsy argument, that you were born again in baptism. No one denies that you were then made the children of God and heirs of his kingdom. But, despite this, you are now undoubtedly the children of the devil. Therefore, you must be born again! Do not allow the devil to make you quibble over the wording, when the fact itself is clear. You have heard what it means to be children of God; if your soul lacks these scriptural marks, whether baptized or unbaptized, you *must* receive those marks or perish everlastingly. If you have been baptized, your only hope is this—that you who

were made children of God by baptism, but are now children of the devil, may yet receive "power to become the sons of God," to receive again what you have lost, even the Spirit of adoption.

Amen, Lord Jesus! May he who prepares his heart yet again to seek your face, receive again that Spirit of adoption. May he have power so to believe in your name as to become a child of God; to know and feel that he has "redemption in your blood, even forgiveness of sins"; that he "cannot commit sin, because he is born of God." May he now be "begotten again to a living hope," so as to "be purified as God is pure." May the Spirit of love and glory rest upon him, and cleanse him, and bring him to "perfect holiness in the fear of God!"

19

THE GREAT PRIVILEGE OF THOSE THAT ARE BORN OF GOD

Whoever is born of God does not commit sin.
—1 JOHN 3:9

1 ... It has often been supposed that being born again, born of God, was the same as being justified; that the new birth and justification were only different expressions of the same reality. It is true that whoever is justified is also born of God, and whoever is born of God is also justified; both these gifts are given to every believer at the same moment. In one point of time, his sins are blotted out, and he is born again of God.

2 ... Though it is true that justification and the new birth are, in point of time, inseparable, yet they are easily distinguished, as being things of a widely different nature. Justification implies a *relative* change; the new birth an *actual* change. In justifying us, God does something *for* us; in begetting us again, he does a work *in* us. Being justified changes our outward relation to God, so that from enemies we become children of God; being born again changes our inmost souls, so that from sinners we become saints. The one restores us to the *favor* of God, the other to the *image* of God. The one takes away the *guilt* of sin, the other the *power* of sin. So, although they occur simultaneously, they are of wholly distinct natures.

3 ... Not clearly discerning the wide difference between being justified and being born again has caused great confusion among many who have written on the subject, especially when they have tried to explain this great privilege of the children of God—that "whoever is born of God does not commit sin."

4 ... In order to understand this, it is necessary to clarify exactly who it is "who is born of God," and in what sense he "does not commit sin."

I / 1 ... First, what is the meaning of the phrase, "whoever is born of God"? Considering all the scriptural passages which contain this phrase, we learn that it means far more than being baptized or any such outward change. Instead, it means a vast inward change, a change wrought in the soul by the Spirit of God, a change in our whole existence. From the moment we are born of God, we live in a different way than we did before, in a different world, as it were.

2 ... When we undergo this great change, we may truly be said to be born again, because of the close resemblance between natural and spiritual birth. Natural birth provides an explanation of spiritual birth.

3 ... The baby not yet born requires air, like every living thing; but he does not feel the air, or anything else, unless in some vague way. He hears very little, his ears being closed; he sees nothing, his eyes being shut, and surrounded by utter darkness. There are some faint beginnings of life, as birth draws near, and some motion to indicate that he is a living being, but no vital senses. Consequently, the baby has no interaction with this visible world, nor any conception of things that occur in it.

4 ... The reason why the unborn baby is a stranger to the visible world is not because that world is far off; indeed, it is quite near, and surrounds him on all sides. The reason is, partly, that his senses are not yet fully developed, to interact with that world; and, partly, that there is a barrier between, which blocks his understanding of that world.

5 ... But no sooner is the child born into the world, than everything changes. He now feels the air with which he is surrounded, as fast as he breathes it in and out to sustain his life. This leads to a continual increase of strength, motion, and sensation, all the senses being now awakened to their proper objects.

His eyes are now open to see light, and light reveals an infinite variety of things which he never knew existed; his ears are open to an endless diversity of sound. Every sense is focused on the objects peculiarly suitable to it. Interacting now with the visible world, he acquires more and more knowledge of it.

6 ... So it is with him who is born of God. Before the great change is wrought, he is not aware of the all-surrounding, all-sustaining God; he does not feel him, he does not sense his presence. He does not perceive that divine breath of life, without which he could not exist; nothing of God makes an impression on his soul. God is continually calling to him, but he hears not; he sees not the things of the Spirit, utter darkness covering his soul. Yes, he may have some faint dawnings of life, some small beginnings of spiritual motion; but as yet he has no spiritual senses to grasp spiritual objects. Consequently, he cannot "discern the things of the Spirit; he cannot know them, for they are spiritually discerned."

7 ... Therefore, he has hardly any knowledge of the invisible world, and hardly any interaction with it. Yet it is not far off; it

completely surrounds him. That other world is not far from any of us; it is above, beneath, and on every side. But the natural man discerns it not; partly because he has no spiritual senses, partly because he knows not how to penetrate the barrier [between him and the spiritual world].

8 ... But when he is born of God, born of the Spirit, how his whole existence changes! His soul is now fully aware of God; he feels God all around him and within. The Spirit (breath) of God is now breathed into the newborn soul; and the same breath which comes from God, returns to God. As it is continually received by faith, it is continually returned by love, by prayer, praise, and thanksgiving—all of which constitutes the breathing of the newborn soul. And by this new kind of spiritual respiration, spiritual life is both sustained and increased daily, together with spiritual strength, motion, and sensation. All the senses of the soul are now awake and capable of discerning spiritual good and evil.

9 ... "The eyes of his understanding" are now open, and he "sees him who is invisible." He sees "the exceeding greatness of his power," and his love toward those who believe. He sees that God is merciful toward him a sinner, that he is reconciled through the Son of God's love. He clearly perceives the pardoning love of God and all his "great and precious promises." "God, who commanded light to shine out of darkness, has shone in his heart, with the knowledge of the glory of God in the face of Jesus Christ." All the darkness is gone, and he abides in the light of God's presence.

10 ... His ears are now open, and the voice of God no longer calls in vain. He hears and obeys the call from heaven; he knows the voice of his Shepherd. All his spiritual senses being now awakened, he has direct interaction with the invisible world; and thus, he knows more and more of the things which before he could not even imagine. He now knows the peace of God, joy in the Holy Spirit,

and the love of God shed abroad in the hearts of believers. The barrier to the knowledge and love of God being now removed, he who is born of the Spirit "dwells in God, and God in him."

II / 1 ... Second, in what sense does the born-again believer "not commit sin"? One who is born of God continually receives into his soul God's breath of life, the gracious influence of his Spirit, and continually returns it. He who thus believes and loves, who by faith experiences God's touch on his spirit, returns the grace he receives in unceasing love, praise, and prayer. While the believer continues in this state, he does not commit sin; indeed, so long as God's nature "remains in him, he cannot sin, because he is born of God."

2 ... By sin, I mean *outward* sin, as commonly understood; an actual, voluntary transgression of God's revealed and written law; any commandment of God, known to be such at the time it is transgressed. But "whoever is born of God," while he abides in faith and love, in the spirit of prayer and thanksgiving, does not and cannot commit sin. So long as he thus believes in God through Christ, and loves him, and pours out his heart before him, he cannot purposely transgress any command of God, either by saying or doing what he knows God has forbidden. So long as God's nature remains in him, that loving, praying, thankful faith compels him to refrain from whatever he knows to be an abomination to God.

3 ... But here a difficulty immediately appears, one that many consider an absolute contradiction, one that causes them to deny the plain teaching of scripture and give up the privilege of the children of God.

It is a plain fact that those who have been truly born of God (the Spirit having infallibly testified to it in scripture) have, nonetheless, committed sin—even gross, outward sin. They have transgressed the plain, revealed laws of God, saying or doing what they knew he had forbidden.

4 ... David, for example, was undoubtedly born of God before he was anointed king. He knew in whom he believed; "he was strong in *faith*, giving glory to God." "The Lord is my Shepherd," he said, 'feeding me, leading me, walking with me, so that I fear no evil.' David was full of *love:* "I love you, O Lord, my strength, my rock and defense, my salvation and refuge." He was a man of *prayer*, pouring out his soul before God in all circumstances, abundant in praise and thanksgiving: "You are my God; I will thank you and praise you." Yet such a child of God could and did commit sin—the horrid sins of adultery [Bathsheba] and murder [Uriah].

5 ... And even after the Spirit was more largely given, even after "life and immortality were brought to light by the gospel [of Christ]," there were still similar sad instances, undoubtedly included in scripture for our instruction. Barnabas, for example, sold all he had for the sake of poor believers; he was entrusted by the church at Antioch, along with Paul, to carry their offering to Judea; he was solemnly chosen to accompany Paul in his first mission to the Gentiles, to be his fellow-laborer in every place. Nevertheless, Barnabas had such a sharp dispute with Paul, that he departed from the work to which he had been called by the Holy Spirit.

6 ... An even more astonishing instance than David or Barnabas is the great Peter himself, the first of the apostles, one of the three closest comrades of Jesus. As Paul relates it in Galatians, Peter had come to Antioch and was freely sharing table fellowship with the Gentile converts there, since the Lord had dramatically convinced him that he "should not call any man common or unclean." But when a Jewish delegation from Jerusalem arrived, he separated himself from the Gentile believers, for fear of his reputation among

the Jews. Other Jewish believers followed his lead, including Barnabas. When Paul saw this glaring inconsistency with the gospel message, he confronted Peter: "If you, being a Jew, live like a Gentile (no longer following the ceremonial law of Moses), why do you expect the Gentiles to live like Jews?" Here also is a plain, undeniable sin committed by one who was truly born of God. How can this be reconciled with the plain, obvious assertion of John, that "whoever is born of God does not commit sin"?

7 ... I answer, as many before me have answered: So long as "he who is born of God *keeps* himself," which he is able to do, by the grace of God, "the wicked one touches him not." But if he does not *keep* himself, if he does not abide in faith, he may commit sin like any man.

It is not as contradictory as it seems, how even the children of God can fall from their first steadfastness, and yet the great truth of God in scripture remain unshaken. The believer who falls did not keep himself by that grace that was sufficient for him. He fell, step by step: First, into *passive inward sin*—not "stirring up the gift of God within him," not "watching unto prayer," not "pressing on to the prize of his high calling." Then, into *active inward sin*—inclining to wickedness in his heart, giving in to some evil desire or inclination. Finally, he loses his faith in a pardoning God, and consequently his love of God, and then, being weak like any man, he is capable of committing even *outward sin.*

8 ... To explain this with a specific example: David was born of God and knew God by faith. He sincerely loved God, and could say, "Whom have I but thee?" But still there remained in his heart the corruption of nature, which leads to all evil. David was on his rooftop, probably praising God, when he looked and saw Bathsheba. He felt temptation, a thought which tended to evil. The Spirit did not fail to point this out. David undoubtedly heard

the warning voice, but yielded somewhat to the thought, and the temptation began to prevail. His spirit was tainted; he saw God, but more dimly than before; he loved God, but not to the same extent, not with the same passion. Though God's Spirit was grieved, he warned him again, though his voice grew fainter and fainter. But David would not hear. He looked now, not to God, but to the forbidden object of his temptation, till nature was superior to grace, and kindled lust in his soul. His spiritual senses ceased, and God vanished from his sight. His faith and love of God ceased, that supernatural and gracious relationship, and David galloped headlong into sin.

9 ... You can see the inevitable progress from grace to sin, step by step: (1) The divine nature of loving, conquering faith exists in him who is born of God. And "he keeps himself," by the grace of God, and therefore "cannot commit sin." (2) A temptation arises; it does not matter whether it is from the world, the flesh, or the devil. (3) The Spirit warns him that sin is near and encourages him to more prayer. (4) He gives way, somewhat, to temptation, which becomes even more pleasing to him. (5) The Spirit is grieved; the man's faith is weakened, and his love of God grows cold. (6) The Spirit reproves him even more sharply. (7) He turns away from the severe voice of God and listens to the soothing voice of the tempter. (8) Evil desire spreads in his soul, till faith and love vanish. He is now capable of committing outward sin, the power of the Lord being departed from him.

10 ... To explain this with another example: Peter was full of faith and the Holy Spirit, and thus keeping himself, he had a clear conscience toward God and man. Walking thus in godliness, he willingly ate with his Gentile brethren, knowing that what God had cleansed could not be called unclean. But when the Jewish brethren arrived, a temptation arose in his heart, to fear the opinion

of those who were still zealous for the Law and regard the praise and favor of these men more than the praise of God.

He was warned by the Spirit that sin was near. Nonetheless, he somewhat yielded to it, even to a sinful fear of man, and his faith and love were proportionately weakened. God reproved him again, but he would not hear the voice of the Shepherd; giving himself up to slavish fear, he quenched the Spirit. So, God disappeared, along with faith and love, and Peter committed the outward sin: Behaving unrighteously, not "according to the truth of the gospel," he separated himself from his brothers in Christ, and by his evil example, he caused the Gentile converts to entangle themselves again under that "yoke of bondage," from which Christ had set them free.

This is how it is that one who is born of God, who cannot commit sin, can and will commit all sorts of sin, without restraint, if he fails to keep himself, [by the grace available to him].

III / 1 ... From the preceding, we may answer, first, a question which has often perplexed sincere believers: Does sin precede or follow the loss of faith? Does a child of God first commit sin, and thereby lose his faith? Or does he first lose his faith, before he can commit sin? I answer: Some sins of omission, some inward sins, must precede the loss of faith; but the loss of faith must precede the committing of outward sins.

The more any believer examines his own heart, the more will he be convinced of this: That faith working by love, in a soul watching unto prayer, allows neither inward nor outward sin. Nevertheless, we are even then liable to temptation, especially those sins that easily beset us. If the soul is firmly and lovingly fixed on God, the temptation soon vanishes; but if not, we are lured away from God by our own desires, entrapped by the promise of pleasure. That desire, conceived in us, brings forth sin; that inward sin destroys faith and casts us headlong into the snare of the devil, so that we may commit any sin whatever.

2 ... We may answer, second, what the life of God in the soul of a believer is; what it consists of, and what is implied by it. It necessarily implies the continual inspiration of the Holy Spirit; God's breathing into the soul, and the soul's breathing back what it first receives from God; a continual action of God upon the soul, and a reaction of the soul upon God. It implies the unceasing presence of a loving, pardoning God manifested to the heart and perceived by faith; an unceasing return of love, praise, and prayer; an offering up of all the thoughts of our heart, all the words of our mouth, all the works of our hands, all our body, soul, and spirit, to be a holy sacrifice, acceptable to God in Christ Jesus.

3 ... We may answer, third, that the reaction of the soul (whatever it might be called) is absolutely necessary for the continuance of the divine life within. Plainly, God does not continue to act upon the soul, unless the soul reacts upon God. God first showers us with the blessings of his goodness, [before we are even aware of it, or in any way deserve it]. He first loves us and reveals himself to us. While we are yet far off, he calls us to himself and shines in our hearts. But if we do not then love him who first loved us; if we will not respond to his voice; if we turn away from the light of his glory; then he will gradually withdraw, leaving us to the darkness of our hearts. He will not continue to breathe into our soul, unless our soul breathes back to him; unless our love, praise, and thanksgiving return to him as a well-pleasing sacrifice.

4 ... Finally, let us follow the direction of the great apostle: "Be not haughty, but fear." Let us fear sin more than death or hell. Let us have a careful (but not cringing) fear, lest we should rely on our own deceitful hearts. "Let him who stands take heed lest he

fall." Even he who now stands fast in the grace of God, in the faith that overcomes the world, may nevertheless fall into inward sin, and thereby "make shipwreck of his faith." How easily then will outward sin regain its dominion over him! Man of God, be always on guard, that you may always hear the voice of God, that you may pray, always and everywhere, pouring out your heart before him! So shall you always believe, always love, and never commit sin.

20

THE LORD OUR RIGHTEOUSNESS

This is the name by which he shall be called, 'The Lord our Righteousness.'

—JEREMIAH 23:6

1 ... How many and how terrible are the disputes which have arisen about religion! Not only among the children of the world, who never knew what true religion was, but even among the children of God, who have experienced "the kingdom of God within them," "righteousness, peace, and joy in the Holy Spirit." How many of these believers, in every century, instead of joining together against the common enemy, have turned their weapons against each other, wasting their own precious time, hurting each other's spirits, weakening each other's effectiveness, and hindering the great work of their Lord! How many weak ones have been confused and discouraged by it all; how many have left their faith! How many sinners have been confirmed in their disregard for all religion, and their contempt for those who profess it! And how many great souls have mourned these senseless controversies!

2 ... Would every lover of God and neighbor not do all in his power to remedy this disastrous situation; to remove contention from the children of God, and restore peace among them? What price would he not pay to promote this reconciliation? And even if we cannot end the conflict, reconciling all the children of God

to each other, we surely can make some small contribution toward it. Happy are they who, in any way, promote peace and goodwill, especially among good men, among those who follow the Prince of Peace and endeavor to "live peaceably with all men."

3 ... It would be a giant step forward, if only we could bring good men to truly understand each other. Many disputes arise purely as a result of opposing parties misunderstanding, then attacking each other, when there is no real difference between them. Yet it is often difficult to convince them of this, particularly when their passions are aroused. Difficult, but not impossible, when we attempt it, not in our own strength, but in dependence upon God, who makes all things possible. How easily is he able to clear the confusion, enlighten hearts, and enable them to understand each other, and "the truth as it is in Jesus!"

4 ... One important example of this issue is contained in the scriptural phrase, "The Lord our righteousness." This truth is deeply embedded in the very essence of Christianity; it is the foundation which supports Christianity's entire framework. This truth is, in Luther's words, "an article on which the Church stands or falls." It is a pillar of the faith which alone brings salvation, that catholic (universal) faith found in all the children of God, which, "unless a man keep it whole and undefiled, he shall perish everlastingly."

5 ... Might you not expect that, however they differed in other truths, all Christians would agree on this truth? But this is far from the case! There is hardly any truth on which they are so little agreed, on which they seem so widely and irreconcilably divided. I am convinced that they only *seem* to be divided. The disagreement is more in words than in sentiment, more in language than in judgment. And the division is not only between Catholic and Protestant, but also among Protestants—even among those who

believe in justification by faith and in every other fundamental doctrine of the gospel.

6 ... But if the difference be more in wording than in opinion, and more in opinion than in Christian experience, how can believers so vehemently contend with each other? There are several reasons: The main reason is not really understanding each other; the other reason is being too keenly attached to their own opinions and modes of expression.

In order to lessen the conflict, I hope, by the help of God, to show (1) what the righteousness of Christ is; (2) when and how his righteousness is imputed [credited] to us; and conclude with a short application.

I / 1 ... What is the righteousness of Christ? It is both his *divine* righteousness and his *human* righteousness.

His *divine* righteousness belongs to his divine nature, as he is "God over all, blessed forever"; the supreme and eternal God, "equal with the Father, concerning his deity." This is his eternal, essential, unchanging holiness; his infinite justice, mercy, and truth; in all of which, he and the Father are one.

But I do not think that the *divine* righteousness of Christ is involved in this conflict. I think that few, if any, would claim that *this* righteousness is imputed to man. Those who believe in the imputation of righteousness, understand it primarily in terms of Christ's *human* righteousness.

2 ... The *human* righteousness of Christ belongs to him in his human nature, as he is the "mediator between God and man, the man Christ Jesus." This righteousness is both internal and external. His *internal* human righteousness is the very image of

God stamped on his soul; a copy of God's righteousness, so far as it can be imparted to a human spirit. It is an imprint of the divine purity, the divine justice, mercy, and truth. It includes Christ's love, his reverence, his submission to the Father; his humility and gentleness; his love for lost humanity; and every other holy and heavenly disposition—and each of these to the highest degree, without defect or taint of unholiness.

3 ... As to his *external* human righteousness, he did absolutely no wrong, committed no sin of any kind, never spoke an improper word, never did an improper deed. Thus far, it is only a *negative* righteousness, though perfect, never achieved by any man, but Christ alone. But his *positive* righteousness was perfect too: He did all things well; every word and every deed, in every circumstance, throughout his life, was exactly "the will of him who sent him." He did the will of God on earth, as angels do in heaven. His obedience was complete; "he fulfilled all righteousness."

4 ... But his obedience implied more than this: It implied *suffering,* suffering the whole will of God—from the time he entered the world, till "he bore our sins in his own body" upon the cross, till having made full atonement for the sins of the world, he bowed his head and died.

The suffering of Christ has been called his *passive* righteousness; the former, his *active* righteousness. But since the active and passive righteousness of Christ were never, in fact, separated from each other, we need not separate them in our thinking or speaking. When we affirm that Jesus is "the Lord our righteousness," we mean both together.

II / 1 ... But when may we truly say that the Lord is our righteousness? When is the righteousness of Christ imputed [credited] to us, and in what sense is it imputed? Every man in the world is either a believer or an unbeliever. To all true believers, the righteousness of Christ *is* imputed; to all unbelievers, it *is not*.

But *when* is it imputed? When they believe. In that very moment, the righteousness of Christ is theirs. It is imputed to *all* who believe *when* they believe. Faith in Christ, according to scripture, and the righteousness of Christ are inseparable. There is no true faith, no justifying faith, without the righteousness of Christ as its object.

2 ... It is true that believers may not all speak alike; they may not all use the same terminology. We should not expect or require that they do. A thousand circumstances may cause them to differ from one another; but a difference in expression does not necessarily imply a difference in understanding. Different persons may use different expressions, yet mean the same thing. Nothing is more common than this, though we seldom make sufficient allowance for it. Even the same persons, when speaking of the same thing at different times, fail to use exactly the same words. How then can we be so rigorous in requiring others to use the same expressions we do?

3 ... And we may go further: Men may differ from us in their opinions, as well as their expressions, and still share the same precious faith. They may have a distinctive understanding of the blessing we share; they may not express themselves as clearly as we do, yet have the same Christian experience that we have. There is a wide difference in the natural capacities of men, and that difference is magnified by a difference in education. These differences affect men's opinions on many subjects; why would their opinions on religion not also be different? Though their opinions and their expression may be confused and inaccurate, their hearts may well be right with God, through Christ their righteousness.

4 ... Let us then make the allowances for others which we would desire for ourselves. Who is not aware of the amazing power of sound teaching? Considering that, who could expect a Catholic to think or speak clearly on this subject [of imputed righteousness]? Yet, when Bellarmine [an Italian Jesuit and cardinal] lay dying, he was asked which of the saints he would turn to; he replied, "It is safest to trust in the merits of Christ." Is there any doubt that, despite many wrong opinions, he had a claim on the righteousness of Christ?

5 ... But in what sense is this righteousness imputed to believers? All believers are forgiven and accepted, not because of anything worthy in them, or anything worthy they could ever do, but strictly because of what Christ has done and suffered for them. "Not by works of righteousness which *we* have done, but by his mercy *he* saved us." "By grace are you saved through faith; not through works, lest anyone should boast." We are "justified freely by his grace, through the redemption that is in Jesus." And this is not only the means of *obtaining* God's favor, but of *continuing* in it. It is how we come to God at first; it is how we come to God ever after. We walk in this new and living way, till our spirit returns to God.

6 ... This is the doctrine I have constantly believed and taught for twenty-eight years. It was this that I published openly in 1738, and many times since, in these and similar words, extracted from the Homilies of our Church [of England]: "These things necessarily go together in our justification: on God's part, his great mercy and grace; on Christ's part, the satisfaction of God's justice; on our part, faith in the merits of Christ. God's grace shuts out man's righteousness, as deserving justification." "That we are justified by faith alone, is meant to take away all merit from our works, and to wholly ascribe the merit and deserving of our justification to Christ only. Our justification comes freely from the mercy of God. Since all the world was not able to pay any part of our ransom [from sin], it pleased God, despite our undeserving, to offer Christ's body and blood on our behalf, to pay our ransom, and satisfy his justice. Christ is, therefore, the righteousness of all them that truly believe in him."

7 ... The Hymns, published and re-published [by the Wesley brothers] across the years, proclaim the same understanding of imputed righteousness. To take one of many, for example: *Jesus, thy blood and righteousness My beauty are, my glorious dress. Midst flaming worlds in these arrayed, With joy shall I lift up my head.'* The entire hymn expresses the same sentiment, from beginning to end.

8 ... In my sermon on Justification by Faith [V], published twice during the last twenty years, I express the same thing in these words: "In consideration that the Son of God has 'tasted death for every man,' God has now 'reconciled the world to himself, not imputing to them their trespasses.' For the sake of his beloved Son, of what he has suffered and sacrificed for us, God now intends to grant, on one condition only [faith], a condition which he himself enables us to perform: the remission of punishment for our sins, our reinstatement to his favor, and the restoration of our dead souls to spiritual life—all as a down-payment on his promise of eternal life."

9 ... This is all more fully and exactly articulated in my treatise on Justification, published last year: "The imputing of Christ's righteousness is the bestowing on *us,* the crediting to *us,* of all the righteousness which belongs to Christ, with all the privileges, blessings, and benefits that are purchased by it. A believer may be said to be justified by the imputed righteousness of Christ. As Calvin states in his Institutes: 'Christ, by his obedience, procured and merited for us the grace and favor of God the Father.' 'To say that we are justified by the grace of God, or that Christ is our

righteousness, or that righteousness was procured for us by the death and resurrection of Christ—they all mean the same thing: that the whole righteousness of Christ is the meritorious cause of our justification; that [immediately] upon our believing, God credits *us* with *Christ's* righteousness.'"

10 ... Perhaps some may argue, "But you affirm that *faith* is imputed to us for righteousness." Yes, Paul affirms that, again and again; so I affirm it too. Faith is imputed for righteousness to every believer, and that faith is faith *in* the righteousness of Christ. It all means exactly the same thing: We are justified by faith in Christ, not by our own works; we are forgiven and accepted, only for the sake of what Christ has done and suffered.

11 ... "But is a believer not *clothed* with the righteousness of Christ?" they ask. Of course he is. The words of the hymn [above] speak of Christ's righteousness being the believer's "glorious dress." The meaning is clear: For the sake of his righteousness, active and passive, we are forgiven and accepted by God.

"But must we not cast off the filthy rags of our own righteousness, before we can put on the spotless righteousness of Christ?" Certainly. We must repent, before we can believe the gospel. We must despair of dependence on ourselves, before we can truly depend on Christ. We must cast off all confidence in our own righteousness, before we can have true confidence in his. We must cease trusting in anything we do, before we can thoroughly trust what he has done and suffered. First, we must receive the sentence of death on ourselves; then, we can trust in him who lived and died for us.

12 ... "But do you not believe in *inherent* [actual, in contrast to imputed] righteousness?" Yes, in its proper place; not as the *ground* of our acceptance by God, but only as the *fruit* of it; not in the

place of Christ's imputed righteousness, but only as a consequence of it. I believe God *implants* righteousness in everyone to whom he *imputes* it. I believe that God *sanctifies,* as well as *justifies,* all who believe in him. Those to whom the righteousness of Christ is imputed, are also made actually righteous by the Spirit of Christ, renewed in the image of God, "after the likeness in which they were created, in righteousness and true holiness."

13 ... "But do you not put faith in the place of Christ and of his righteousness?" No; I am careful to put each of these in its proper place. The righteousness of Christ is the whole foundation, the sole foundation, of our hope. By faith, the Spirit enables us to build on that foundation. God gives this faith, and, the moment we believe, we are accepted by God, not for the sake of our faith, but for the sake of what Christ has done and suffered for us. So, each of these has its proper place, and neither clashes with the other. We believe, we love, we endeavor to walk blamelessly in all the commandments of the Lord; [but despite this evidence of our sanctification, we continue to rely wholly and solely on the *imputed* righteousness of Christ]. As the [Wesley] hymn states it: *"His passion alone, The foundation we own; Ourselves we forsake, And refuge we take in Jesus's righteousness."*

14 ... I no more deny the righteousness of Christ than I deny the deity of Christ! Neither do I deny imputed righteousness! These are both unkind and unjust accusations. I always did, and do still affirm, that the righteousness of Christ is imputed to every believer. Who *does* deny this doctrine? All nonbelievers, whether baptized or unbaptized; all who believe the glorious gospel of Christ to be a cunningly devised fable; all Socinians and Arians [non-orthodox Christians who held a low view of Christ]; all who deny the full deity of Christ, and therefore deny his divine righteousness, supposing him to be a mere mortal, and deny that his human righteousness

can be imputed to any man, believing that all men are accepted by God on the basis of their own righteousness.

15 ... The human righteousness of Christ, at least the imputation of it, as the whole, sole meritorious cause of the justification of sinners before God, is likewise denied by Catholics, at least by those who are true to the doctrine of their church. But undoubtedly there are many of them whose experience goes beyond their doctrine; who, though they are far from expressing themselves correctly, yet feel what they know not how to express. Yes, though their understanding of this great truth be as crude as their expression of it, yet with their hearts they believe. They rest on Christ alone, both for present and eternal salvation.

16 ... Along with the Catholics, are even some members of the Reformed churches, those usually called mystics. One of the chief of these, in this century, was the Englishman, William Law, who absolutely and zealously denied the imputation of the righteousness of Christ. Robert Barclay likewise ridiculed the doctrine, saying, "Imputed righteousness! Imputed nonsense!" The Quakers hold to the same opinion. In fact, most of those who claim to belong to the Church of England are either totally ignorant of this concept, or deny imputed righteousness, along with justification by faith, as being destructive of good works. To these we may add a considerable number of Anabaptists, together with thousands of Presbyterians and Independents, recently influenced by the writings of Dr Taylor. (I will not judge these, but leave them to the great Judge.) But will anyone dare to claim that all these mystics, all these Quakers, all these Presbyterians and Independents, all these Anglicans, who are not clear in their opinions or expressions, are thereby void of all Christian experience? That they are all in a state of damnation, "without hope, and without God in the world"? No! However confused

their opinions, however incorrect their language, are there not many of them whose heart is right toward God, and who truly know "the Lord our righteousness"?

17 ... Thank God, we are not among those who are confused in understanding and careless in expression. We use the theological language of imputation and believe in the spiritual reality of imputation; but we are not willing to force it on others. Let them use whatever expression they believe to be most scriptural, provided that their heart relies only on what Christ has done and suffered, for their pardon, grace, and glory. I cannot express this better than James Hervey [contemporary Anglican clergyman]: "We are not particular about the phrasing. Only let men be humbled as repenting criminals at Christ's feet, let them rely as dependents on his merits, and they are undoubtedly on the way to a blessed immortality."

18 ... Is there any reason to say more? If we keep to this understanding, all contention about language is silenced. Who can disagree with Hervey? He is a man of peace, offering accommodation to all the warring parties. I wholeheartedly accept his offer. And whoever refuses to do so is an enemy of peace, a troubler of Israel, a disturber of the Church.

19 ... My one concern is this: that men would use the imputed righteousness of Christ as an excuse for their own unrighteousness. It has been done thousands of times. A man is reproved for a life of drunkenness, for example. "O," says he, "I pretend to no righteousness of my own; Christ is my righteousness." Another is solemnly warned that "the unjust shall not inherit the kingdom of God." He replies, with brazen assurance, "Though I am personally unjust, I have a spotless righteousness in Christ." And so, though a man be far from the practice or temperament of a Christian; though he have not the mind of Christ, nor walk as Christ walked;

yet he insulates himself from the conviction of sin by appealing to the righteousness of Christ.

20 ... Having seen so many deplorable instances of this, I myself am very sparing in the use of these expressions. As your brother in Christ, I would urge you, who use them frequently, to warn your hearers against this damnable abuse. Warn them (they may listen to *you!*) against "continuing in sin that grace may abound." Warn them of the solemn decree of God, that "without holiness no man shall see the Lord," while they vainly lay claim to Christ's holiness. Warn them that if they remain unrighteous, the righteousness of Christ will profit them nothing! Convince them that the righteousness of Christ is imputed to us so that "the righteousness of the law may be fulfilled in us," and so that we may "live soberly, righteously, and godly in this present world."

It only remains for me to offer a brief exhortation to my brothers in Christ. First, I would address those of you who strongly *oppose* the concept of imputed righteousness, who condemn all those who accept it as 'antinomians' [Christians who exaggerate grace to the detriment of the moral law]. But is this not bending the bow too much in the opposite direction? Why quarrel with them for using the phrases they like? And if they quarrel with you for the same reason, do not imitate the bigotry which you blame. Why be angry at a verbal expression? Perhaps it *has* been abused—most expressions have been! However, the abuse may be corrected, and the use remain. Above all, be sure to retain the truth behind these words: "All the blessings I enjoy, all I hope for in time or eternity, are given wholly and solely for the sake of what Christ has done and suffered for me."

Second, I would address those of you who strongly *support* the concept. Do you not honestly believe that I go far enough in your direction? What more would you demand of me? I accept your entire premise: that believers have every blessing only through the righteousness of God our Savior. I happily allow you your preferred expressions, only asking that you warn your hearers against the abuse, which you are as deeply concerned to prevent as I am. I myself frequently speak of imputed righteousness. But allow me some freedom of conscience here; allow me to use the phrase just as often as I judge it preferable to other expressions; and do not be angry with me when I fail to use it every two minutes. Do not call me a Papist [Catholic] or accuse me of being an enemy to the righteousness of Christ. Be patient with me, as I am with you. Do not cry out hysterically that I am subverting the very foundations of Christianity; whoever does this does me great wrong. May the Lord have mercy on them. The fact is that I lay the same foundation of faith that you lay; and "no other foundation can be laid, but Jesus Christ." I build inward and outward holiness on that foundation, just as you do. Do not allow any distaste or unkindness or coldness of heart toward me. Even if there is a real difference of opinion between us, where is our common Christianity, if we cannot think and let think? How much more, if it is only a difference of expression? Or even more, if it is only a matter of frequency? We surely cannot allow this to become a bone of contention! Let us not allow such trifles as these to give our common enemies an opportunity to ridicule and blaspheme! Let us, at long last, join hearts and hands to serve our great Lord! As we have "one Lord, one faith, one hope," let us strengthen each other in God, and with one heart and voice declare to all mankind, "The Lord our righteousness."

Preached at the Chapel in West Street,
Seven Dials, London, November 1765

Acknowledgments

I was born into Methodism. We were every-Sunday Methodists. To the degree that any Methodist kid learned to revere Wesley, I did. I attended a Methodist college and seminary, but my historical and theological interests then were more in the Reformation period. In seminary, I did take classes with the renowned Wesley scholar, Albert Outler. But it was a little book, *John Wesley's Theology Today,* by Australian ecumenist, Colin Williams, which first helped me identify the distinctive Wesleyan message and understand it within the broader Protestant context. In graduate school, my focus, again, was on the Reformation period, both Continental and English. I returned to Florida and to pastoral ministry during those heady days when our churches were growing apace. My scholarly reading about Wesley and my reading of Wesley himself (his Journal and Sermons) took precedence now over the Reformation, but, alas, poor Mr. Wesley had to compete with the everyday demands of parish and family life. So, I never became a Wesley expert, but I can say that Wesley greatly influenced and inspired my life and ministry. And when, in mid-career, disillusioned by a misuse of Methodist authority, I flirted with what I hoped would be a less authoritarian denomination, it was John Wesley, personally, who drew me back from the brink! I have been ever after grateful to him!

When, in retirement, I stumbled (read the Foreword) into editing Wesley's sermons, very few people knew what I was doing. My wife Barbara was patiently indulgent of my hours in the study. As I edited more and more of the sermons, I shared what I was doing with members of my clergy covenant group, several of whom were particularly encouraging. My friend and former bishop, Tim Whitaker, one of our church's finest souls and keenest intellects, looked at some of my early work; in his ever-meticulous way, he critiqued my efforts and challenged me to persevere. Florida colleagues, Jay Therrell and Jeremy Rebman, leaders in the Wesleyan Covenant movement, also read and commented on my work. Finally, I discovered that Bob Tuttle, retired seminary professor and author of books on Wesley, was living in my own town; he too was graciously complimentary and encouraging of my efforts.

Finally, the work finished, it was time to think about publishing. But where to start? I knew absolutely nothing about it. Providentially, Sue Holbrook, an author in my local church, led me to her book consultant, Suzanne Fox, an experienced author in her own right. Suzanne introduced me to the mysteries and intricacies of the publishing world, without expecting that I would comprehend much of it. She was right. Patiently she led me, demandingly she pushed me, through the various stages of producing a printed book. Her brother, Andy Fox, voracious reader and active Methodist, was kind enough to read it all the way through, with attention to details. During this process, Suzanne was in constant contact with CJ Madigan, book designer, who apparently delights in the necessary minutiae of publishing that would drive most people to distraction.

So, though I relied on no one in my actual editing of Wesley, there were many, named and unnamed, who provided the necessary background, inspiration, encouragement, and technical expertise that brought my efforts to published completion. I acknowledge my debt to all.

About the Editor

Charles E. Weaver is a native Floridian. His education includes a BA in History from Millsaps College; an MTh from Perkins School of Theology, Southern Methodist University; and a year of graduate studies in History at the University of Virginia. He is a retired member of the Florida Conference of the United Methodist Church. He received his first pastoral appointment at age twenty; he served as pastor for thirty years, district superintendent for five, and assistant to two bishops for nine. He is married to Barbara, a public schoolteacher and administrator; they have three married sons and eight grandchildren. The Weavers live in Vero Beach, Florida, and worship with a Global Methodist congregation.

About the Book

This book is set in Baskerville, a typeface originally designed in the 1750s by British businessman John Baskerville. Baskerville began his career teaching handwriting and carving gravestones. After making his fortune in the manufacture and sale of lacquered goods, Baskerville became a printer in Birmingham, England. Baskerville made use of his wealth to produce elite book editions characterized by higher-quality printing, inks and paper than were customary at the time. The innovative typefaces and styles Baskerville created with his punchcutter, John Handy, engendered controversy among his contemporaries but were admired by Benjamin Franklin among others. Though Baskerville himself practiced no religion, he designed and printed a notable folio edition of the Bible after becoming the official printer of the University of Cambridge in 1758. The serif typeface that bears his name has been adapted and reinterpreted by many twentieth-century foundries and type designers.

The typeface used on the book cover, IM Fell, was designed by Igino Marini based on the type punches assembled by John Fell, Doctor of Divinity, in the 17th century. Fell, who served as the

Bishop of Oxford and the Dean of Christ Church, took as his mission the creation of a "learned press" at Oxford University; as part of this endeavor, he assembled an extraordinary group of type punches and matrices before his death in 1686. Fell left the collection, said to be the oldest in England, to Oxford University. He requested that all of its components be kept together, and the university has honored his wishes.

The portrait used on the book's cover depicts Wesley as he appeared two years before his death. Wesley sat for the noted British painter George Romney on four successive Mondays in late 1788 and early 1789. He was struck by the rapidity of Romney's work and noted in a letter that the painting "was thought to be a good likeness." Though Wesley appears in many depictions created both during and after his lifetime, the Romney portrait is the only one for which he is known to have posed repeatedly. In addition, he engaged an engraver to make copies of the portrait to share with friends and supporters.

The version used here is owned by the National Portrait Gallery in London, which now identifies it as "a good early copy of the portrait by George Romney." The work now generally accepted as the original portrait is in the collection of the Philadelphia Museum of Art.

Printed in Great Britain
by Amazon